N

THE
DEHUMANIZATION
OF MAN

SOME OTHER TITLES BY ASHLEY MONTAGU:

On Being Human
Man's Most Dangerous Myth: *The Fallacy of Race*
Darwin, Competition, and Cooperation
The Natural Superiority of Women
Immortality
Prenatal Influences
Man in Process
The Humanization of Man
The Dolphin in History
Man's Evolution
The Idea of Race
The Human Revolution
The Anatomy of Swearing
Sex, Man and Society
The Ignorance of Certainty
Touching
The Elephant Man
The Nature of Human Aggression
Human Evolution
Growing Young

SOME OTHER TITLES BY FLOYD MATSON:

The Idea of Man
The Broken Image
The Human Connection (with Ashley Montagu)
Hope Deferred (with Jacobus tenBroek)
Prejudice, War, and the Constitution (with J. tenBroek and E. N. Barnhart)
Being, Becoming and Behavior (editor)
The Human Dialogue (co-editor with Ashley Montagu)

Ashley Montagu

and

Floyd Matson

THE
DEHUMANIZATION
OF MAN

McGraw-Hill Book Company

New York · St. Louis · Toronto
Mexico · Hamburg · San Francisco

1 2 3 4 5 6 7 8 9 D O C D O C 8 7 6 5 4 3

ISBN 0-07-042845-X

Library of Congress Cataloging in Publication Data

Montagu, Ashley, 1905–
    THE DEHUMANIZATION OF MAN

    1. Alienation (Social Psychology) 2. Anomy.
3. Civilization. 4. Humanism. I. Matson, Floyd W.
II. Title
HM291.M64   1983   320.5'44   83-11276
ISBN 0-07-042845-X

Book design by Grace Markman

To the memory of Erich Kahler

Acknowledgments

The authors are grateful to their eagle-eyed friend, Dr. Phillip Gordon, for his careful reading of the proofs, and to Gladys Justin Carr, Editor-in-Chief and Chairman of the Editorial Board, and Leslie Meredith, Associate Editor, both of McGraw-Hill, for their patience and courtesy.

CONTENTS

The books we need are the kind that act upon us like a misfortune, that make us suffer like the death of someone we love more than ourselves, that make us feel as though we were on the verge of suicide, or lost in a forest remote from all human habitation—a book should serve as the axe for the frozen sea within us.

—Franz Kafka

PREFACE

HIS BOOK is concerned with an invisible dis-ease, an affliction of the spirit, which has been ravaging humanity in recent times without surcease and virtually without resistance, and which has now reached epidemic proportions in the Western world. The contagion is unknown to science and unrecognized by medicine (psychiatry aside); yet its wasting symptoms are plain for all to see and its lethal effects are everywhere on display. It neither kills outright nor inflicts apparent physical harm, yet the extent of its destructive toll is already greater than that of any war, plague, famine, or natural calamity on record—and its potential damage to the quality of human life and the fabric of civilized society is beyond calculation. For that reason this sickness of the soul might well be called the "Fifth Horseman of the Apocalypse." Its more conventional name, of course, is *dehumanization*.

The present represents a preliminary inquiry into various of the symptoms, sources, products and side-effects of dehumanization in the modern world—with primary reference to America, where the condition is apparently most pervasive and where the evidence of its devastation is most readily available. Our purpose is the modest one of providing, not a complete etiology and certainly not a sure cure, but a tentative diagnosis of the "dehuman syndrome" and a report on the extent of its proliferation. It should be emphasized that this is not an encyclopedia of all that ails our civilization—of the sum total of its discontents. Far from it. We have chosen to be selective rather than comprehensive, indicative rather than definitive. Many of the most conspicuous, and some of the most serious, of contemporary aberrations and atrocities are absent from our discussion—not by oversight but by design. This is not a survey but a reconnaissance, a probe; and in our probing we have sought, for the most part, to avoid the busier beaten paths of cultural criticism. The decision to stay off the common thoroughfares where possible, and to go instead through certain half-deserted streets, is of course partly expedient—it cuts down the mileage—but it is also a choice based on our sense of the imbalance of contemporary social analysis and commentary, with its preponderant (and wholly justified) attention to political derelictions and other clear and present dangers. Although we do not presume, like Captain Kirk of the Starship *Enterprise,* to go boldly where no man has gone before, we have attempted to go where too few explorers have gone before; or where, in our opinion, they have not gone quite far enough or brought back sufficient hard evidence of the dangers and demons that lurk out there—beyond the circle of light, behind the cool facades and beneath the paved streets of the social order, in the widening cracks of civilization: at the modern heart of darkness.

Our concern in this book is mainly with the brute facts of dehumanization in contemporary life and culture: with dehumanizing acts and dehumanized actors. Accordingly, following an introductory overview of the problem we begin (in Chapter One) with an appraisal of the dehuman syndrome and its contagious carriers—the "living dead"—and we conclude (in Chapters Six and Seven) with an extended report on the new invasion of barbarism into the once-pleasant suburbs of popular culture. But that is only part of the story. It is a premise of our book that there is a direct continuity, in any period of history, between thought and action—between the tower and the street. Neither in the person nor in the nation are mind and body disconnected; the realm of ideas and the world of affairs are joined in continuous and reciprocal interaction, and neither can be understood without reference to the other. Therefore, our attention will alternate between the "group mind" (or public consciousness) and the "body politic," reflecting the complementarity of theory and action. It was ever thus. Behind the genocide of the Holocaust lay a dehumanized thought; beneath the menticide of deviants and dissidents, in the Gulags of Russia and the cuckoo's nests of America, lies a dehumanized image of man: in fact, it is the same thought and the same image. The late historian and philosopher Erich Kahler—to whom this book is dedicated—clearly perceived that inhuman connection and the importance of its systematic investigation:

> For instance, the horrors of the Nazi regime, its use of the most up-to-date techniques for atrocities of the lowest, sub-human, indeed sub-bestial kind, such happenings are in some way related to the subtlest intellectual experiences manifesting themselves in the arts and the sciences. What made its appearance in the fascist states, in fact even in the First World War—the sudden slump of humanity from an overwrought civilization into that strange, systematized bestiality, *ce crime collectif absolument neuf, . . .* —this and the subsequent co-existence and co-development of both tendencies, over-civilization and dehumanization, have, as far as I know, scarcely been studied methodically. Yet they are, so it seems to me, the basic, the most serious events of our age.[1]

"If one were to nominate the prevalent feeling today," observed a syndicated columnist a few years ago, "the guess, alas, might be helplessness." And, after cataloguing various of the dreary specifics of defeat and frustration in everyday life, he mused: "Human beings have always felt their limits, but have people ever felt so helpless as they do in this most powerful of centuries?"[2]

This familiar paradox—the collective sense of immense powerfulness, of "superpower," matched by the personal sense of intense powerlessness—is not peculiar to the present age, of course; but it appears to many observers to be more pervasive in scope and more profound in impact than at any earlier time. To be sure, the names for this devitalized condition vary, and the explanations differ even more; what is widely shared is the amorphous feeling of a kind of spiritual enfeeblement, an inability to cope. For most persons the dead weight of powerlessness is experienced directly as a private burden, a debilitating factor in the increasingly stressful task of getting through the day—and making it through the night. This is the observational level of the psychologist and psychotherapist, whose testimony on the subject is unambiguous: "As soon as powerlessness is referred to by its more personal names," according to Rollo May in his classic account of *Power and Innocence,* "many people will sense that they are heavily burdened by it."[3] And the late Erich Fromm, through a long career of sustained psychosocial analysis, consistently identified the characteristic syndrome of modern humanity as one of enervated "passiveness," a state in which the individual "feels powerless, lonely, and anxious . . . [with] little sense of integrity or self-identity."[4] To the concerned historian or sociologist, on the other hand, the intuition of helplessness is translated into what Christopher Lasch has termed "a general crisis of western culture" reflecting the exhaustion of political ideas and the bankruptcy of traditional institutions, which finds expression in "a pervasive despair of understanding the course of modern history or of subjecting it to rational direction."[5]

Similar commentaries on the state of helplessness, both personal and cultural, might be indefinitely recited; but the melancholy refrain is too familiar to need further confirmation. The immediate evidence of its reality, within us and around us, is sufficiently compelling. If it is perhaps too much even now to declare that most men and women lead lives of quiet desperation, it is plain that many of us, much of the time, feel alone and afraid in a world we never made. Our subjective feelings of helplessness—of the absence of choice, the futility of effort, the loss of control, the failure of nerve—are graphically reinforced by the printouts from the laboratories of behavioral science. Thus the psychiatric code words for powerlessness—depression, anxiety, impotence, rage—describe a condition so common as to seem epidemic among us. Likewise the political correlates—voter apathy, cynicism, distrust of authority—loom like cancers on the body politic. And the sociological indicators—anomie, inertia, deviance, delinquency and drift—are the stuff of contemporary textbooks in Mass Society, Social Problems, and Collective Behavior.

Nor is there any reassurance to be found in the state of the arts, either elite or popular. The theme of alienation, connoting powerlessness and pessimism, has been a staple of our literature and drama (and a near-fixation of our visual arts) for so long that it has become a platitude; but it shows no signs of fading away on that account. If anything the literary imagination has grown even darker, and the plots have thickened, in the years of anxious narcissism that followed the collapse of the ardent counterculture and the failure of radical idealism in the late sixties; Bob Dylan has given way to Woody Allen.

The "Force" (that lovely symbol of power joined to innocence) may still be imagined to reside in recycled Arthurian legends or in galaxies far away; but the last American hero has long since vanished from our stage and screen—and even on TV (the last refuge of the forced smile) he appears only in reruns. It is the heyday of the *antihero*—the schlemiel, punk, jerk, trickster, and sad sack—who goes through the motions of his loser's role more in sorrow than in anger and whose sole claim upon our sympathies is that we recognize in him not the worst, but merely the least of ourselves. The funhouse mirror of the lively arts gives us back a distorted image that is meant to be a caricature, but in our anxiety and self-doubt we are more than half-prepared to believe in it anyway—to suppose that we might, after all, have come to look like this. Perhaps Pogo was wrong: it is not the Enemy that we have met but only the Victim; and, so far as we can tell in this bad light, he is us.

The course to be followed in this book may be briefly outlined. It is not insistently consecutive; the reader might begin with any chapter, circling back or forging ahead as his or her own interests dictate. But a certain pattern is intended. The introduction, "Modern Times," provides a preliminary sketch of the broad background, historical and theoretical, within which the culture of dehumanization has grown and festered; this background is seen to be dark and troubled, like a Ryder landscape, filled with anonymous crowds and distorted figures, shot through here and there with rays of light from the pens of unreconciled spirits who did not go gentle into that good night. Chapters One and Two are more contemporary, describing separate versions of the dehuman condition today—one of them terminal and the other merely incipient. The first of these takes the characteristic form of the Malevolent Robot, illustrated by G. Gordon Liddy and others; while the second assumes the friendlier image of the Cheerful Robot, as personified by Hugh Hefner and institutionalized in the peculiar pornography of sexological science.

Chapter Three has to do with another debased science—that of behaviorist psychology and its ingenious experiments in the field of dehuman engineering, all for the purpose (as Aldous Huxley recognized half a century ago) of producing good behavior in a craven new world. This is the longest chapter in the book, and perhaps the heaviest; but we venture to think it will not be found dull. It is followed by a related discussion (Chapter Four) devoted to a more subtle form of mind control, that which is practiced daily upon us all by the media merchants of persuasion in their magic theater of illusion. It is a tale of mass seduction.

Chapter Five, on the "Counter-Counterculture," traces the dehumanization of the promising youth movement of the sixties—from its pristine vision of the flowering of America and the sensitizing of the world to its tragic denouement in the hallucinatory politics of atrocity (Left and Right). The collapse of the counterculture, as we see next, left in its wake more than broken dreams and fallen idols; it spawned a decadent culture of nihilism and a mystique of vicarious violence ("terrorist chic") which have found fullest expression in Hollywood genre films, in the musical wave of punk-rock, and in the wide, snide world of competitive sport. These current events, and their relation to the decline of culture, form the subject matter of Chapters Six and Seven.

Finally, in a brief epilogue, we carry our probe beyond the present and seek to estimate the odds on a genuinely alternative future: the evolution of *Homo Humanus*. The odds are shown to be long; and of course the race is handicapped. Nevertheless our confidential tip to the reader is to join the action and get a bet down on the longshot to win. After all, it's the only game in town.

MODERN TIMES: THE CULTURE OF DEHUMANIZATION

I have seen
The old gods go
And the new gods come.

Day by day
And year by year
The idols fall
And the idols rise.

Today
I worship the hammer.
—*Carl Sandburg, "The Hammer"* (1910)

So the new leisure has brought its seeming opposite, restless-
ness. And because these cannot be reconciled the great emptiness
comes.

—*Robert MacIver*

D EHUMANIZATION is as old, or nearly so, as the species *Homo Sapiens*; and the legends of its first appearance are representative versions of how evil entered the world of man. In the grander
myths, such as the one best known to the Western world, a state of
innocence and harmony, an existence without guilty secrets or dirty
tricks, is abruptly ended by a fall—a crisis precipitated by the tempta-
tions of a nascent and assertive ego. For some modern myth-makers,

like Jean-Jacques Rousseau, the state of original bliss was demolished by the arrival of civilization—that is, of industry, agriculture, and the institution of property. Karl Marx, an Old Testament prophet turned secular humanist, proposed the same thesis less romantically, focusing attention on private property and the pursuit of power through class struggle as the explanation of man's inhumanity to man. It was by way of Marx (and his repudiated mentor Hegel) that the modern concept of alienation came to be elaborated into a central and permanent feature of social theory. For Marx it was the peasant and worker successively—the losers in the struggle of power after power, the "victims of oppression and the wretched of the earth"—who were the most thoroughly alienated. But it was not only these who were the psychic losers in the processes of social change which have occasionally erupted at critical points in human history; it was all who absorbed the tremor and felt the shock. Thus an Egyptian scribe, some four thousand years ago, recorded the dislocations of such a turning point:

> Robbers abound. . . . No one ploughs the land. People are saying: "We do not know what will happen from day to day." . . . The country is spinning round and round like a potter's wheel. . . . No more do we hear any one laugh. . . . No public office stands open where it should, and the masses are like timid sheep without a shepherd. . . . Artists have ceased to ply their art . . . The few slay the many. . . . Impudence is rife. . . . Oh that man could cease to be, that women should no longer conceive and give birth. Then, at length, the world would find peace.[1]

From its beginning, civilization brought its discontents. For, as Lewis Mumford has pointed out, it introduced not only the division of labor and the "megamachine" of exploited masses but the degradation of all life to the level of merchandise to be bought and sold—not only labor but "love" itself. Custom gave way to law, the folkways to the social order; for the price of security and material progress, something of humanity was lost or placed in continuous jeopardy. At bottom, as Mumford writes, "the goods of civilization have been achieved and preserved—and this is a crowning contradiction—largely by methodical compulsion and regimentation, backed by a flourish of force. In that sense, civilization is one long affront to human dignity."[2]

At a late point in the waning of the Middle Ages, a fifteenth-century French poet, Eustache Deschamps, uttered the theme of self-alienation which was to characterize the modern age already struggling to be born:

> Why are the times so dark
> Men know each other not at all,
> But governments quite clearly change
> From bad to worse?
> Days dead and gone were more worth while,
> Now what holds sway? Deep gloom and boredom,
> Justice and law nowhere to be found.
> I know no more where I belong.[3]

To know where one belonged, in the Middle Ages, was to know who one was; identity was not personal but communal, a matter of affiliation, status, and role. One was a Baker or a Smith, perhaps a Goldsmith, or one was Mat's son; that was all the ID that was needed either for external recognition or internal self-assurance. Not to know where one belonged was to be truly alien, unprotected and unacknowledged, a homeless mind without a sense of self. It was Raymond Williams, in *The Long Revolution,* who reminded us that the term "individual" in its medieval usage meant only one of a class (as when we speak of an individual pearl or paramecium); not until the latter part of the sixteenth century, when feudal institutions and obligations were largely dissolved throughout Europe, when status had given way to contract and the entrepreneur was buying out the lord of the manor, did the modern sense of the individual *qua* individual—of man-in-person, man for himself—come into currency. Before that time it is fair to say that there were people in the world, even personages, but no *persons.* (Even after that time, to be sure, not all people were recognized as persons; for centuries to come women and children, as well as slaves, were regarded as property, while disparaged minorities [such as Jews, Orientals, the aged, the blind, and the poor] were perceived both legally and psychologically as nonpersons. But the concept of the individual "in his own right," however limited in scope, had become a part of the general consciousness; the age of individualism was underway.)

The Alienation of Affection

The discovery of the individual, the creation or invention of "modern man," was also paradoxically the source of the first portent of alienation, the first sense of peril to the integrity and dignity of the human person. Almost simultaneously, the new consciousness of individual personality which was born in the Renaissance and celebrated by the Enlightenment was counterbalanced by the consciousness of opposing forces bent upon the destruction of personality. Perhaps only the modern mind could conceive of alienation because it was only the modern who minded. More seriously, the sense of alienation was a product of that great transformation (in Karl Polanyi's phrase) which marked the end of a world and a way of life that had existed for millennia and had set the framework for all of human thought and valuation. That something was lost in its passing, never to be known again but often dreamed of, has been cogently suggested by Peter Laslett in his study of England before the industrial age, *The World We Have Lost*:

> The word alienation is part of the cant of the mid-twentieth century and it began as an attempt to describe the separation of the worker from his world of work. We need not accept all that this expression has come to convey in order to recognize that it does point to something vital to us all in relation to our past. Time was when the whole of life went forward in the family, in a circle of loved, familiar faces, known and fondled objects, all to human size. That time has gone for ever. It makes us very different from our ancestors.[4]

It was not only that men and women were uprooted from ancient ways which made the trauma of the industrial revolution so unlike all previous transformations. The new world was not merely somewhat different: it was actively hostile to the old world in its deepest impulses and most characteristic expressions. The transition from the age of faith to the age of the machine was not just another of those historic shifts from familiar customs to novel conditions; rather, to take a metaphor from science and its fictions, it was like a space odyssey from a known universe of positive energy forces, passing through a "black hole" of electromagnetic reversal, into an opposite universe powered by negative current. It was the devout minds and poetic souls who were first to feel the difference in the air; at the very outset of the transformation, after Copernicus but before Galileo and Newton, there were early warning signals from such monitors of the spirit as John Donne:

> . . . [the] new philosophy calls all in doubt,
> The Element of fire is quite put out;
> The Sun is lost, and th' earth, and no mans wit
> Can well direct him where to looke for it.
> 'Tis all in peeces, all cohaerance gone;
> All just supply, and all Relation.[5]

In the seventeenth century, when the "mechanical philosophy" of Newton had begun to take effect upon the minds of men, there were many who felt the same confusion and despair as Donne; who recognized the implications of what Alexandre Koyré has called "the scientific and philosophical destruction of the cosmos."[6] Another philosopher of our own time, E.A. Burtt, has conveyed the feeling of those who resisted the reconstitution of the universe in thoroughly mechanistic terms and the resultant view of man as "a puny irrelevant spectator":

> The world that people had thought themselves living in—a world rich with colour and sound, redolent with fragrance, filled with gladness, love and beauty, speaking everywhere of purposive harmony and creative ideals—was crowded now into minute corners in the brains of scattered organic beings. The really important world outside was a world hard, cold, colourless, silent and dead.[7]

Of course not everyone felt that way. The astonishing discoveries of modern science, the age of invention and enterprise, the ambience of Enlightenment, the revolutionary politics of liberty and equality, and ultimately and most reassuringly the century of progress and the triumph of technology, were doubtless experienced by most men and women of the rising middle classes as the steady unfolding of a vista of endless promise—and not only of promise but of demonstrable achievement. The ambiguous quality of that achievement—the ethics of the "bitch-goddess Success," the rugged edges of individualism, the Emersonian fear that "Things are in the saddle,/And ride mankind"—might be caviled at by intellectuals and Tories; but the entrepreneurial classes of Europe and America were not likely to be impressed by these doubts even where (on Sundays or in the fortnightly periodicals) they attended to them at all. Those who had the solidest case to make against the human costs of industrialization—the moles at work in the "dark satanic mills," the pauper hordes whom Engels observed in Liverpool and Manchester, the sewer rats of Victor Hugo, the street urchins of Dickens, the appalling English case studies of Mayhew, Booth, and the Hammonds—were acknowledged only at second hand and for the most part sentimentally; their protest was obscene but not heard.

But whether the imperatives of the modern world—money, mechanism, and materialism—were approved or disapproved, they carried the day and called the tune: they replaced the organic pulse with the artificial metronome. The earliest symbol of the new order, as Mumford has demonstrated, was the clock—which made its appearance in the town squares of Europe in the fifteenth century and commenced its inexorable regulation of the cycles of life and labor, in direct conflict with the natural and immemorial rhythms of the seasons and of the earth's own movement around the sun—the obsolete imperatives of the agrarian world.[8] We can only guess how this must have felt to those caught up in the wrenching phase of transition; but a peculiar and profound form of dehumanization was taking place, involving the loss of a sense of subjective control or even participation in the conduct of daily life. The old ways had been experienced as the commands of nature, hence of human nature; to submit to nature's laws was a form of self-direction. There might be tyranny in the elements, in the vagaries of weather and disaster; but, like death, these things were a part of life and could be borne with dignity. The new imperatives were not only external, imposed from without; they were also *nonhuman*, "alien," detached from human feelings, and in a real sense "against nature." Henceforth human life would not move with the tides, but proceed like clockwork.

Ballet Mecanique

A vivid illustration of the loss of community and solidarity in the modern world—what might be termed the breaking of the human connection—was presented by Paul Halmos a generation ago in his account of the decline of the choral dance. Although the choral forms of dance, in which the group as a whole took part, had their origins in prehistoric times, they remained a lively feature of village life through the Middle Ages. Their functions, once largely ritualistic, were at all times related to the needs for active participation, spontaneous expression, and the sense of belonging. "In the choral dance," writes Halmos, "an inarticulate consensus and an absolute fraternity are reaffirmed from time to time, thus tightening up group cohesion and conserving solidarity. In it the individual member finds a reassurance that he is not alone."[9] The choral dance fell victim to the general dislocations of the Industrial Revolution; it gave way gradually to more exclusive and privatized forms: "The group is 'broken up' into independent couples: the minuet, allemand, passepied, bourree, gigue are mixed dances with a strong choral framework; the cotillion-quadrille type of so-called 'square dances' represents the link between the choral and couple dances."[10] The modern couple forms, miscalled "social dancing," were in reality antisocial; as Halmos shrewdly observes, they occurred typically through the act of "going out"— outside the familiar group—and they involved little interaction with other couples in the lonely crowd of the dance floor. Meanwhile, the professionalization of dance through the modern spirit of technique, creating the "split world of performers and audiences," further alienated the individual from expression and participation: "the hypertrophy of audiences," remarks Halmos, "is just another symptom of desocialization . . ."

In the twentieth century, the desocialization of the dance has reached extreme dimensions. Even the attenuated interaction of the couple dances, which at least preserved the semblance of contact, has been undermined by the characteristic dance fads of the post-rock era which come more and more to represent solo exhibitions by self-absorbed narcissists engaged in the private transports of Saturday night fever. More poignantly and pointedly, the urban institution of the commercial dance hall has long since become a refuge for the terminally lonely and outcast who may, for a price and for an hour, enjoy the illusion of being king or queen of the Stardust Ballroom. The Mephisto waltzes of the taxi-dance emporium, the rituals of Roseland, resemble nothing so much as modern versions of the medieval *Dans Macabre* or *Totentanz*: the "Dance of Death" in which the Grim Reaper in the form of a dancer forces all alike—old and young, poor and rich—to join him in the very last dance (to the tune of "Goodnight, Sweetheart"). The desocialization of the dance, through such parodies of expression and travesties of companionship as these, has been paralleled by the dehumanization of the dancers—not only in the taxi-dance halls but in the endless diversity and perversity of commercial exploitations of performance and observance: among them the dance "marathons" of the depressed thirties, the caged "go-go" girls of rock-'n-roll bars, the mechanical drills of precision chorus lines, the "exotic" dancers and topless prancers of the big resorts, the simulated epileptic seizures of male rock stars (from Elvis the Pelvis to Mick the Jagger). There is an old Chinese maxim which avers: "One may judge of a king by the state of dancing during his reign." Thus Paul G. Cressey, following a detailed study of the taxi-dance hall, came to view it as a microcosm of the modern condition. "In the last analysis," he concluded, "the problem of the taxi-dance hall can be regarded as the problem of the modern city"—whose dominant characteristics are "mobility, impersonality and anonymity."[11]

If the decline of the choral dance, and the degradation of dance itself, may be taken as a symbol as well as symptom of the alienated society, there is another and more familiar image which came to dominate the consciousness of the nineteenth century as a kind of iconic and kaleidoscopic projection of its deepest impulses and grandest aspirations. It is, of course, the image of the Great Machine—a montage of scientific designs and popular mechanics, of experimental discovery and practical invention, coalescing into a vision of the modern Prometheus unbound: the *deus ex machina*, alternately embodied in the hissing demon of Steam, the purring spirit of the Dynamo, the great turning wheels and thrusting pistons of the factory, all of it as overpowering and inscrutable to ordinary intelligence as the ways of the Almighty. "Why need I speak of steam," wrote Ralph Waldo Emerson in 1870, "the enemy of space and time, with its enormous strength and delicate applicability, which . . . can twist beams of iron like candy-braids, and vies with the forces which up-heaved and doubled over the geologic strata?"[12] And Henry Adams, standing awestruck in the great hall of dynamos at the Paris Exposition of 1900, formulated his famous vision of the huge electrical machine as a "symbol of infinity" and a wholly new moral force as powerfully representative of the twentieth century as the Virgin Mary had been representative of the thirteenth:

> As he grew accustomed to the great gallery of machines, he began to feel the forty-foot dynamo as a moral force, much as the early Christians felt the Cross. The planet itself seemed less impressive, in its old-fashioned, deliberate, annual or daily revolution, than this huge wheel, revolving within arm's-length at some vertiginous speed, and barely murmuring—scarcely humming an audible warning to stand a hair's-breadth further for respect of power—while it would not wake the baby lying close against its frame. Before the end, one began to pray to it; inherited instinct taught the natural expression of man before silent and infinite force. Among the thousand symbols of ultimate energy, the dynamo was not so human as some, but it was the most expressive.[13]

Yet neither Emerson nor Adams, awed as they were by the new symbols of force, were quite overawed. Unlike the more "progressive" spirits of their age, who thought to see ultimate salvation in science and universal happiness through technology, their intuitions of the potential sacrifices that would be demanded by the mechanical Moloch veered off into nightmare. "These arts," conceded Emerson, "open great gates of a future, promising to make the world plastic and to lift human life out of its beggary to a godlike ease and power." But he was no more enamored of a world turned plastic than was the fictional character, Benjamin, in the 1967 movie *The Graduate*, when taken aside by an excited businessman and vouchsafed the one key word that could open the great gates of his own future: "Plastics!" Emerson remained a doubter and a worrier: "Yes, we have a pretty artillery of tools now in our social arrangements: we ride four times as fast as our fathers did; travel, grind, weave, forge, plant, till, and excavate better. We have new shoes, gloves, glasses, and gimlets; . . ." And there will surely be more; and more is surely better. But here the Emersonian tone of prophecy turns just a little sour: "Man flatters himself that his command over Nature must increase. Things begin to obey him. We are to have the balloon yet; and the next war will be fought in the air. We may yet find a rosewater that will wash the Negro white."[14] Yes, we have a pretty artillery of tools; but where are they taking us? They are taking us (this was 1870) toward a coming war to be fought in the air; but where is the invention that will take us toward peace on earth? We may concoct a formula to whiten the black man's skin; but where is the formula to dignify blackness and end race hatred? Salvation, said Emerson, is not to be found in our machines and their ingenious sciences; but something else, something more ominous, may be found to be growing there:

> Many facts concur to show that we must look deeper for our salvation than to steam, photographs, balloons, or astronomy. These tools have some questionable properties. They are reagents. Machinery is aggressive. The weaver becomes a web, the machinist a machine. If you do not use the tools, they use you. All tools are in some sense edge-tools, and dangerous.[15]

It was the same with Henry Adams; except that his disaffection from the new age ran deeper. Adams had never accepted the nineteenth century; he could scarcely be expected to embrace the twentieth. Yet, as readers of his great personal odyssey are aware, he made a harder and nobler effort to understand the scientific revolution just then beginning to unfold, and the mysterious new forces of energy it was on the way to unleashing, than any philosopher or scientist of his time. He strove valiantly to be objective, as he had sought to be in his highly esteemed histories; but now, approaching seventy, he was writing a personal history, indeed a "confession" on the order of Augustine and Rousseau, and even his elaboration of the purported scientific "law of acceleration" and the "dynamic theory of history" turned into an eloquent *cri de coeur*. In the year 1904, looking backward upon the century of commerce and corruption, and looking forward into the century of nuclear war and nuclear waste, Adams assumed almost against his will (and certainly against his training) the voice of a prophet in the classical tradition, warning of the doom ticking away for all of mankind in the yet untapped and barely recognized energies at the heart of matter. As his biographer, Ernest Samuels, has commented:

> In a time of alienation and deepening crisis, the denun-ciatory voice of Henry Adams has a singularly contemporary relevance. . . . Even in his own day he saw the eighteenth century American dream of unlimited opportunity and in-definite progress turning into a waking nightmare of the moral dilemmas of a capitalist society. He saw too that though science was indeed making tremendous advances in the conquest of Nature, winning every battle in that age-old contest, the odds were growing that a dehumanized mankind might lose the war.[16]

In a famous chapter of the *Education,* entitled "The Dynamo and the Virgin (1900)," Adams presented his dark vision of the Western world divided against itself by "two kingdoms of force which had nothing in common but attraction." One was symbolized by "the Virgin, the Woman," whose extraordinary magnetic power had given unity and energy to the Age of Faith: "Symbol or energy, the Virgin had acted as the greatest force the Western world ever felt, and had drawn man's activities to herself more strongly than any other power, natural or supernatural, had ever done . . ."[17] The force of the Virgin had been centripetal, unifying, nurturing and conserving; and it had also been astonishingly creative, inspiring the production of "four-fifths of [man's] noblest art." But that force had been dissi-pated with the decline of the church and its replacement by the secular religion of science and business; even as a symbol the Virgin had only a few appropriate shrines left (notably at Chartres), and nothing of her spiritual power and moral force had ever successfully crossed the ocean to America. Adams saw the new century as enthral-led by the other kingdom of force, symbolized by the Dynamo: a force not centripetal but centrifugal, conveying not unity but multi-plicity, proliferating its seed of power and swiftness and material plenty at such a rate as to leave humanity dizzied, anxious, unreason-

able, and afraid. Scanning this probable future, and tracing the uncontrolled acceleration of energy through the recent centuries of the
modern world, Adams was led to a remarkable prediction—set down
in 1905 in a letter to another historian:

> The assumption of unity, which was the mark of human
> thought in the Middle Ages, has yielded very slowly to the
> proofs of complexity. The stupor of science before radium is a
> proof of it. Yet it is quite sure, according to my score of ratios
> and curves that, at the accelerated rate of progression since
> 1600, it will not need another century or half century to turn
> thought upside down. Law in that case would disappear as
> theory or *a priori* principle and give place to force. Morality
> would become police. Explosives would reach cosmic vio-
> lence. Disintegration would overcome integration.[18]

That dark vision of apocalypse to come was singularly at odds with
the main current of thought and opinion in the first decade of the new
era which all the great expositions and world's fairs, from Paris in
1900 to St. Louis in 1904, were celebrating rapturously as the utopian World of Tomorrow. But there were other voices to be heard,
here and there, crying in the wasteland. One of these, a poet, was
writing out of a land which had known the force of the Virgin and
was experiencing in full measure the almost equal and opposite force
of the Dynamo. Perhaps it was not precisely a mechanical monster
which the Irishman William Butler Yeats would envision as a rough
beast, a vitalized Sphinx, slouching towards Bethlehem to be born;
but it might well have been, in view of Yeats' famous assessment of
the condition of man in the new century:

> . . .
> Things fall apart; the centre cannot hold;
> Mere anarchy is loosed upon the world,
> The blood-dimmed tide is loosed, and everywhere
> The ceremony of innocence is drowned;
> The best lack all conviction, while the worst
> Are full of passionate intensity.[19]

The Dehumanization of the Self

The victory of the mechanical equation over the organic principle was only the start of the modern process of dehumanization. It seemed to pit man against the machine, by splitting the world into a private human sphere and a mechanical public domain; if he had become an automaton at work, the individual might still be autonomous at home. But that apparent division of life into convenient spheres of interest, as Jacques Ellul in particular has argued, was itself a myth providing false comfort. It was not only the workplace that was mechanized; the machine was in the garden as well. That which connected man and machine, undergirding them both, was the modern spirit of *technique*—the technological imperative.

> As long as technique was represented exclusively by the machine, it was possible to speak of "man *and* the machine."
> . . . [Man] was in a position to assert himself apart from the machine; he was able to adopt a position with respect to it.
> But when technique enters into every area of life, including the human, it ceases to be external to man and becomes his very substance. It is no longer face to face with man but is integrated with him, and it progressively absorbs him.[20]

The mechanization of life could be complete only with the mechanization of man—that is, with his total and willing absorption into the system as a functional unit, a smoothly working part. The human subject, as an end in itself, must become an object, a means to other ends. The last refuge of the secret self, the deepest hidden recess of spontaneity and freedom, must be infiltrated, subjugated, and recycled into conformity with the technological society. Man, in effect, had to be emptied out of essential humanity—in order to be restocked with artificial needs and scientifically conditioned reflexes.

The dehumanization of man, initiated from without, would be finally accomplished when the individual accepted his fate and completed the process from within, by a voluntary act of compliance and conversion. As long as he held out, as long as he continued to struggle, the victory was not total; the process of dehumanization would be consummated in the moment when it was no longer felt or comprehended by its victim, no longer opposed but welcomed. What was required, in short, was the unconditional surrender of the self. As we shall see in subsequent chapters, this capture and possession of the self has taken a variety of forms: among them the engineering of behavior, the seduction of the mind, the savaging of play, the brutalization of culture. And there have been at least two distinct versions of self-dehumanization, which might for convenience be designated as "hard" and "soft." The first, much the more dramatic and conspicuous, takes the form of the Malevolent Robot, the "living dead" (to be examined in Chapter One). The other form, more subtle but scarcely less abject in its self-surrender, is the smiling model of adjustment and accommodation to which C. Wright Mills gave the name of the "Cheerful Robot" (to be discussed in Chapter Two). Despite their obvious differences, these two versions of the dehuman syndrome share a number of significant traits. Both represent psychological defense mechanisms, although one is apparently adaptive (well-adjusted) and the other notoriously maladaptive (pathological); both tend to be compulsively conformist in behavior, hence intolerant of ambiguity and suspicious toward deviance; and both exhibit a markedly diminished capacity for genuine feeling. As a notable psychiatric study of the phenomenon has put it, "Self-directed dehumanization empties the individual of human emotions and passions."[21] But the emptiness soon comes to be filled with substitute gratifications: in the one case "fun," and in the other violence. The hard and soft varieties of self-dehumanization are, of course, two sides of the same coin, mirror images of the same shriveled figure. One image is that of the Good Citizen, who pays his taxes, cultivates his garden, and minds his own business; the other image is that of the Bad Character (although it also may take the form of the Good Soldier, as witness William Calley, Gordon Liddy, and Adolf Eichmann). It is the hard case who assaults and kills another on the street, in full public view; it is the soft case who watches silently from his window. The one takes part in a gang rape, carried out on the pool table of a neighborhood tavern; the other looks on from his bar stool. These two are more than brothers; they are alter egos, who may exchange roles at any moment. We do well to be concerned about them both.

David Mamet's play *Edmond*, first produced in 1982, constitutes a riveting case study of the hardening of the soft shell of self-dehumanization. The protagonist, an altogether respectable and seemingly reasonable citizen of the middle class, descends through a series of trivial frustrations into a murderous hell of his own making. The author's point is that Edmond is not one of "them" but one of *us*, any one of us in the next bad moment or the moment after that. As critic Jack Kroll has put it:

> Edmond is the rock-bottom man, the man who's died inside, who can't be either happy or unhappy, only enraged at his own emptiness. So kill a president, kill a pop star, taint a Tylenol, saw the beaks off some pelicans. Or look at your wife, and feel the blank rage of nothingness. Get drunk, get high, get sick. Look at the woman, the black man, the white man, the other—and feel the civil smile on your face twist into the snarl of hate. Feel the surge of lust that curdles into the urge to kill. Tell the cop you don't know why you did it, you don't know *that* you did it. It was a misunderstanding. It was the devil. It was the genes. It was the bad smell of your life. It was the good smell of your life. Feel the shocked satisfaction as you're reborn into the comfort of monsterhood.[22]

The Flight from the Self

It was the pioneer American sociologist Charles Horton Cooley who coined the term "the looking-glass self," at the turn of the century, to describe his theory of the formation of character through social interaction (in effect, we not only see ourselves as others see us, we *become* ourselves as others see us). In the light of subsequent social theory and cultural history, Cooley's metaphor takes on a much more literal meaning than he intended—one that he would surely have repudiated out of hand. In actuality what one sees in the looking-glass is not a self at all, of course, but the reflection of a self—a "mirror image" without substance or life, which moreover "lies" by literally reversing what it supposedly reflects. In Cooley's day there must have seemed little harm in the application of such a loose and inaccurate figure of speech; no one then was likely to mistake the phantom image for the solid reality. We had not yet arrived at the Pictorial Age, with its revived idolatry of graven images. The "graphic revolution" which photography had ushered in was well along technically, but its psychological impact was not yet widely felt or understood. Today we are the heirs and creatures of that videographic revolution; it has transformed both our outlook on the world and our insight into ourselves. Not only are we surrounded, distracted, bombarded and massaged by audio-visual images, we are infatuated with them, addicted to them, and seduced by them. The stages and techniques through which this mass seduction has taken place will be the subject of later discussion (Chapter Four). Our concern at the moment is with the deeper background of cultural consciousness in which the tyranny of the image has begun to undermine our relation to reality, deplete our conception of ourselves, and convert our conduct of life into a succession of improvised and insincere theatrical turns on the stage of the "Imagic Theater." (Soon each of us, when asked the question "What do you do?" may reply: "I do impersonations.")

The extent to which, in the present age of electronic reproduction and re-creation, the image has overcome reality and replaced it with a more vivid and "believable" reality of its own, has been convincingly demonstrated by numerous scholars—notably by Susan Sontag in her provocative interpretation of photography and by Daniel Boorstin in his classic account (appropriately entitled *The Image*) of the graphics revolution and its denouement of the staged pseudo-event.[23] What is less well recognized is that it is not only our acknowledgment of outer reality—the existence of the phenomenal world—that is confused and undermined by the triumph of the image and the conversion of life into theater; it is also our hold on inner reality, our apprehension of the self, and with it the capacity to take responsibility for our actions. When all the world's a stage, and all the men and women merely players, then none of us is responsible for the script and the continuity. Indeed our very success in the part is gauged by our ability to "efface" our real self, to remove our existential presence from the stage, to absorb the role and be absorbed by it. And when our performance is truly convincing, we may succeed on other levels as well; we may get away with murder. In fact the theatrical model of behavior, with its abolition of self and abdication of responsibility, is implicit in the opinions of psychiatrists and the judgments of courts in numerous insanity cases; thus John W. Hinckley, Jr., found not guilty of attempted assassination by reason of insanity, was evidently acting out as faithfully as he could the role of a fictive character named

Travis Bickle in the motion picture *Taxi Driver*. (When asked why he had accumulated a large cache of handguns, Hinckley is said to have replied: "Ask Travis.")

In Cooley's own science of sociology, the updated concept of the looking-glass self—the insubstantial image which appears only when bidden and then is merely a pose—has in recent decades become an unacknowledged premise, if not a dominant paradigm, of the discipline. The irrelevance of the self, not to say its immateriality, is a tacit assumption shared by nearly all major theoretical denominations—making plausible the claim that sociology is the most self-less of the behavioral sciences. What Robert W. Friedrichs has termed the "flight from the self" in modern social thought has an extended history—the exodus may have begun with the earliest formulators of a "social physics"—but in recent times it has taken on the character of a mass evacuation. One influential school of thought—the dramaturgical theory associated with Erving Goffman—has gone so far as to regard society literally as theater and to portray individual action as dramatic performance, or more precisely as play-acting, with all the mummery and makebelieve which that entails. Regarded in this theatrical light (and shadow), the "presentations of self in everyday life" come very soon to seem all presentation and no self. (Indeed Goffman has gone to considerable pains to deflate the very idea of the self as having any existential reality. For example: "The self, then, as a performed character, is not an organic thing that has a specific location, whose fundamental fate is to be born, to mature, and to die; it is a dramatic effect . . .")[24] At some point in the elaboration of this sociological esthetics, shadow overwhelms substance and appearance consumes reality; no distinction is any longer perceptible between the theater of life and the "life" of the theater. The inference is not, of course, that the two spheres are equally real (what is real about a theatrical fiction?); rather it is that both are equally spurious—or at least, in the preferred language, equally absurd. (Not coincidentally, two sociologists of this persuasion, who authored a book on *The Drama of Social Reality,* also published *A Sociology of the Absurd.*)[25]

The dissolution of the personal self as we had thought we knew it (as agent, subject, or center), and its reconstitution as "dramatic effect" or role performance, carries with it an important consequence which removes the theory from the ivory tower of academicism and brings it down to the earthy level of manipulative persuasion, social gamesmanship, and the brokerage of power. Much of the work of Goffman and his followers gives the impression of a sophisticated updating of Machiavelli's unsentimental handbook for the man who would be king. Thus, as one critic has pointed out, their works are replete with terms appropriate to the single stance of opportunism, of making it in the rat race: "Terms that denote this stance have included the following: management, strategies, tactics, devices, mechanisms, maneuvers, stratagems, practices. . . . In other words, there is here a stripped down and modest version of game theory."[26] The game theory is modest anyway in its scope of reference; Goffman's primary interest has been in the strategic encounters of everyday life, the little games people play of "impression management" and one-upmanship; and it should be acknowledged that in the understanding of this interpersonal and informal social world, until lately neglected by scholars (other than anthropologists far from home), Goffman's microsociology has made a valuable contribution. But it is not quite so modest in its assumption that what is salient about the events of human interaction, what is most to be remarked and celebrated, is the art of successful manipulation and mastery. Since these ends are more likely to be brought about by deception and dissimulation than they are by openness, trust, or other ethical constraints, the literature of social dramaturgy gives tacit encouragement (if not academic absolution) to the spreading mood of abrasive cynicism abroad in the land, and to the popular prophets of aggressive self-advertisement whose own dramatic versions of the competitive game and how to win it (through flimflam or intimidation) constitute the informal social gospel of the modern executive suite. As Alvin W. Gouldner, a notably dissenting sociologist, has observed: "Goffman thus declares a moratorium on the conventional distinction between make-believe and reality, or between the cynical and the sincere." More than that, his theory reflects and reinforces the new economy "centered on mass marketing and promotion, including the marketing of the self."[27] That is the crucial dereliction of this fashionable social theory: having stripped the self of reality and responsibility, and having turned it into a charade of affected poses, it can do no better than to send it out to market, equipped with a smile and a shoe-shine. If self-prostitution means the death of the salesman, what's the difference: it goes with the territory.

Goffman's social dramaturgy, for all its peculiarity and idiosyncrasy, is in this respect in the forefront of the main stream running through the field. As suggested earlier, there has always been a built-in bias against the self (and more explicitly against the human as individual) in sociology, if only by virtue of its perfectly proper concern with larger institutions and structures, with the social and collective dimensions of life. In many of its classic formulations, at the hands of the nineteenth-century European system-builders of the "grand tradition," the very notion of individuality, of a distinctive personal self, was forcefully put down wherever it ventured to raise its phantom head. For most of these early masters—Comte, Gumplowicz, Ratzenhofer, Durkheim—all that was real and rational in history was the organic aggregate, variously identified as the Group, Race, Class, Nation, or simply as Society. Thus the influential Gumplowicz thundered:

> *The great error of individualistic psychology is the supposition that man thinks. . . .* A chain of errors; for it is not man himself who thinks but his social community . . .
> The individual simply plays the part of the prism which receives the rays, dissolves them according to fixed laws and lets them pass out again in a predetermined direction and with a predetermined color.[28]

There was, however, another reason, apart from "sociologism," for this occupational resistance to the recognition of the individual in his own right: namely, scientism. When the grand tradition emigrated to America, around the turn of the century, there was some pragmatic objection to its sweeping theoretical gestures—but scarcely any to its heavily positivist methodology. Most American sociologists interpreted their mission as the construction of a science of society modeled on that of the queen of sciences; hence the recurrent popularity of the formidable appellation, Social Physics. Unhappily (or happily, as the case may be), no such exact science has ever emerged; but it has not been for want of trying on the part of successive generations of seekers after the physicalistic grail. Whether their constructs followed the path of systematic grand theory (culminating in the magisterial work of Talcott Parsons) or went down the narrower trails of laborious microresearch which C. Wright Mills was to term

"abstracted empiricism," there was little tolerance for any manifesta-
tion of the ghostly self in their machines. With the rise to long-term
dominance of the Parsonian system theory following the second
world war, what little was left of the personal self became indefinitely
lost to view in an intricate maze of interlocking roles, functions, and
overarching structures—constituting an abstract and monolithic Social System which came to look (in the eyes of those professional
dissidents who remained unawed by the majesty of it all) like nothing
so much as Dostoevski's Crystal Palace. (One of the earliest critics,
Wayne Hield, said of the Parsonian world that in it "Man is a helpless
creature to be adapted and adjusted to the *status quo* or what is
called 'social control.'" To which Gouldner later added: "Man is a
hollowed-out, empty being filled with substance only by society.")[29]

It was largely through the agency of "role" that modern
sociologists came to dissipate, deplete, and finally collapse the old-
fashioned idea of the self. In one of its earliest (and possibly its wisest)
formulations, that of G. H. Mead's symbolic interactionism, "role"
was merely a loose construct pointing to the common practice of
"taking the role of the other" in ordinary acts of communication.
Unfortunately the simple term "role" seems to carry an irresistible
connotation of theatricality; and it was not long before "role-taking"
became translated into "role-playing," which in turn led us directly
into the theater of makebelieve and mock performance. In this putting on and taking off of public faces, the self could never make an
appearance—or, rather, it could make *only* an appearance. To be
sure, some images might be held to be more effective than others, and
some performances more successful, but none could be held to be
"truer" than any other. It didn't matter; the question of truth, of
reality, was rarely brought up. There was no one in the theater (as
there had been in a classic silent film of horror) with an urge to strip
off the mask in order to see who the phantom of the opera really was.

The triumph of the image and the exile of the self in sociology may
seem to be an arcane matter of interest only to academicians; but, in
fact, it finds a remarkably close parallel in the general drift of public
consciousness toward the embrace of illusion and the retreat from
reality (see Chapter Four within). In both cases, appearances (as in
the photograph and the TV image) have riveted our attention and
forced a suspension of disbelief; and in both cases there is an inclination to accept the performance at "face value," to prefer the instant

replay to the original action, and to pass unprotestingly through the looking-glass into a far, far better world than we have ever known—no matter if it turns out to be the underworld of Plato's cave, and if those figures we see before us are only flickering shadows, poor players that strut and fret their hour upon the screen and then are seen no more: until the reruns.

1

THE DEHUMAN SYNDROME: PROFILES OF THE LIVING DEAD

The trouble with Eichmann was precisely that so many were like him, and that the many were neither perverted nor sadistic, that they were, and still are, terribly and terrifyingly normal.
—*Hannah Arendt*

Hence, as long as one believes that the evil man wears horns, one will not discover an evil man.—*Erich Fromm*

SOCIAL SCIENTISTS in recent years have made an important discovery: they have discovered evil. To some that may seem the equivalent of reinventing the wheel; for as we all know the apprehension of evil is as old and universal as myth, perhaps as old as humankind, and it has been both learnedly and luridly addressed by poets and preachers, by theologians and philosophers, through the ages. But, until our own time, it had not been the concern of scientists; there were no Manicheans in the laboratories. That posture of indifference to the good, the bad, and the ugly should not surprise a modern reader; the concept of "evil," even apart from its archaic vocabulary, clearly entails a value judgment, and there could be no place for such emotive concerns in any of the sciences—whether of nature, man, or society. The conventional attitude was neatly summed up in the declaration of sociologist Robert Bierstadt in the fifties that "the scientist, as such, has no ethical, religious, political, literary, philosophical, moral, or marital preferences. . . . As a scientist he is interested not in what is right or wrong or good or evil, but only in what is true or false."[1]

That is no longer the prevailing attitude among social scientists—or, for that matter, even among physical scientists. It was still possible at the end of the last century for an eminent physicist (Lord Kelvin) to proclaim without fear of professional contradiction that a scientist must "follow the Truth wherever it may lead, though the heavens fall." But that, as Lewis Mumford has pointed out, was before the Atomic Dawn—before stars fell on Hiroshima. The old confidence of the scientists in their anointed mission of truth-seeking, and their Olympian status above the mortal storm, became a casualty of applied quantum mechanics. The appropriate epitaph for the Kelvinist faith was pronounced in 1948 by J. Robert Oppenheimer, architect of the nuclear bomb, who said: "In some sort of crude sense which no vulgarity, no humor, no overstatement can quite extinguish, the physicists have known sin: and this is a knowledge which they cannot lose."

This altered state of consciousness—the acknowledgment of a moral concern—is especially evident in the social sciences today where the subject matter is widely seen (despite the continuing protests of those who call themselves technologists of behavior) to be no more nor less than suffering humanity. The turnabout has its own intellectual history, of course; but it may have been first signaled to the general public by the appearance in 1963 of Hannah Arendt's controversial *Eichmann in Jerusalem,* which was unapologetically subtitled *A Report on the Banality of Evil.* The forbidden Topic A of social science, now out of the closet, was further legitimized by a succession of studies bearing the same imprimatur (among them two by the sociologist Ernest Becker, *The Structure of Evil* and *Escape from Evil,* and another by William Irwin Thompson, *Evil and World Order*).[2] More recently an impressive attempt to construct a systematic "sociology of evil" has been undertaken by Stanford Lyman in *The Seven Deadly Sins: Society and Evil,* which sets forth a rhetoric of social criticism designed to "take evil as a topic in its own right, seeking to uncover its historical backgrounds, describe its social forms and architectonics, and examine its supports and strengths."[3]

The point of Hannah Arendt's classic case study of the mass exterminator, Adolf Eichmann, was that evil in the present century
wears a new face—that it does not look like evil, speak like evil, or
hear like evil as we had thought we knew it. It no longer wears horns;
instead it wears the face of banality, of everyday normality; and "this
normality," as Arendt emphasized, "was much more terrifying than
all the atrocities put together, for it implied . . . that this new type of
criminal . . . commits crimes under circumstances that make it
well-nigh impossible for him to know or to feel that he is doing
wrong."[4] The new face of evil—blandly ordinary, commonplace,
sincere—is not even a mask: for no mask is needed where there is
nothing to hide, no guilt or shame, no awareness of sin. Thus President Richard Nixon, after the entire sordid and vicious skein of
Watergate-related crimes had come unraveled, could go on television
to announce to the American people: "I am not a crook." And thus a
young convicted murderer, when asked whether he was sorry for his
deed, could respond: "Am I sorry? Are you nuts? Of course I'm sorry.
You think I like being locked up?"[5]

Along with its new face, evil has acquired a new voice. Modern sin,
as Lyman has observed, no longer speaks with the sibilant and seductive serpent's tongue: "It speaks in monotones, impersonally, technically, without apparent feeling or moral recognition . . ."[6] It may
relate atrocities, either inflicted or imagined; but it adopts the accents
of a recorded answering service or a routine weather report. The
reason is that, knowing no evil, this voice speaks no evil; all matters
are equally trivial, and all events (tomorrow's weather or yesterday's
murder) are equally unimportant. Erich Fromm, reporting on his
psychoanalytic experience with what he terms the "necrophilous"
(death-oriented) personality, had this to say:

> A somewhat less identifiable trait of the necrophilous per-
> son is the particular kind of lifelessness in his conversation.
> This is not a matter of what the conversation is about. A very
> intelligent, erudite necrophilous person may talk about things
> that would be very interesting were it not for the way in
> which he presents his ideas. He remains still, cold, aloof; his
> presentation of the subject is pedantic and lifeless.[7]

Even on the subject of greatest interest to him, the delivery or
fantasy of death, he speaks with unaltered banality. Here is a charac-

teristic conversation, from the transcript of a psychologist's interview with a fourteen-year-old boy who had murdered a woman by setting her on fire (to collect a "commission" of $500):

Q. Did you have a good night's sleep?
A. Yeah.
Q. In the morning, what happened then? . . . Did you feel upset at all, after you had poured gasoline on the woman and she burned to a crisp?
A. No. She didn't burn to a crisp.
Q. She didn't burn to a crisp?
A. No. She lived a week before she died. It was just like on every other day . . .
Q. Did you cry afterwards?
A. No. To tell you the truth, I had no feeling after I did it.
Q. No feelings at all?
A. No, I forgot all about it until they caught me.[8]

A slight variation on this voice of banality, one which allows for a touch of affect, is that of the technician of the killing ground who discusses his trade openly with evident pride in his professional skills. Thus G. Gordon Liddy, unrepentant mastermind of the Watergate caper and other more lethal feats of derring-do, tells in his autobiography of the pleasures of apprenticeship as a G-man:

At the FBI Academy I enjoyed two kinds of training the most: firearms and "defensive tactics." The latter was a blend of the more lethal techniques of several martial arts . . . I learned how to take a gun away from anyone foolish enough to hold it close enough for me to reach it, and to tear off his trigger finger in the bargain. I learned to kill a man immediately with no more than a pencil; to maim, to blind, and, generally, to employ my body's "personal weapons" against an opponent's "vulnerable areas."[9]

These are, of course, extreme versions of the dehuman syndrome—the mental state of the individual whose self-dehumanization has reached a point of such virulence that it feeds on the dehumanization of others. The alienated stranger who has become so estranged from himself and the world that he no longer feels a human emotion still strives for a human response—if only that of revulsion and outrage. In his absurdist novel, *The Stranger,* Albert Camus dramatized the condition of the outsider whose retreat from humanity is so complete that he can murder without hesitation and without feeling—other than the hope that his act may gain for him at last the recognition he has been denied. "For all to be accomplished," he says at the end, "for me to feel less lonely, all that remained to hope was that on the day of my execution there should be a huge crowd of spectators and that they should greet me with howls of execration."[10]

Bored to Death

In his sociological analysis of the Seven Deadly Sins—sloth, lust, anger, pride, envy, gluttony, and greed—Lyman has devoted particular attention to the cardinal sin of sloth. The term "sloth," he points out, was originally a medieval translation of the Latin word *acedia* (or *accidie* in Middle English), meaning essentially "without care." Physically, *acedia* connotes the familiar traits of "slothfulness": indolence, laziness, indifference to work. But there is much more to it than that. Psychologically, *acedia* or sloth is characterized by a number of symptoms centering upon *affectlessness,* defined as "a lack of any feeling about self or other, a mind-state that gives rise to boredom, rancor, apathy, and a passive inert or sluggish mentation."[11] To be without affect is to know no affection, to have no sympathy, to owe no loyalty and admit no obligation—either to others or to oneself. In this state of inertia, of suspended motivation, the victim of sloth becomes the archetypal drifter, both mentally and socially adrift, rootless, self-exiled, "wandering forever and the earth again" (in Thomas Wolfe's phrase). Lacking purpose, his slothful movement becomes mere motion; unable to find direction, he seeks only distraction. As Lyman points out, the characteristic attribute of this cardinal sin, and the most potentially destructive, is *boredom.* "It is in the variety of individual and collective outbursts that boredom produces the many faces of its peculiar evil," he writes. "Boredom finds its quintessential feeling in the anguishing sense that one is 'full of emptiness,' possessed by a longing that knows no object, and indeed converted from being to nothingness."[12]

Boredom, however, may be too mild and mundane a term for this modern sickness of the soul. Michael Selzer, in his graphic survey of the seventies' pop-cultural styles in depravity and violence, *Terrorist Chic,* has concluded that the proliferation of degradation cultists and cheap-thrill afficionados in America heralds an ominous downward turn in modern culture—a radical deterioration of civility and sensibility which has gone beyond mere boredom or ennui to a near-cataleptic state of consciousness which he designates the "anorexia of experience": an incapacity to absorb experience, accept commitment, or sustain relationship beyond the immediate moment. Desensitized to the normal range of feelings, overdosed on sensual stimulation, beyond even the pretense of caring, the subjects of Selzer's informal case histories have one by one turned to scenarios of pain and cruelty—inflicted, imbibed, or simulated—as a last desperate device to restore, if only momentarily, the sense of being alive.

> The terrorists, and Terrorist Chic too, now appear as products of a phenomenon far more dangerous than the boredom engendered by bourgeois monotony and affluence, merely. Boredom can be appeased by something interesting. *The incapacity to find anything interesting*—that is to say, the incapacity to experience—is, however, a condition for which no remedy appears available. Boredom may be a product of the industrial revolution. The condition we are talking about here, though, is a product of postindustrial society—of modernity.[13]

For some of these dis-interested and dis-eased individuals, the inability to absorb experience or to find a focus in reality appears to be related to the condition of cognitive dissonance which social psychologists have traced to the breakdown of mental powers of information-processing in an age of massive and massaging media. When the weight and profusion of sensory input overloads the circuits of the brain, information turns into *noise*—a blooming, buzzing confusion of signals which has the effect of what was once called a "narcotizing dysfunction." Thus one of Selzer's subjects, an avant-garde photographer with a penchant for the art of violence, declares that ordinary reality which lacks sensation "has a very numbing effect on me, and I like to feel I'm alive. I like to have things poking at me, and making me feel, like, Christopher, wake up, you're alive!" The interview continues:

"Is that why you're involved with violence?"

"The seventies is a period of great physical violence, but also of emotional violence—there's so much of that around. I need constant probing by my friends and people and lovers to tell me that life is real interesting and that there is no need to chuck it all away, and that it is worth living." . . .

"But why have you gone in this particular direction?"

"Because it keeps me awake. I'm just always in a zombie state, it's hard for me to keep awake because I'm numbed by the TV and the magazines and everything else. It hypnotizes me. I find myself reading *People* magazine and wasting time reading shit like that. Wasting time watching some TV show that draws me in. It's, like, my way of escaping from all that input and information coming at me from all around, but it's just as hypnotizing in its own way, which is actually much worse than the effect of real life. So between the real world and that crap I find myself like a zombie. Sometimes I let myself be beaten. I don't really like that, but it wakes me out of a zombie state. . . . I don't really like it, because it hurts; but that's not actually the main thing, because sometimes it goes beyond that and then I realize I'm awake and that's fine . . ."[14]

It is fine, for the moment, to realize one is awake—no matter how painful or humiliating the stimulus—but as it turns out even this apparent awakening is only another illusion and diversion, a slightly altered state of unconsciousness. "For while he needs these stimuli to make him feel alive and awake," as Selzer remarks, "the more he obtains of them the less alive and awake he actually feels, and he ends up, as he expressed it, being 'lulled' and 'hypnotized' by them."[15] His reference to himself as a zombie is peculiarly appropriate; for in West Indian folklore (and in the recycled fakelore of American popular culture), a zombie was a human corpse raised from the grave by a sorcerer or supernatural power and made to walk the earth, like the somnambulist of Dr. Caligari's cabinet, seeking to bring to others the death it craves for itself.

The familiar cycle of life-imitating-art-imitating-life is nowhere more strikingly evident than in this resurrection of the zombie—the return of the living dead—to the theater of popular drama and the stage of social reality. On one side is the conspicuous trend within the behavioral sciences toward the identification and analysis of increasing numbers of alienated human beings, inhabiting various classes of society, in such terms as "the living dead" (Yablonsky); "corps of living corpses, legions of zombies" (Lyman); necrophiliacs consumed by "a passionate attraction to all that is dead, decayed, putrid, sickly . . . the passion to transform that which is alive into something unalive" (Fromm).[16] On the other side there is the enormously successful career of the zombie, the living dead, in popular films. While this dehuman creature had numerous antecedents in earlier movies—in the form of vampires, golems, somnambulists, and assorted monsters—the figure of the zombie first appeared on the screen in the 1930s and became a B-movie staple in the following decade (e.g., Val Lewton's *I Walked With a Zombie*). The immense popularity of this Caribbean version of the "undead," the walking corpse, found reflection in a host of absurdist cinematic spinoffs (such as *Zombies on Broadway*), provided a new word for Webster's Dictionary and a name for a potent rum punch, gave way in the fifties to more novel variations on the same theme (notably *Invasion of the Body Snatchers*), and underwent a powerful revival in the late sixties in the form of director George Romero's cult-classical *Night of the Living Dead*—a movie of such potent shock effect that it inspired an even more ghoulish sequel in the seventies (*Dawn of the Dead*). We shall have more to say about the contemporary cinema of terror and violence in Chapter Six; for present purposes the relevance of the zombie is in the coincidence of its arrival as a phenomenon of popular culture at the same time as social pathologists were discovering the term as a metaphor to describe a new and spreading type of deviant personality—a dehumanized human who has arisen not from the rural graveyard but from the urban junkyard, the accidental waste product of the asphalt jungle, the neon wilderness, and the air-conditioned nightmare. The discovery of the real-life zombie was not merely a case of life (and social science) imitating art; rather it was the other way around. The dramatistic image of the living and walking dead, today as forty years ago, derives its power to fascinate, its dreadful credibility, from the *frisson* of recognition it evokes in us.

For it is not only in our nightmares that we have seen these empty faces and rigid forms before: we have seen them on the street, in broad daylight, as faces in the crowd, strangers on a bus, anonymous figures in the background of the cityscape. They exist in fact, they are really out there; but in their lifelessness, their absence of affect and their vacancy of expression they assume an air of unreality, like manikins or marionettes. The illusion of their being the "living dead" is not pure fantasy; they correspond in actuality to our deepest human intuition of their nature and their portent. Thus Lyman, referring to the proliferation in our midst of "asocial formations of strangers, marginal men, disaffiliated persons, lonely crowds, and uprooted masses" who share an attenuation of the normal human capacity for feeling, observes:

> These people are not dead in the conventional sense, nor indeed are they very likely to kill themselves in acts of release from a dreadful ennui. However, they might form corps of living corpses, legions of zombies, who, because of their defection from living, prey upon those who have not yet fallen into the cavern of contemporary despair.[17]

The Automation of Humanity

The dehuman syndrome, as it has become increasingly manifest in postmodern society, has come under scrutiny by various students of social pathology. Marxist critics have tended to regard it as the contemporary expression of their classical theory of the alienation of labor under capitalism—the separation of the worker from the product, and the reward, of his labor.[18] Freudian analysts have been disposed to relate the condition to individual life-histories involving narcissism, infantile regression, and instinctual aggression (Thanatos).[19] Sociologists in the tradition of Durkheim, Weber and Simmel have emphasized the salient characteristics (bureaucratic organization and individual atomization) of industrial mass society.[20] Through all of these differing approaches, there has run a common thread of explanation which may be summarily described as *technological dehumanization*: i.e., the reduction of men to machines.

It is an old apprehension, to be sure, older even than the industrial world—and one that has furnished a recurrent theme of fantasy and science fiction ever since Mary Wollstonecraft Shelley entertained her circle of emigré English esthetes in 1818 with a nightmare vision of the first "cyborg" (cybernetic organism). The wider and more subtle influences of the technological imperative upon human nature and conduct will be examined in Chapter Two. What concerns us here is the pathology of mechanization, and specifically the emergence of a new type of social character which appears to be not so much deviant as *mutant*—an organic combination of man and machine. It is this freak product of cultural evolution to which sociologist Lewis Yablonsky has given the apt name of "robopath." The creatures of a society which worships mechanical efficiency, regularity and predictability, robopaths are individuals "whose pathology entails robot-like behavior and existence . . . they are people who simulate machines."[21]

If the robopaths among us were few in number, or if they were only the harmless swarmers of the lonely crowd, there might be reason for humane concern but little cause for alarm. But the apprehension of social scientists like Yablonsky is that their growing incidence in the population is taking on the proportions of an epidemic—and, what is still more disturbing, that their characteristic behavior is marked by hostility, acompassion, and aggression. In short, the robopaths are not only machine-like in their behavior: they are walking engines of destruction. "In a society of robopaths," declares Yablonsky, "violence reaches monstrous proportions, wars are standard accepted practice, and conflict abounds."[22] Moreover, the condition of robopathology is seen to be so rampant as to suggest that it may become the "classic disease of this era"—a contemporary variant on the established modern disorders of neurosis, psychosis, and sociopathology. "The twenty-first century," Yablonsky warns, "may be characterized by an epidemic of robopathology."[23]

As suggested earlier, a common trait of the robopathic personality is automaton behavior—rigidly conformist, compulsively orderly and efficient, unemotional and unspontaneous, and unquestioningly obedient to authority. Thus, as Yablonsky puts it, "robopaths are efficient functionaries and bureaucrats. They meld into social machines, as functional cogs, in part because as [Karl] Capek stated, 'they never think of anything new and they have no soul.'"[24] Whatever the authority they obey or the cause in which they enlist, they can be relied upon to carry out any command and to perform any act to which they are assigned without reservation, reflection, or remorse. They may be ordered by their superior officer, as was Lieutenant William Calley, to "waste" an entire Vietnamese village—including infants, the old and the infirm. It is all in the day's work:

> I did not sit down and think in terms of men, women and children. They were all classified the same, and that was the classification we dealt with—just so many enemy soldiers. I felt then, and I still do, that I acted as I was directed, and I carried out the orders that I was given, and I do not feel wrong in doing so . . .[25]

They may be commanded by their leader, in this case Charles Manson, to invade a Hollywood home not previously known to them and murder all of its occupants:

> Q. "Did Tex tell you why you four were going to Terry Melcher's former residence?"
>   Matter-of-factly, with no emotion whatsoever, Susan [Atkins] replied, "To get all of their money and to kill whoever was there."
> Q. "It didn't make any difference who was there, you were told to kill them; is that correct?"
> A. "Yes."[26]

Or they may, like Gordon Liddy, be awaiting instructions from appropriate government officials to kill a bothersome journalist (Jack Anderson) and/or a former CIA official (Philip Agee) who had tattled on the Company. In the case of Liddy, the thought processes are coolly rational:

> I also fail to see any distinction between killing an enemy soldier in time of declared war and killing an enemy espionage agent in a "cold" war, or even killing certain U.S. citizens. For example, were I back in my ODESSA position and were given the instruction from an appropriate officer of the government, I would kill Philip Agee if it were demonstrated (as it has often been argued) that his revelations have led directly to the death of at least one of his fellow CIA officers, that he

intended to continue the revelations, and that they would lead to more deaths. Notice that this killing would not be retributive but preventive. It is the same rationale by which I was willing to obey an order to kill Jack Anderson. But I would do so only after satisfying myself that it was: (a) an order from legitimate authority; (b) a question of *malum prohibitum*; and (c) a rational response to the problem.[27]

The strange career of G. Gordon Liddy, related in graphic and meticulous detail in his autobiography, is a case very much in point. This self-appointed hit man for CREEP (the Committee to Re-Elect the President) embodies more obviously than most the characteristics of what Erich Fromm has labeled the "monocerebral orientation" to life. "This cerebral-intellectual approach," according to Fromm, "goes together with the absence of an affective response." In such people feelings are reduced to the crude form of passions, "such as the passion to win, to prove superior to others, to destroy, or the excitement in sex, speed, and noise." And something more:

> The monocerebral man is characterized by another very significant feature; a special kind of narcissism that has as its object himself—his body and his skill—in brief, himself as an instrument of success. The monocerebral man is so much part of the machinery that he has built, that his machines are just as much the object of his narcissism as he is himself . . . In a symbolic sense it is not nature any more that is man's mother but the "second nature" he has built, the machines that nourish and protect him.[28]

The Mechanical Will of G. Gordon Liddy

When Gordon Liddy was a small child he regarded himself as a weakling and a coward, afraid of nearly everyone. What turned his fears into shame, and his shame into self-loathing, was Liddy's sense that his cowardice was somehow a betrayal of the family honor—that tradition of brave deeds rehearsed in his mother's bedtime reminiscences and heroically embodied in his earliest role model, Uncle Ray, who had battled his own way up from the streets through college and law school to a reputation as one of the bravest of J. Edgar Hoover's G-men. Resolving to shed his shameful self-image, little Gordon embarked upon a systematic campaign to make himself strong, fearless, and combat-ready. As it turned out this was to be a lifelong campaign, full of bold triumphs but never quite satisfactorily resolved; there would somehow always be need of further proofs and tougher tests. Liddy's best-selling autobiography, *Will*, published in 1980, is the detailed record of that continuous effort to prove his manliness—to himself, to his family, to his comrades in the field, to his implacable foes lurking in the shadows, to J. Edgar Hoover, to Attorney General John Mitchell (whom he was to call "General"), to President Richard Nixon (his ultimate role model), and to the world.

Liddy's education in self-mastery began in parochial school, where the nuns introduced him to *authority*. "First, God. And then: the flag." The daily ceremony of pledging allegiance to the flag was an event of dignity and precision.

> We stood at rigid attention, facing the flag in lines straight enough to rival those of the massed SS in Leni Riefenstahl's *Triumph of the Will*. . . . At the words *to the flag* we shot out our right arms in unison, palms down, straight as so many spears aimed directly at the flag. It was the salute of Caesar's legions, recently popular in Germany, Italy, and Spain.[29]

The act did wonders for the boy Liddy; not only did he enjoy the mass salute but he soon became unexcelled in the speed of his thrust and the iron steadiness of his arm. The habit became so ingrained, he tells us, that in later life whenever the pledge has been recited or the anthem played he has had to suppress an urge to snap out his right arm.

Not surprisingly, Gordon soon discovered his real childhood hero, one even more impressive than his G-man uncle: Adolf Hitler. Told about the Fuehrer by a German housemaid in the mid-thirties, he began to listen (against his father's wishes) to Nazi broadcasts and especially to Hitler's speeches. "He sent an electric current through my body and, as the massive audience thundered its absolute support and determination, the hair on the back of my neck rose and I realized suddenly that I had stopped breathing."[30] The example of Hitler had a particular inspiration for Liddy; if the Fuehrer could raise an entire nation out of weakness and fear to strength and glory, then Gordon could do the same for himself. First he must face down his fears, one by one, and master them. "*Suffering. That was the key.*" Through enduring suffering and conquering his fears, he "would build incredible willpower! The world opened up to me. *I could become anything I wanted to be!* The thought took my breath away."[31]

One of the childhood fears which Liddy undertook to conquer was of awesome mechanical forces, such as those contained in the great dirigibles and steam locomotives still prevalent in the thirties. Though frightened he was fascinated by these great machines and drawn to their Moloch-like powers, wishing he could be like them and imbibe their terrible force. He confronted them directly, first the dirigible and then the locomotives, standing virtually in the path of their roaring engines, trying to breathe their power into his own body and soul.

> What extraordinary power they had! Machines could go on forever. They never got tired, never hurt, just kept putting out all that power, day after day, week after week, year after year, world without end, amen. A flash of inspiration struck me. *I would make myself into a machine.*[32]

And so he did. He began to run long distances, forcing himself through thresholds of pain. When his lungs felt as if they had burst he kept repeating, over and over, "I am a machine, a machine feels no pain. I am a machine, a machine, a machine." He imagined the roar of a locomotive and ran on until he "ran out of fuel," just like a machine. Deliberately, through the autoconditioning process of self-hypnosis, he was reconstructing himself in the form of a robot.

Another of Liddy's childhood fears was of rats, which he dealt with in a style that was to become characteristic. Encountering a dead rat one day, he devised a test that would dispel his fear of the rodents forever. First he made a little fire; then he carried out his plan.

> For the next hour, I roasted the dead rat. Then I removed the burned carcass with a stick and let it cool. With a scout knife I skinned, then cut off and ate the roasted haunches of the rat. The meat was tasteless and stringy. Finished, I dismantled the

little fireplace and buried the rest of the carcass. . . . I smiled as the thought occurred to me: from now on rats could fear *me* as they feared cats; after all, I ate them too.[33]

But there was still a problem, not of fear any longer but of *feeling*—of human emotion. The young Liddy discovered one day, after shooting a squirrel in a rather messy way, that there was a residue of sentiment connected with the kill. That would never do for an efficient machine, especially a killing machine. "I was furious with myself," he writes, "not because I'd caused the pain, though I regretted that, but because I hadn't been able to kill without emotion. How could I expect to be a soldier in the war? I had to do something to free myself from this disabling emotionalism." He found the answer just across the street, where a neighbor was raising and butchering chickens for the market. Liddy eagerly volunteered to help slaughter the animals. At first he was a clumsy killer; but he persevered in his steadfast way until he achieved a cool mechanical perfection of the art:

> I got better at it, and over a period of time I killed and killed and killed, getting less and less bloody, swifter and swifter, surer with my ax stroke until, finally, I could kill efficiently and without emotion or thought. I was satisfied; when it came my turn to go to war, I would be ready. I could kill as I could run—like a machine.[34]

Through later years Liddy continued to harden his will and sharpen his mettle, by imposing on himself a succession of tests to resist pain. A favored technique, gleaned from the wisdom of the East, was that of burning himself for increasing periods of time—first with lighted cigarettes, then with matches and candles. Soon he was exhibiting small permanent scars. "Still I persisted, always using my left hand and forearm so as never to incapacitate my right—my gunhand." Finally, after burning a finger so severely he almost lost its use, he gave up the exercise; but it had served its purpose. "Since my will was now so strong I could endure a long, deep, flesh-charring burn without a flicker of expression, I wasn't concerned. . . . I was ready for anything." Years later Liddy's little trick of playing with fire came in handy when he wished to convince an attractive young woman of his ability to keep a confidence, no matter what.

> I told her to light her cigarette lighter and hold it out. She did and I locked my gaze upon her eyes and placed my hand, palm down, over the flame. Presently the flesh turned black and when she smelled the scent of burning meat, Sherry Stevens broke from my gaze and pulled the lighter away from my hand. She seemed frightened badly so I took pains to calm her, wrapping an ice cube against the burn with a napkin and returning to my dinner.[35]

It was not only Gordon Liddy's will that was being systematically mechanized; it was his heart as well. When it became time for him to select a wife, mere rationality was not sufficient; this existential decision must be guided by biological science and statistical probability. He analyzed his prospective mate with the same "mathematical precision" that had been brought to bear by the fictional Captain Queeg of *The Caine Mutiny* in solving the mystery of the stolen strawberries.[36] The young woman's ancestry (Dutch-Irish) checked out, and her parents possessed the appropriate physical and intellectual credentials; she herself was a veritable Rhine maiden. When he had garnered the necessary vital statistics, writes Liddy, "I knew she was the woman I wanted to bear my children. A Teuton/Celt of high intelligence, a mathematical mind, physical size, strength, and beauty, she had it all. I fell in love."[37]

Love was not enough, of course. Production was all-important. Liddy embarked on a program of producing six children in six years. Why so many? The answer was a combination of probability statistics and a guard against the contingency of having to throw out a weakling from the litter. Liddy reckoned that "children can be lost to sickness, accident, or war and six would raise substantially the probability that at least some offspring would survive. Just as important, I recognized that a child can lose itself through failure of the will to achieve and that having six would make it easier to accept and write off such a living death as well."[38] But he eventually decided, out of consideration for the maternal machinery, to slow down the production rate: "Although one of the reasons I had chosen Frances to be the mother of my children was her size and strength, which should have enabled her to bear half a dozen high-performance children, I certainly had not intended to risk damage by pushing her to design limit."[39]

Liddy's adventurous career, as the world knows, culminated in his employment by CREEP to engage in a succession of undercover "tricks" which were not merely dirty but frequently lethal—at least in intention. Despite the tone of braggadocio that marks his autobiography, and the conspicuous emphasis on his efficiency and rationality, the evidence of Liddy's own narrative reveals him to have been an almost total bungler and nearly as much a fool as he was a knave. The image of the overly diligent and dedicated sleuth that emerges from these pages bears a distinct resemblance, not to Sherlock Holmes or James Bond, but to Peter Sellers' preposterous Inspector Clouseau. Virtually none of Liddy's devious and painstaking schemes for the break-in of offices, the purloining of documents and the destruction of files, the demolition of buildings, the killing of some enemies and the drugging or disgracing of others, worked out according to plan. The most notorious of them—the Watergate break-in and the burglary of the office of Daniel Ellsworth's psychiatrist—not only backfired completely but failed to turn up the slightest incriminating evidence. Many of Liddy's scenarios were too outrageous even for the White House Plumbers to stomach; others simply flopped or fizzled out. There is something absurd and ludicrous—enhanced by Liddy's solemnly self-serving narration—about the antic plots of his motley gang of spooks (significantly code-named ODESSA: "It appealed to me because when I organize, I am inclined to think in German terms and the acronym was also used by a World War II German veterans organization belonged to by some acquaintances of mine, Organisation Der Emerlingen Schutz Staffel Angehörigen: ODESSA").[40] This band of unmerry pranksters were like nothing so much as "Yippies" of the Right: morally if not mentally retarded adolescents psyched up on the sowing of mischief and the spreading of confusion among His Majesty's Disloyal Opposition.

The black humor of the Liddy gang's conspiracies and capers is as irresistible as it was unintended. Thus, for example, when it was decided to "get" the columnist Jack Anderson because of his exposures of CIA activities, Liddy confides to us that one of his group (the secret agent and novelist E. Howard Hunt) "urged the use of LSD on the steering wheel of the 'target's' automobile to cause him to hallucinate at a public function and thus be discredited." But this neat trick was not to come off, because, as Liddy tells us in his deadpan way, "Dr. Gunn shot down that idea on the ground that CIA experience with the drug had demonstrated the unpredictability of individual reaction."[41] The exquisitely named Dr. Gunn did not, however, "shoot down" Liddy's suggestion of the final solution of the Anderson problem ("the logical and just solution")—i.e., that "the target be killed. Quickly." The only problem was choosing among a host of ingenious murder techniques. Among those discussed and reluctantly discarded was "Aspirin Roulette"—the smuggling of a poisoned headache tablet into the target's medicine cabinet. Another, suggested by the ghoulish Dr. Gunn, "involved catching the target's moving automobile in a turn or sharp curve and hitting it with another car on the outside rear quarter. According to Dr. Gunn's mathematical calculations, "if the angle of the blow and the relative speeds of the two vehicles were correct, the target vehicle would flip over, crash, and, usually, burn."[42] It was finally decided, rather unimaginatively, simply to have Anderson murdered on the street by obliging Cubans and make it look like an ordinary everyday mugging fatality. Liddy was also willing, he tells us, to do the job himself. But in the end all of the brainstorming and game-planning was in vain; Liddy's superiors over at CREEP got cold feet and canceled the contract.

Liddy went on to mastermind the Watergate caper and other botched pieces of skullduggery, to get caught and convicted, to serve four years in a variety of challenging prison situations, and following parole to embark upon a lucrative new career as an author and lecturer—especially in demand on college campuses where large numbers of students, to whom Watergate and the Nixon presidency are already matters of historical folklore, have come to regard him as a kind of real-life incarnation of the legendary vigilante-enforcer portrayed repeatedly on the screen by Clint Eastwood and Charles Bronson.

As to how G. Gordon Liddy regards himself, if any doubt remains, the following excerpt from his autobiography provides an unambiguous answer. It describes a scene in the courtyard of Danbury prison following a legal skirmish in which prisoner-lawyer Liddy had bested the warden and the associate warden, both of whom were disliked by the inmates.

It was after working hours when I approached the rear of the grandstand from which softball and other games in the prison yard are watched. I was greeted and hailed by passersby for the victory. . . . About thirty black prisoners were congregated behind the grandstand and on nearby benches. When the black men saw me they grinned and raised their fists in salute, shouting, "Hey, hey!" The closer I got the more excited they became and when I was upon them some were on their feet, right arms and fists outstretched, shouting. A feeling of immense power came over me. The martial music and roaring crowds that thundered through the shortwave forty years before rang through my mind again with undiminished strength as I answered the blacks' salute with the one I'd learned before the American flag so long ago in 1938: my right arm shot out, palm down, and was answered by a roar of approval. In that moment I felt like a god.[43]

The Pathology of Obedience

The dehuman syndrome—with its atrophy of feeling, obsessive concern for efficiency and rationality, and compulsive obedience to authority—is most clearly identifiable in the virulent stages of the disorder, when there appear to be few limits to the actions a "robopath" will venture in the service of what he takes to be his mandate, his mission, or his orders. If he is (in Yablonsky's term) a robopathic leader—like Adolf Hitler, Charles Manson, or the Rev. Jim Jones—he possesses what Oriental tradition called a "mandate from heaven" and what Western tradition knew as "divine right"; he has internalized the source of authority and is obedient to its inner voice. If he is a robopathic follower, much the commoner form—like Adolf Eichmann, Lt. Calley, Gordon Liddy, and the members of the Manson family—he is only doing what he takes to be his duty; he is obeying orders, following instructions to the letter, carrying out legitimate commands to the best of his ability. Given the appropriate symbols and trappings of authority, as in the soothing bureaucracy of the "chain of command," he is freed to perform his instrumental role with efficiency, skill, and a clear conscience—which is to say that he has delegated his conscience to higher authority and is automatically relieved of the distressing questions of moral responsibility and individual choice. Within these secure parameters he may still exercise considerable ingenuity and take genuine pride in his accomplishments; his highest aspiration is to be a "good soldier" and to be so recognized. His moral sense has not been abandoned but rather transformed: it has become a technical ethos, a morality of means. As the psychologist Stanley Milgram puts it:

> . . . his moral concern now shifts to a consideration of how well he is living up to the expectations that the authority has of him. In wartime, a soldier does not ask whether it is good or bad to bomb a hamlet; he does not experience shame or guilt in the destruction of a village; rather he feels pride or shame depending on how well he has performed the mission assigned to him. [44]

According to Milgram, it is not the abandonment of morality—which may be more loudly proclaimed than ever—but the abdication of responsibility for individual choice and behavior that characterizes the key problem of modern social and cultural pathology. The buck stops nowhere; acts are no longer initiated but routinely carried out. "The person who assumes full responsibility for the act has evaporated," says Milgram. "Perhaps this is the most common characteristic of socially organized evil in modern society." [45]

Milgram's own concern for the spread of nonresponsibility and compulsive conformity in American society is the outgrowth of a famous series of psychological experiments conducted under his direction at Yale University in the early 1960s. The purpose of the studies, which extended over several years and involved nearly a thousand subjects, was essentially to discover the limits of obedience (and the capacity for disobedience) to authority. Various scenarios and situations were experimented with, but the prototype setting was one in which volunteer subjects, in the role of "teachers," were induced to administer a cumulative series of supposed electric shocks to other apparent volunteers (actually trained accomplices) assigned the role of "learners." So far as the teacher-subjects were aware, the shocks they gave were real (at the outset of the experiment they watched the "learner" being strapped into an impressive-looking "electric chair"). The rationale for administering the shocks was that they were engaging in an experiment to test the effect of punishment on learning; whenever the "learner" in the next room returned wrong answers to questions from a memory test, he was to be given an electric shock, progressively more severe with each "mistake." The subject sat before an impressive board of electric switches indicating shock levels from 15 to 450 volts, in eight graded steps, with an ominous sign at 375 volts reading "Danger—Severe Shock," and with the last two switches forbiddingly marked "XXX."

In the room with the "teacher"-subject was the "experimenter" (a disguised member of the research team), appropriately garbed in a white coat, clearly representing a scientific authority figure. It was his role to instruct the subject on the procedure, to supervise his performance, and (the crux of the matter) to order him to continue the experiment and to increase the shocks whenever he should hesitate or refuse to go on. Meanwhile the "learner," out of sight in an adjoining room, provided audible feedback to the simulated shocks from a script of graduated responses ranging from mild grunts through angry protests to a final "agonized scream." At the upper level of the series of jolts the "learner" could be heard pounding on the wall and shouting, "Stop it, you're killing me!" Even then, should the subject attempt to break off, the "experimenter" would coolly instruct him to continue, resorting if necessary to the ultimate verbal prod: "You have no other choice, you *must* go on." Following his final scream of agony, the "learner" would fake unconsciousness or death by ceasing to make any sound—whereupon the subject was blandly told to count "no response" as an incorrect answer and to continue to administer shocks of lethal dosage (450 volts) to what, for all the subject knew, was the already dead body of his partner.

These contingency plans for the extreme levels of electric shock had been devised originally by Milgram for what he assumed might be a few rare cases of peculiar meanness or total lack of feeling among the volunteer subjects, who comprised a random sample of the city's population. Milgram was totally unprepared for what happened. In a typical experiment, involving forty subjects, *all forty* complied with instructions by shocking their "victims" up to a dosage of 300 volts—beyond the level of the "agonized scream." Fourteen subjects broke off at about that point; but twenty-six others, or 65 percent of the total group, continued to press the buttons and increase the shocks up to the maximum of 450 volts (well past the stage labeled "Danger: Severe Shock"). These subjects hesitated at various points; some pleaded with the experimenter to call it off, and many of them threatened to quit—but in the face of authority and repeated orders to continue, they went on to the bitter end. Milgram found their behavior both "surprising and dismaying." As the experiments developed, he began to wonder to what lengths such subjects might go at the behest of a master's voice:

> What is the limit of such obedience? At many points we attempted to establish a boundary. Cries from the victim were inserted; they were not good enough. The victim claimed heart trouble; subjects still shocked him on command. The victim pleaded to be let free, and his answers no longer registered on the signal box; subjects continued to shock him.[46]

Moreover, these subjects who were willing to shock their experimental partner unto death—to commit homicide on order—were not certified psychopaths or convict volunteers: they were "good people," ordinary law-abiding citizens drawn from a wide spectrum of classes and callings ("Typical subjects were postal clerks, high school teachers, salesmen, engineers, and laborers"). They were not driven by hate or hostility, but on the contrary expressed only compassion for the unfortunate captive they were injuring. It gave them no pleasure; they would rather not have to do it; but orders were orders, and a commitment was a commitment. (Besides, they had accepted a modest payment for their cooperation.) Someone would have to do it; it was in the interest of science; the responsibility was not really theirs but the experimenter's. "I merely went on," said one subject later: "Because I was following orders . . . I was told to go on. And I did not get a cue to stop."[47] This general attitude of almost total compliance, of reflexive conformity, led Milgram to a set of generalized conclusions which transcend the boundaries of his experimental studies. The first represents a validation of Hannah Arendt's concept of the banality of evil: "This is, perhaps, the most fundamental lesson of our study: ordinary people, simply doing their jobs, and without any particular hostility on their part, can become agents in a terrible destructive process."[48] And by lending themselves to that force of evil they also destroy a part of themselves: their autonomy, their unique identity, their humanity. For what is it finally that we have seen in these experiments, asks Milgram? It is not aggression or anger or explosions of rage, as theorists of the "naked ape" and the "imperial animal" might have predicted. No:

> Something far more dangerous is revealed: the capacity for man to abandon his humanity, indeed, the inevitability that he does so, as he merges his unique personality into larger institutional structures . . . when he merges his person into an organizational structure, a new creature replaces autonomous man, unhindered by the limitations of individual morality, freed of humane inhibition, mindful only of the sanctions of authority.[49]

We might say of this ordinary person, simply doing his job—no, not simply doing his job, but doing it as efficiently and meticulously as possible, entirely absorbed in his work, modestly proud of his skill, deferential, glad to be of use—we might say of him what Melville's obsessed Captain Ahab said of himself: "All my means are sane; my motives and object mad."

2

THE CHEERFUL ROBOT
AND THE
TECHNOCRACY
OF SEX

I N THE PRECEDING CHAPTER we encountered the spectral figure of the
"living dead," the robopathic or necrophilous personality—a peculiarly virulent strain of the dehuman syndrome which might be
given the name of the Malevolent Robot. This zombie-like creature
is, in reality as well as in fantasy, an embodiment of evil and an
apparition of terror. But the Malevolent Robot, though its breed is
increasing, is far less significant statistically than its more familiar and
commonplace sibling: the complacently diminished human identified
by sociologist C. Wright Mills in the late fifties as the "Cheerful
Robot." As the name suggests, this novel personality type—which
Mills perceived as the natural byproduct of technological society—is
characterized less by alienation and discontent than by adaptation
and contentment; he is not the disaffiliated stranger but the Organization Man. In his bland amiability and comfortable adjustment, he
might appear superficially to pose no problem at all, either to society
or to himself. Indeed his is a much more subtle form of the syndrome
of dehumanization; not only does he not wear horns, he almost seems
to wear a halo. But appearances are often deceiving; the happiest
expressions in any crowd are likely to be found on the faces of those
who have been sedated, those who are high on drugs, those who are
severely retarded, and those who have been lobotomized.

Writing at a time when social scientists were becoming newly concerned with the spread of technical organization and mechanical routine into all aspects of life, Mills was especially fearful for the survival of freedom and reason—of the autonomous individual—under the conditions of mass society and mass culture.

> We do not know how profound man's psychological transformation from The Modern Age to the contemporary epoch may be. But we must now raise the question in an ultimate form: Among contemporary men will there come to prevail, or even to flourish, what may be called the Cheerful Robot?[1]

Mills's concern was not so much for the hapless victim of coercive brainwashing, reduced to a robot state involuntarily through chemical, psychiatric, or surgical intervention. Rather he was alarmed by what he took to be an emergent type of socially adjusted and willingly compliant individual for whom both routine and the distraction from routine were not only acceptable but "meaningful"—and to whom therefore the burdensome issues of personal freedom and independent thought have become irrelevant and even vaguely suspect. "It will no longer do," wrote Mills, "merely to assume, as a metaphysic of human nature, that down deep in man-as-man there is an urge for freedom and a will to reason." Too many men have seemed prepared to shrug off their own freedom and to go willingly into the mindlessness of compulsive conformity, ritualized behavior, and automated existence. In the affluent society, under the glittering cornucopia of the national supermarket and the pervasive atmosphere of fun and games—in the alternating cycle of distraction and tranquilization—might there be a corresponding deterioration in the human capacities of reflection and resistance, of active choice and intelligent response, even of individuality itself? It was time, Mills observed, to pause in our celebration of material and technological progress and to confront the other side of the coin: the counterproductive waste products and pathogenic potentialities of technology in the field of human life.

> In our time, must we not face the possibility that the human mind as a social fact might be deteriorating in quality and cultural level, and yet not many would notice it because

of the overwhelming accumulation of technological gadgets? Is that not one meaning of rationality without reason? Of human alienation? Of the absence of any free role for reason in human affairs? The accumulation of gadgets hides these meanings. . . . That is why we may *not*, without great ambiguity, use technological abundance as the index of human quality and cultural progress.[2]

Thus Mills concluded that "the ultimate problem of freedom is the problem of The Cheerful Robot"—both to understand the conditions of his ascendancy among us and to find ways to pull the plug on the automated assembly line and reverse the engines of his manufacture.

The Man from Glad

Mills's prophetic vision of the Cheerful Robot was closely duplicated, a few years later, by the philosopher Herbert Marcuse in his own vivid image of the "Happy Consciousness"—a sort of benign cancer of the mind generated by advanced industrial society, which has had the effect of replacing the individual conscience with a programmed consciousness that resonates only to pleasurable stimuli and registers only degrees of satisfaction. This genial conditioned reflex screens out the murmurs of the still small voice, turns up the volume of the situation comedy, joins in the canned laughter, and in short is "the token of declining autonomy and comprehension."[3] The Happy Consciousness stands for the depleted state of awareness of Marcuse's famous construct of "One-Dimensional Man," a more radical and systematic formulation of Mills's affable automaton. Marcuse carried the psychobiography a step farther, maintaining that unidimensionality was the guiding principle of postindustrial society itself, which had attained the capacity to control and manipulate not only the technical resources of production but the human resources of consumption—transforming the independent citizen into a dependent consumer by deflecting genuine needs away from constructive and critical channels of expression into the vacuous maze of packaged distraction and attenuated lust. The resultant Happy Consciousness, wrote Marcuse,

reflects the belief that the real is rational, and that the established system, in spite of everything, delivers the goods. The people are led to find in the productive apparatus the effective agent of thought and action to which their personal thought and action can and must be surrendered.[4]

More than that: ". . . in this transfer, the apparatus also assumes the role of a moral agent. Conscience is absolved by reification, by the general necessity of things." In short, the real is not only rational but thoroughly admirable. The material has become the ideal; quantity is quality. The circle of necessity has been completed; the system, in delivering the goods, also delivers the Good.

There is an obvious irony in the frequent recurrence of the imagery of "gladness"—as with the happy consciousness of the cheerful robot—in the critical literature of the past generation concerned with problems of mass society and technological alienation. In his classic survey of suburban society in the fifties, *The Organization Man*, William H. Whyte, Jr. gave special attention to the "happy blocks," those ideal-typical residential groupings which were the most closely knit and which appeared to be marked by a spirit of unrelenting *Gemütlichkeit*.[5] Similarly Alan Harrington, in his autobiographical case study of an organization man, *Life in the Crystal Palace*, insisted that the 500 members of his corporation's headquarters "are a happy family. I say this without irony, not for the reason that I am in the public-relations department, but because it is the truth. We give every appearance of happiness."[6] (After three years of such euphoria, Harrington fled from the palace in a state of spiritual nausea; but on the testimony of his book few others shared his disenchantment or even understood it.)

To a superficial observer, the appearance of so much bliss (manifested in smile buttons, glad hands, team play, Muzak, and general good fellowship) might seem a convincing refutation of the downbeat findings of social scientists hooked on alienation, anomie, and *Angst* in the contemporary industrial milieu. And indeed one such observer, the pop journalist Tom Wolfe, has redefined the Happy Consciousness as the authentic spirit of good times and happy days: in his view it was not, after all, the vacant grin of the robot but the radiant expression of the free soul, liberated by technology and affluence, extending his ego and expanding his consciousness in a new enactment of rugged individualism. Writing in the late sixties (of all times), Wolfe excoriated the intellectual critics of modern life and culture who insisted on raking over stale problems of alienation, repression, poverty, war, and the like. With their eyes fixed on the gutter, he declared, they have overlooked the *real* revolution going on in front of them: the "Happiness Explosion." Everywhere Wolfe went in search of his upbeat human-interest stories, and everywhere he looked on the social scale (from the "proles" to cafe society), he found people strenuously enjoying the fruits of their newfound affluence and leisure. Even the old myth of the "happy worker," seemingly demolished by Harvey Swados a decade before,[7] was revived and rehearsed in the pages of *The Pump House Gang.* "What struck me throughout America and England," Wolfe exclaimed, "was that so many people have found such novel ways of doing just that, *enjoying,* extending their egos way out on the best terms available, namely, their own."[8] To Wolfe these were all "happy winners," whether they were merely "happy workers" (alias "the happy people"), somewhat wealthier "happy mass fops" (stylized Hair Boys of the fast-car set), or the most happy fellow of all in Wolfe's collection: multimillionaire Hugh Hefner, the Playboy King, who has elaborated a pretentious "Philosophy" of what might be called happy hedonism. Ensconced in his updated crystal palace of electronic playthings and pneumatic playgirls, Hefner proclaimed his own true happiness to Wolfe in curiously aggressive terms:

> "You know," he says, "people get the idea I'm a Barnum or something, putting on a show. People come by here, and you can tell—they want to find a flaw in it all. They want to think I can't be happy. They want to think it's got to be a lousy, unprofitable life I'm leading. Well, I can tell you something. It's a *damned full life!*"[9]

Hefner is not only the most conspicuously "happy" of Wolfe's joyful company of ego-extenders, he is also the most powerfully symbolic. For Hefner is, in Wolfe's celebrant title, "King of the Status Dropouts." What that means is that he leads an army of the newly affluent, drawn from the middle and lower-middle classes, who have opted to defy the traditional system of social ranking and status in favor of making their own rules and blazing their own trails. They are the postmodern people of plenty, the heirs of technological abundance:

They are the new middle class with few of the old Babbitt status drives; a *lumpen* middle class. . . . They have been stuck with the old European status system, the way their forebears always had been. But then—beautiful, bounteous, glorious war!—World War II started off a chain of good times and advances in electronic technology that is now enabling millions to live the full life as status dropouts: dropping out of conventional status competition in order to start their own league—in the privacy of the home, as it were.[10]

The keys to this kingdom are technology (the glittering technology of the electric age) and the money to buy it with. All of Wolfe's heroes—whether they are motorcyclists or laid-back surfers or custom-car builders or disco denizens—are really heroes of consumption; and his superheroes (like Hefner, surfboard king Hubie Alter, and record king Phil Spector) are entrepreneurs of leisure. They are pre-eminently the creatures and servitors of technological society; and although Wolfe strives in his mock-urbane manner to present them as its stars, its "happy winners," they come through almost without exception as its victims. Thus Hefner, the ridiculously rich and raffish recluse, attended by harems of bunnies and swarms of sycophants, nevertheless hides from the world and even from his entourage in an enormous rotating bed—as secure, self-contained, and vibrant as the womb—in which he acts out, over and over, the infantile, if not quite innocent, fantasies of a depraved child.

> To account for Hefner's astonishing success—well, the *Playboy* aura of sex, by itself, is not enough. One must add another picture that has been shown often enough in *Playboy*—a large, *secure* bed, settled in a windowless corner, with smooth mellow walls, in a heavy wooden frame, low, smooth, modern—surrounded by smooth mellow-wood cabinets, with sliding panels that slide back to reveal *dials*. No girls anywhere in the picture! Just paradise; a bed, a fortress of smooth wood, windowless walls, and dials.[11]

Hefner, so Wolfe tells us, not only remains holed up in his mansion for months at a time, he seldom leaves the great bedroom and its greater bed-womb. From that technological epicenter, with its star-wars console of dials and gadgets, Hefner surveys the world and commands his play-full empire. The tableau he presents is supposed to be marvelously impressive and monarchical ("a damned full life"); instead it is distinctly depressing and even morbid in its indecent exposure of a totally narcissistic personality luxuriating in his aliena- tion from the outside world, from the light of day, from ordinary reality, possibly from sanity itself. For all its illusion of glamor and persistent happy talk, this is in the end a sad story of a warped and diminished human life. It bears a striking resemblance to the self- destructive saga of that other modern mogul of the entertainment world, who also feared to leave his bed: Howard Hughes.

It should be said that Wolfe, despite his evident infatuation with the Hefner lifestyle, is not without an intuitive awareness of the absurdist side of the story, with its conspicuous overconsumption and its technological fetishism. So Wolfe ends his profile, appropriately, on a note of fantasy suggestive of what might be the ultimate journey of the Consumer King, or the King of Whirl:

> And one can almost see the ultimate—appealing!—the Con- sumer King, his smile pulled on, his eyes lit up, his head back, sinking back into the middle of the biggest, roundest bed in the history of the world, reaching his hands back . . . just a bit, to the dials, and then—
>
> . . . rrr . . . rrr . . . rrr . . .
>
> —that great bed starts turning, into an orbit of its own, with the Ampex videotape on right there, coming over the screen, a videotape of a *very beautiful thing* that happened right there in that room, at the center of the world, the perfect moment, renewed with every revolution of the bed, every revolution of a . . . *controlled* universe, with one's own self as king, dropped, not *out,* but *in,* to the perfect rotation, around and around, in ever-decreasing concentric circles, to- ward . . . nirvana, *ambrosia,* while, following one's own perfect orbit, out there, for all to see, is the . . . *Playboy beacon!*—up on top of the yes! Playboy Building, sweeping the heavens of America with the two-billion-candlepower beam of American Hefnerism and the perfect . . . bliss . . . rrr . . . rrr . . . rrr . . .[12]

The Technocracy of Sex

The symbol of the *bed,* for Hugh Hefner, is clearly a many-faceted thing. If it is first of all representative of the snug and rhythmic harbor of the womb (and last of all, one may guess, of this recluse's tomb as well), it is also more literally the electronic control center of both his industrial enterprise and his recreational enterprise (i.e., sex). The two enterprises are interrelated in various ways. Hefner's economic empire (the Playboy industry) is based on sex as commodity; while his own private indulgence in sex, on that enormous bed, is as manipulative and strategic as a management coup. Both his money-making and his love-making are exercises (apt word) of power, finesse, and expertise; and indeed they seem to give him equal, not to say equivalent, satisfaction. Hefner's mansions (in Chicago and Beverly Hills) are not-so-stately pleasure domes which are repeatedly displayed in his publications, thereby serving as models of envy and emulation by humbler devotees of the Playboy Philosophy. That philosophy itself, by the way, constitutes a kind of sexual economics; it is based squarely on the principle of laissez-faire, of winning and scoring in the flesh market, of getting and spending the accumulated capital of nature's sperm bank as though it were guaranteed by the Federal Reserve System. Hefner has succeeded, as it were, in eating his cheesecake and having it too: he has not only made a big business out of sex but he has contrived to make a sexy thing out of his business. (The early psychoanalyst Wilhelm Reich would have appreciated the Playboy Philosophy; at one time in his own career he sought to establish "sex-economic" cadres, and later on he actually marketed an Orgone Box guaranteed to produce orgasmic potency [or your psychic investment back].)[13]

In an advanced technological society, thoroughly dominated by the principles of quantification and efficiency, it is not really surprising— it is only sad—that the sphere of sexual relations, once thought to be the last bastion of human spontaneity and personal privacy, should become the laboratory for scientific experiment and technical expertise. It is not surprising because, whatever may still be said for *love* as a mystery and a noumenon, the "act of love" is a palpably physical phenomenon, a behavioral event (with a beginning, middle and end) subject to the full repertoire and paraphernalia of the psychotechnician's black bag—capable of measuring not only quantity but duration, sequence, extensity, intensity, side effects, sound effects, oscillations, palpitations, pointer readings of every kind: an audiovisual concert of galvanomic indicators. Given the combination of biological technology and behaviorist psychology, both of which were in place early in the present century, the door to the boudoir had surely to be forced open sooner or later—simply in the interest of science. To be sure, it might be claimed that the first surreptitious entry of the scientific observer into the bedroom was not that of the behaviorist but of the psychoanalyst. It was Sigmund Freud, at the turn of the century, who with his own master key opened the locked door to the secret chamber of the heart, or at least of the loins. However, the psychoanalyst did not directly observe the act of love but rather overheard it in retrospect; he was not really a voyeur but only an eavesdropper. Such second-hand carnal knowledge, further befouled by mentalist interpretations, could not satisfy the empirical curiosity of the disciples of Ivan Pavlov and John B. Watson—whose scientific faith lay in what James Joyce (not one of them) called the ineluctable modality of the visible. For the behaviorist the act of love, the physical performance, had to be *seen* to be believed—that is, to be certified, documented, compared, computed, and (the technical objective) improved upon.

The ultimate in direct frontal scanning and meticulous recording of the sequential episodes of the sexual act, in all its manifold variations and combinations, awaited the appearance in the sixties of the team of Masters and Johnson—who were to set an all-time observational record of ten thousand orgasms over ten years. But the foundations of modern "sexology" had been prepared many decades earlier, by researchers in Europe and America seeking to extend the mechanistic assumptions of biology and physiological psychology to the sphere of sexuality. Each nation, as Stephen Kern has wryly noted in *Anatomy and Destiny,* appears to have made its contribution to the new science along lines consistent with popular notions concerning national character. Thus the Germans were the most systematic, comprehensive and relentless in their investigations—led by the redoubtable Richard von Kraft-Ebing—and in effect inaugurated the science of sex through the coinage of the term *Sexualwissenschaft* (by Iwan Bloch in 1906). The romantic French, with a few notable exceptions (such as Charles Féré and Alfred Binet), preferred to regard the subject of love-making as an art best interpreted and appreciated by their own great artists and writers (like Rousseau, Balzac, Zola, Rodin, and Proust). "The English," remarks Kern, "produced a great number of empirical and practical 'how to do it' manuals for young men and women."[14] And the Americans, as we shall see, perfected both the statistical method and the experimental approach which were to lead to the immensely influential and problematic contributions of Alfred Kinsey and his successors Masters and Johnson.

From the beginning there was a dual purpose to the scientific study of sexuality; it sought to be both pure and applied, theoretical and therapeutic. On one side, it held that human sexuality, as a biological function, warranted a degree of scientific specialization comparable to that accorded the eye, ear, nose and throat. On the other side, there was a strong technological imperative—a zeal to increase productivity and efficiency, to optimize performance and maximize input and output through the application of technique. In America especially, with its competitive ethic of success and its cult of popular mechanics, the science of sexology could not long remain pure and disinterested; it progressed irresistibly toward the development of an applied technology of sexual prowess and achievement ("a bigger bang for a buck"). This thoroughly practical and strategic approach to the most intimate of personal relations received its penultimate reinforcement at mid-century with the successive publication of the Kinsey Reports on male and female sexuality. The scientific background which Professor Kinsey brought to his monumental studies of human behavior was that of an entomologist with a specialized knowledge of the habits (courting and otherwise) of the gall wasp; his lack of any training or experience whatsoever in the sciences of human behavior was widely regarded as a positive asset, since it would presumably protect him from the taint of subjective anthropomorphism and guarantee the objectivity of his researches. As it turned out the Kinsey Reports exceeded the expectations of the most rigorous of experimental psychologists and zoologists; he and his associates were as scrupulously detached in their observations as they were mathematically elegant in their charts and measurements. It might be said that nothing sexual was alien to them; when their work was done virtually no twist or turn of human sexual activity was left unclassified, no practice unrecorded, no spasm uncounted. What Freud had qualified, Kinsey quantified.

The public was enchanted. Both Kinsey Reports, despite their formidable textbook character and their dense thicket of statistics and technical formulations, were immediate bestsellers, and Professor Kinsey became an overnight celebrity—somewhat on the order of Pasteur, Madame Curie, and the Dr. Ehrlich of the Magic Bullet. It seemed a great victory for science, a pioneering breakthrough in the unraveling of the mysteries of sex. But in reality the "Kinsey revolution" was something less than that, and something more; the significant innovations contained in the Reports were not scientific (their findings were incremental rather than novel) but sociological, cultural, and moral. Kinsey presented his researches as entirely disinterested and unbiased, as "objective data" and an "accumulation of scientific fact," as merely a "report on what people do, which raises no question of what they should do." But, of course, the Reports, with their enormous and enduring popular vogue, did raise the question of what people should do (in or out of bed)—and answered the question in decisive terms. The Kinsey Reports were not the first shot in the modern sexual revolution (Havelock Ellis and Freud share the credit for that); but they represented a landmark in the struggle to liberate sexual behavior alike from the morality of puritanism (guilt) and the mythology of romanticism (love). For the essence of Kinsey's answer to the question of what people should do was simply: if it feels good, do it—the oftener the better, the more the merrier, any which way you can. As Lionel Trilling observed in his classic analysis of the first Kinsey volume, "the Report is partisan with sex, it wants people to have a good sexuality. But by good it means nothing else but frequent."[15] Kinsey's sober-sided tomes, in fact, provided the empirical counterpart, the scientific validation, of the Playboy Philosophy of Hugh Hefner. And if Kinsey, like Hefner, helped to remove the dark shrouds of guilt and shame from the domain of sexual expression, he also helped to dissipate its atmosphere of tenderness, caring, and concern. He accomplished the depersonalization of sex.

He did so by first reducing quality to quantity—and then, by a greater alchemy, converting quantity into quality. The first operation was straightforward enough, following a well-established behaviorist method (known to humanistic philosophers as the Reductionist Fallacy, or the flimflam of Nothing But). Sexual intercourse was defined strictly in quantitative terms as a form of physical behavior, no more and no less; feelings became states of excitation, context was perceived as duration, and relationship was reduced to coupling. The total experience of what an earlier generation had known as intimate relations was nothing but these measurable reactions and reflexes. (What was good enough for the gall wasp, as someone remarked of the second Report, was good enough for the gal WASP.) The voluminous statistics were indeed impressive, even startling; each of the two Reports was greeted by the public as a Book of Revelation. Long before the crasser opportunism of Dr. David Reuben, Americans learned from Dr. Kinsey everything they always wanted to know about sex—except its human dimension. They learned, for example, that the average American husband had achieved 1,523 orgasms before marriage and the average wife 223; in short, there were no equal rites in premarital sex. It was also learned that 6.3% of all male orgasms resulted from homosexual contacts (this was the big news in 1948), 69.4% from heterosexual encounters, 24% from masturbation or nocturnal emissions, and 0.3% from contact with animals. (What was not widely recognized, though the facts were there, was that these reports on the sexual behavior of "the human male" and "the human female" were in reality only reports on the sexual behavior of a very limited and unrepresentative sample of American men and women. Not only were the findings not universally applicable, the sample populations themselves were distinctly atypical of the society from which they were drawn. Thus of Kinsey's 5,940 women subjects more than 75% had gone to college and nearly 20% had graduate training.)[16]

The net result of Kinsey's quantification of sexual experience was at once to downplay its immeasurable subjective aspects (the whole area of feeling, not to say of loving) and to place a premium on numbers, frequencies, schedules, and comparative performance. Now that the facts were in it became possible for the first time to rate one's actual prowess against the "norm"—to increase the frequency of intercourse if one was sub-par or perhaps to cut back on the action if one was conspicuously excessive. The latter option, however, was unlikely in view of Kinsey's evident enthusiasm for a quantitatively full sex life; what was more likely, for males at any rate, was a compulsion to up the ante, to seek to prove one's competence and to improve one's rating. It is noteworthy that the term "score," used as a synonym for sexual contact, came into circulation at about the same time as the Kinsey Reports. What also came into general circulation was a new degree, even a new form, of anxiety based on worry about the quantity and frequency of sexual activity. Psychoanalyst Rollo May, on the basis of his own clinical experience, observed that "couples place great emphasis on bookkeeping and timetables in their love-making—a practice confirmed and standardized by Kinsey."[17] And another psychoanalyst, John Schimel, remarked: "My patients have endured stoically, or without noticing, remarkably destructive treatment at the hands of their spouses, but they have experienced falling behind in the sexual timetable as a loss of love."[18] The result of this surrender to the technological imperative was not the hoped-for power gain of a Faustian bargain; it has insured neither greater happiness nor even heightened passion. Instead the clock-watching, technique-oriented lover finds that he is scoring more but enjoying it less. As May puts it, "the emphasis beyond a certain point on technique in sex makes for a mechanistic attitude toward lovemaking, and goes along with alienation, feelings, of loneliness, and depersonalization."[19] In his quantification and routinization of the most intimate, giving, and spontaneous act of which humans are capable, Kinsey in effect administered a national robotomy. Stephen Kern has succinctly summarized the human significance of his contribution:

> Beginning in 1948 sexual performance acquired a measurable value unprecedented in the history of human relations. The era of the scientific study of sex had culminated in a new era of the scientific experience of sex. Human sexuality became a competitive event subject to the same kinds of evaluations on the basis of speed, frequency, and endurance previously reserved for athletic events and machine production.[20]

The Pornography of Science

After Kinsey, there was only one further step to be taken before human sexuality could be said to have been brought altogether within what B. F. Skinner has proudly called the "technology of behavior." Freud had introduced systematic theory and causal explanation; Kinsey had provided empiricism and statistics; all that was needed to complete the process was direct observation and controlled experiment. In short, sex must be brought into the laboratory and *performed* there: a scientific passion play, as it were, complete with lights and cameras, producers and directors, and a cast of either one or two performers depending on the script. That, as the world knows, was the impressive achievement of Dr. William H. Masters and Mrs. Virginia A. Johnson at the Reproductive Biology Research Foundation of St. Louis, duly recorded in their books *Human Sexual Response* (1966) and *Human Sexual Inadequacy* (1970). The contribution of Masters and Johnson was not merely technical but dramatistic; in their carefully designed settings, the scientific study of sexuality became a media event.

The association of this singular research product with the dominant symbols of the audiovisual age—the photographic image, the candid camera, the X-rated movie, the technology of special effects, and the zoom-lens closeup of sexual organs—is so thoroughgoing as to warrant its being labeled the pornography of science. The daily performance of sexual theater over the ten years of the initial research project, under the direction of Masters and Johnson, contained all the essential elements of classical drama. Each morning at ten, the volunteer cast (eventually to total 382 women and 312 men) arrived on the lab "set," disrobed, reclined on a couch, and commenced either to masturbate or copulate, according to the production schedule. The ensuing action was recorded by motion picture cameras, using color film, as well as by various measuring devices including an "intrauterine electrode." (There was also another highly ingenious mechanical contraption, to be described below.) Sometimes the actors were "prepped" for the performance by exposure to erotic films and/or literature; it is not revealed whether mood music was ever employed. The element of theatricality in this highly original research is underlined by the information that many of the earliest performers recruited by Masters and Johnson were prostitutes—that is, professionals (mainly female) already trained and practiced in the arts of simulation and dissimulation. There was also drama, of an improvisational sort, implicit in the selective casting of volunteers for intercourse, who often met each other for the first time (creating the *agon* of dramatic tension) and who were frequently chosen on the basis of their reputed superordinary predilection for sex (heroic potentiality).

But the most significant theatrical component of this scientific photoplay was that it transpired within the classical formula of consecutive acts (in this case ordained as four in number), moving progressively from the prologue of foreplay to the dramatic peak of climax, followed by anticlimactic resolution and mop-up. The complete play corresponded to the cycle of human sexual response, as monitored by Masters and Johnson: the first act was defined as the excitement stage, the second act (like most second acts) as the plateau phase; the third act was, of course, "orgasm" (or the grand climacteric), and the last act was "resolution." As to the comparative quality of individual performances, although the researchers eschewed direct dramatic criticism, it is evident from their report that there were a number of star performers, as well as some who were plainly miscast as lovers. For example, there was one sixty-year-old woman who reportedly was capable of 14 to 50 orgasms in a period of 20 minutes. Moreover, "The remarkable fact was her ability to achieve full relaxation as soon as her partner did . . . . Immediately after his ejaculation she relaxed in complete satisfaction."[21]

Masters and Johnson also contrived a striking variation on the standard themes of masturbation and copulation which brought them (however unwittingly) into the company of the great directors of science-fiction cinema. Their filmed observations were sometimes made during what was termed "artificial coition—a laboratory procedure that makes accessible to direct vision and to recording on motion picture film internal changes observable in no other way."[22] This novel procedure was made possible by the construction of what one reporter has called the "great artificial coition machine," the ultimate electronic dildo—in effect, a robot lover, tireless, adjustable, and silently accommodating, an invention beyond the wildest imaginings of Jules Verne or H. G. Wells (but quite within the grasp of Kurt Vonnegut). The great artificial coition machine, according to journalist Patrick M. McGrady, Jr., was kept well hidden within the recesses of the research foundation: "Only staff and volunteers who demonstrably *had* to see it ever saw it. Casual visitors, the press, other professionals—never." It was apparently guarded like a secret weapon, which in a sense it was—the most literal rendition of the phallus-symbolism of industrial machinery ever devised. Reporter McGrady managed to penetrate the tight security and obtain a verbal picture:

> One who had seen it described it to me. The business end was a clear plastic phallus, with glans optics designed by Corning, suitable for photography. It looked just like a

slightly larger than normal erect penis, about 8 inches long. It was driven by a small electric motor. The apparatus was long enough to provide for attachments, and sturdy enough to do the job without wincing. The phallus was gripped by solid metal arms linked to the drive mechanism and cams. Thanks to gear springs, the operator could control the phallus's thrusting to accord with any desired rhythm, from total standstill to a frenzied, pre-ejaculatory staccato. The posterior end of the phallus was open, to provide for attachments such as a camera.[23]

The artificial coition machine of Masters and Johnson was ultimately dismantled and sent to the scrapheap, not because of inefficiency or malfunction but because of adverse publicity or the fear of it. But this single-purpose robot deserves a permanent niche in the Smithsonian Museum of Technology—or at least in the Ripley arcade exhibits of unbelievable inventions just slightly ahead of their time. For, while it is no mere phallic symbol but an actual working replica of *penis erectus,* it is vividly symbolic of the state of mind and entire conceptual framework of contemporary sexologists for whom the subject of human sexuality is comprehended in strictly mechanistic terms. The very definition of sexual behavior, of lovemaking, is derived from their instrument readings—which give the measure of physiological responses in exhaustive and exact detail but are blind and deaf to the murmurs of the heart, the silent dialogue of lovers, the invisible communion of I and Thou. No wonder that the preference of the researchers was for prostitutes for whom feeling was irrelevant to the performance and for couples who were strangers to each other; the arrangement conveniently minimized the risk of "involvement," of the intrusive and dysfunctional influence of *caring,* or indeed of any interest at all in the proceedings other than the elementary motivations (some might call them cheap thrills) of erotic curiosity, exhibitionism, pecuniary reward (a fee was usual), and a free lay. What was expressly wanted and what was apparently given was uncomplicated, businesslike, anonymous screwing. It could not even be said of this ritualized scenario that it deserved the title of "Love with the Proper Stranger"; the one natural ingredient that was effectively guarded against, ruled out, and frightened off the premises was love.

In fact, the avowed interest of Masters and Johnson—as of Kinsey before them and of myriad researchers after them—was not in persons but in organs, not in psychology but in physiology. Dr. Masters brought to his work the preoccupations of a trained obstetrician and gynecologist (Mrs. Johnson brought no equivalent training, but learned quickly and efficiently on the job). Their attention was concentrated upon the working parts rather than upon the whole human being; what is described in their reports bears no resemblance to interpersonal relations but only to the collisions and interlockings of organic machines. As psychotherapist George Frankl has commented:

> One can read the detailed descriptions of physiological responses of 694 people during more than 10,000 cycles of sexual excitation, and not know that they are individuals, persons who feel, think, have pleasure or pain; they are depicted as bodies undergoing certain reflexes with not a mind between them.[24]

But if the person remains invisible in this documentary production, all of the pertinent bodily parts are present and accounted for. "Responses of the penis, scrotum and testes, the breasts, clitoris, labia, vagina, cervix, uterus and other parts of the body are all presented and explained."[25] These parts and their physicochemical changes are reported by the authors in a deliberately assumed and steadfastly maintained rhetoric of technical description and clinical detachment. Thus we are told nothing of the feelings of the principals (was there any joy? was there ever ecstasy?) but much about "controlled penile stimulation"; nothing concerning disappointment or chagrin but a great deal about "inadequate erection syndrome." Yet this careful posture of scientific disinterest cannot quite conceal the intense absorption and intellectual excitement—what Michael Polanyi has termed the "heuristic passion"—of dedicated scientists hot on the trail of experimental discovery and continuously on the verge of the "eureka" experience. Their discoveries, in fact, were numerous, if not always apparent to the untrained reader. For example, as a scientific colleague reported: "One of the major discoveries of Dr. Masters and Mrs. Johnson, of course, is the way in which the motion of the inner lips (minor labia) pulls on the hood of the clitoris."[26] On the other hand, there were occasions when the discovery was appreciable even by the layman: "In some individuals [in orgasm] the whole body may be thrown or tossed, or rolled, over a distance of several feet or yards."[27] The voyeurism of the sexological observer derives not from any human interest but from its cancellation—from disinterest itself. His eye is not on the sparrow but on its twitching; he does not witness the frenzy of the naked girl on the couch but the pull of the minor labia on the hood of the clitoris. As psychotherapist Leslie Farber has pointed out in a trenchant critique of the Masters-Johnson experiments, the sexologist has his own sense of right and wrong (procedures), of good and bad (outcomes), but it is of a different order from the ethical standards ordinarily applied to human affairs:

> . . . the ideal Sexologist, as he presses his eye to his research, finds another variety of drama—inordinately complicated in its comings and goings, crimes and resolutions—with its own requirements of right or wrong, good and bad, all writ very small in terms of "droplets" and "engorgements" and "contractions."[28]

It is as if the ordinary range of human vision, its *Gestalt* effect, which is organized to take in patterns and totalities and to find beauty in a whole living form, has been anesthetized; the visual field is truncated and the eye refocused, by dint of training and disciplined concentration, so as to apprehend only the separate bodily parts and their reflexive quiverings. It is an act of visual and psychological dissection which not only cuts off the parts from the whole, the sexual organs from the human being, but also cuts off the observer from any sympathetic identification—any recognition of the presence of an alter ego, a sister or brother, a lover, a *person*, above and behind and within this graphic documentary account of minute organic unfoldings and engorgements, tumescences and detumescences, all of it remote and exotic, vaguely repellent, and altogether alien to any personal experience of sexual activity on the human scale.

The depersonalization involved in this tunnel-vision approach to sexuality is epitomized in the famous Masters-Johnson film of female masturbation which was publicly released and exhibited around the world for several years before it was abruptly withdrawn from circulation. Only the body of the woman is shown, a faceless torso, like a Paleolithic fertility symbol brought to life and set in motion on the couch. Hers is a solo performance, silent and self-absorbed, carried out under the intense scrutiny of the scientific team and the camera lens, and necessarily completed in a single uninterrupted sequence. As David Holbrook has characterized the scene: "Coldly, the scientists observe her moving fingers, the flush on her thighs, her moistening organ, her stiffening nipples, the fine film of sweat covering her whole body afterwards."[29] The headless woman has succeeded in her difficult role, performing ably if methodically under unusual environmental stress; she might be memorialized as the Unknown Soldier in the sexological revolution. But the body in this film lacks more than a face and an identity; it has been shorn of all humanity. Objectivity has made of her an object, a hunk of writhing flesh, an anatomical curiosity to be idly or abstractedly or pruriently watched. The passionless pornography of the laboratory, focusing its camera eye upon the primary erogenous zone and its excitations, has produced a strip of film indistinguishable from countless blue movies on the same subject that were simultaneously on view in adult theaters and pornshops from Copenhagen to Osaka. Indeed the coincidence of this peculiar cinematic exercise and the prevailing pornographic vogues and fetishes of the same period (the late-sixties) is remarkable. At the same time as the M-J film of female masturbation was being discreetly distributed to professional audiences, the most popular theme of the commercial sleaze-film circuit was what was commonly advertised as the "beaver" movie: a relentlessly sustained extreme-closeup view of an anonymous vagina, a moving part abstracted from personal context, variously agitated and fondled by automanipulation. The philosophy of the producers was no doubt different, but the cinematography was virtually the same. Thus the interesting likelihood occurs that, in various cities of the world, toward the end of the decade, two different sets of audiences were watching, with equal intentness and concentration, two almost interchangeable versions of this fashionable subgenre of the skinflick—one of them produced in Paris or New York or Hong Kong, the other produced in St. Louis. It is only a little farfetched to speculate whether, if a whimsical distributor had somehow managed to switch the two beaver films, either audience would have known the difference—or would have minded if they did.

It is commonly accepted that the essence of pornography, as distinct from erotica, is symbolic dehumanization: the reduction of a human subject to the status of an object. A standard device for accomplishing this reduction to thing-ness, in pictorial pornography, is the elimination of features and traces of identity—for example, hiding the face of the model or cropping the picture to remove the head. Often there is a further cropping of limbs or bodily parts considered extraneous to the viewer/voyeur's interest. Concentration upon an isolated area or organ of the body (breasts, buttocks, pubic area, legs, feet, etc.) is, of course, the hallmark of fetishism, a specialist form of the pornographic impulse. Films and picture magazines catering to these interests often avoid portraying the full human form from head to toe, in deference to the localized concerns of the market. To regard the favored anatomical part in its full human context would be more than a distraction; it would be an embarrassment. It might destroy the concentration of the viewer, and with it his fantasy. And to look upon the face of the model-object—worse yet, to have the face look upon *him*—could be shattering. The potential threat to the voyeur in such a visual confrontation is twofold: that of recognizing and that of being recognized. If he recognizes *her* as an individual, by seeing her face, she is instantly rehumanized: she is no longer merely an object, she cannot be used as freely, the fantasy is dissolved. And if, more dreadfully, she seems to recognize *him*, in the instant of eye contact, he is lost: he stands accused and exposed. (As in the nightmare of the peeping tom: one evening, while he keeps his regular vigil outside the window, the woman pauses in her disrobing, perhaps hearing a sound, and glances in his direction. She speaks: "Why, Arnold!")

Of course, the sexologist, in his disinterested concentration on the sexual parts and their natural functions, is not to be identified with the peeping tom or other voyeur. His motives are strictly those of empirical science; he is scrupulously careful to avoid or erase the slightest suggestion of any interest other than that of objective research. Thus Masters and Johnson kept rechecking their data and revising their reports, editing their language and eliminating anything at all suggestive of sexiness or emotionality, of personal presence or of "human interest." They became admittedly preoccupied with the shadowy issue of pornography. For example, they withdrew the masturbation film from circulation at the first sign of unseemly notoriety; they refused to allow any pictures or accounts of the great artificial coition machine (people were beginning to personify it as "Mr. Penis"), and eventually dismantled it altogether. And they devised an expository prose style as densely technical and deliberately monotonous as they could make it.[30] In short, every effort was exerted by the team of sexologists to make their research as objective, detached, unfeeling, and mechanistic as possible.

In so doing, they accomplished the very effect they were striving to avoid. They created a new pornography—the pornography of science. What was pornographic in their sexual experiments and exhibitions was not any momentary lapse of objectivity or fugitive flicker of ulterior interest in the performances before them; they had guarded all too well against the infiltration of ordinary human sensibilities. The pornography of their dogged investigation was in the perfection of its objectivity, its serene insensitivity, its meticulous absorption in anatomical detail and organic function. Just as their masturbation movie with its headless torso reduced the human subject to a physical object, so their cumulative observation of ten thousand anonymous climaxes over ten years succeeded in objectifying the act of love itself, shriveling its meaning and quality to the level of comparative measurements, technical strategies, and mechanical equipment. In bringing the bedroom into the laboratory, as Leslie Farber has pointed out, Masters and Johnson metaphorically brought the laboratory into the bedroom. By virtue of the authority which science vested in them, and because of the enormous popular influence of their bestselling tracts, they made practicing self-experimenters of a generation of true believers. Thanks to them, and to their forerunners and successors, we have become a nation of anxious technicians: every man his own sexologist. The Masters and Johnson tomes were followed, appropriately enough, by the ever-popular "M" and "J" instructional guidebooks (his and hers).[31] Today, for many millions of Americans and Europeans, it is not merely chic to know the score and keep the score—it is a matter of earnest self-improvement and urgent self-therapy.

> Whatever room we choose for our lovemaking [writes Farber] we shall make into our own poor laboratory, and nothing that is observed or undergone in the real laboratory of science is likely to escape us. . . . Whatever detail the scientific will appropriates about sex rapidly becomes an injunction to be imposed on our bodies. But, it is not long before these impositions lose their arbitrary and alien character and begin to change the way we actually experience our bodies.[32]

The way we begin to experience our bodies is as machines, high-tech equipment, as external and controllable as the stereo system which accompanies and reinforces their sexual activity. As amateur sexologists, following the lead of our instructors, we begin to make ourselves into objects—looking on (as it were) at our own performance, checking the contractions and engorgements as they occur, critically appraising the four-act drama from the wings, approximating the difficult skill of participant-observation. Thus, for example, as Farber demonstrates, the solitary onanist who is well-versed in his craft and sullen art becomes "both scientist and experimental subject, science and sex now being nicely joined. In his laboratory room, he may now abstract his sexual parts from his whole person, inspect their anatomic particularities, and observe and enjoy the small physiologic events he knows best how to control."[33]

The psychological consequence of such clinical experimentation with the self (and others), empirically conducted in the bedroom-laboratory, would seem to be not only self-dehumanization but the more specific condition of "low-grade schizophrenia" which Erich Fromm has diagnosed as the characteristic pathology of "cybernetic man" in advanced technological society. The low-grade schizophrenic, while capable of ordinary functioning and even proud of his superior rationality, has effectively cut himself off from his feelings and his body. He has become an object to himself. As Fromm describes his mentality and its social implications, he takes on the familiar features of the Cheerful Robot:

> He turns his interest away from life, persons, nature, ideas—in short from everything that is alive; he transforms all life into things, including himself and the manifestations of his human faculties of reason, seeing, hearing, tasting, loving. Sexuality becomes a technical skill (the "love machine"); feelings are flattened and sometimes substituted for by sentimentality; joy, the expression of intense aliveness, is replaced by "fun" or excitement; and whatever love and tenderness man has is directed toward machines and gadgets. The world becomes a sum of lifeless artifacts; from synthetic food to synthetic organs, the whole man becomes part of the total machinery that he controls and is simultaneously controlled by. He has no plan, no goal for life, except doing what the logic of technique determines him to do. He aspires to make robots

as one of the greatest achievements of his technical mind, and
some specialists assure us that the robot will hardly be distinguished from living men. This achievement will not seem so
astonishing when man himself is hardly distinguishable from
a robot.[34]

High Pornography: The Dehumanization of Art

The pornography of science, with its symbolic dissection of the
human subject into objective and mechanical parts, finds perhaps its
closest contemporary parallel not so much in the base pornography
of the popular arts but, increasingly, in what has been called the
"high pornography" of the fine arts.[35] In the fields of postmodern
painting and sculpture, particularly, there has been a marked and
mordant tendency to focus attention upon isolated organs and anatomical parts, generally sexual, and to present them for close inspection in blown-up enlargements which often give the appearance of
parodying the full-color illustrations in anatomy textbooks. Moreover, the art of the nude has shifted noticeably from the frank celebration of sexuality and the human body which characterized earlier
treatments of the subject to a coolly, almost clinically, detached
perspective which seems the exact visual equivalent of a descriptive
report by Kinsey or Masters and Johnson. What this trend of high
pornography portends is a radical dehumanization of art far exceed-
ing the critical imagination of Ortega y Gasset, whose classic essay of
the forties, "The Dehumanization of Art," first gave currency to the
idea.[36]

By way of background, it should be recognized that there is an
ancient, if not always honored, tradition of the erotic in Western art
(and an even older and distinctly more honored tradition in Asian art,
notably that of India and Japan). It may well be, as Lord Kenneth
Clark has maintained, that an element of the erotic is implicit in all
portrayals of the female nude—if not indeed in all representations of
feminine beauty.[37] Often, of course, the erotic element is entirely
explicit—a central theme of the art work. Even so direct a reference
to human sexuality has been, in some periods and cultures, an admis-
sible ingredient of high art (specifically of the visual arts of painting
and sculpture). The common denominator of erotic art has tradition-

ally been an open avowal and demonstration of the joys of sex: not only its carnal pleasures and earthly delights, its fantasies and transports, but also its playful prologues and tranquil epilogues: in short, both the comminglings of the flesh and the communions of the spirit.

The dark side of Eros is also to be found in traditional art, of course (as witness Bosch and Hogarth); but for the most part it has not been integral to the artistic mainstream but rather has constituted what might be called a counterculture of low art—low enough to be "underground"—which has served different purposes and different audiences. This is the tradition of pornography, which has had as its dominating spirit a parody and mockery of sex—at best a goodhumored burlesque, meaning no harm but "taking off" the pompous veneer—and at worst, which is all too often, giving vent to the submerged imagery and impulse of hostility and fear (Freud's "return of the repressed"), directed both at sexuality itself and at the female sex in particular.

Much of pornography—not all of it, as some zealous feminists would have us believe, but a great deal—embodies male fantasies of the subjugation and control of women, typically illustrated by themes of domination and conquest. The alienated image of woman as the "Other," the totally alien (famously documented by Simone de Beauvoir), reaches back beyond the hags and witches of Occidental mythology, beyond Lilith, to those formidable carved effigies on the prehistoric cave walls which made a totem and taboo of the elemental female icon: the "Venus" V or triangle, and more broadly the stripped-down torso, shorn of all identifying features except gargantuan breasts and pelvis.[38] To be sure, those primitive carvings were ambivalent and ambiguous images; as fertility symbols, as representations of the Earth Mother, they affirmed a life force as positive as the sun. But that did not make them simply benign or wholly reassuring; they were the awed and apprehensive imagings of the cosmic female whom Joseph Campbell has identified as the Queen Goddess of the World. In mythology around the globe, early and late, she has taken alternate forms and incorporated conflicting emotions. "The mother of life," as Campbell observes, "is at the same time the mother of death; she is masked in the ugly demonesses of famine and disease."[39] The mixed male feelings of veneration and aversion, of attraction and repulsion, were evidently merged in those headless, limbless female torsos dating from the Old Stone Age which were turned up in quantity around the Mediterranean by nineteenth-century archeologists—and to which they gave the ironic collective name of "Venus." They did so because, like the most famous of female statues, the Venus de Milo, these archaic figurines were generally limbless. But the symbolism goes deeper than that; for the Greek statue from Milos, as the world has known it since its recovery in 1820, is a conspicuously mutilated version of Venus/Aphrodite (the goddess of beauty and fertility as well as of love). Her arms have been broken off, rendering her defenseless and vulnerable; she is also naked to the waist, as if forcibly disrobed. The basic symbolism of this crippled figure is scarcely that of an all-powerful goddess but rather of the familiar denuded and defenseless female captive whose most celebrated rendering is in Hiram Powers' 1850 statue of "The Greek Slave": a foreign girl stripped naked, bound in chains, mounted on the auction block, passively resigned to her sexual fate.

But there is an even more graphically suggestive imagery in the persistently recurring subject of the female torso in both ancient and modern art. As Norma Nichols has written (in an illuminating study of the changing artistic images of women, *The Mirrors of Eve*):

> . . . there is an additional significance to the female torso: *sans* head it can never be individual, and *sans* feet it can never escape. Many cultures have covered the heads or veiled the faces of their women, and some have bound their feet; a great many more have bound their bodies. The harem slave, for example, might be characterized as a female torso without benefit of surgery. The image of the torso is therefore multifaceted, as befits an icon. It embodies the source of female power and mystery, and so is an object of male worship; but for that very reason it is also an object of fear. The female torso, carved and sculpted and (more recently) painted by men, is moreover its own revenge. In this stripped-down model, woman is permanently and totally immobilized.[40]

The Sadeian symbolism which the female torso makes literal has been expressed in other ways by numerous modern (and postmodern) artists whose work reflects or imitates or mocks the technological imperative of misplaced objectivity and anatomical fetishism.

As the art critic Barbara Rose has pointed out, the treatment of the naked body as an object does not remove it from erotic attention but rather displaces and vulgarizes its eroticism by focusing on awkward and unattractive features of the nude. Among European surrealists of the twenties, for example—notably those who took the Marquis de Sade for their patron saint (as Robert Hughes has graphically reminded us in *The Shock of the New*)—it was a common artistic conceit to portray isolated limbs, breasts, or other parts of the female body in willfully grotesque arrangements.[41] A later and singular case in point is that of the mordant American expressionist Hyman Bloom, who produced in the forties a series of brilliantly colored paintings of corpses and their parts (e.g., *The Leg*) which reflected a degree of professional detachment rivaling that of Quincy the Coroner; the high pornography in his chilling portraits could perhaps be fully appreciated only by another necrophilous personality. Following in somewhat the same biology-lab tradition is the dissective art of the contemporary painter Harold Stevenson, who has chosen to concentrate his esthetic sensibility on single parts of the human body—"gigantic blow-ups of fingers, tongues, and genitalia," as William Gerdts has described them—"painted rosey-colored flesh that appears fascinatingly and at the same time repulsively sticky."[42] A similar fixation on the organic particular is exhibited in the 1962 series of paintings by Larry Rivers entitled "Parts of the Body," in which each anatomical section is accompanied by text-like arrows and lettered signs. Whatever the conscious intentions or less conscious impulses of these artists may have been, they have produced a gallery of images which precisely mirror the clinical pornography of the sexologists—not only in superficial likeness but in the underlying perversity of vision and the derangement of what used to be known as kind regard.

The dehumanization of art in the age of technics has also taken less blatant forms. As Gerdts has demonstrated in his history of the American nude, ". . . a supercool and impersonal treatment of the nude seems to be especially characteristic of painting in the present day, and such total impersonality carries over into contemporary sculpture as well."[43] In the paintings of Ben Kamihara, for example, nude figures are strewn about domestic landscapes with such detached indifference as to appear mere inert objects, hardly to be distinguished from the other furniture of chairs, tables, draperies, and pillows. The artist invites our inspection of his lifeless objects in the manner of a biologist showing off his collection of preserved specimens. This posture of cool impersonality is most conspicuous in the highly regarded work of Philip Pearlstein, whose graceless and often ugly nudes are not only presented as objective fact but are symbolically dissected by the cropping of whatever limbs or parts do not conveniently fit the frame. The accentuation of the negative in such work as Pearlstein's is oddly counterbalanced by what might be termed the desecration of the positive in Tom Wesselman's Pop-art series, "The Great American Nude," which takes a leering look at the female erogenous zones in a cruel parody of poster and pin-up art. "Woman is depersonalized," says Gerdts of this collection, "so that only her erotic components are described—mouth, nipples, pubic hair."[44]

What is distinctive, and disturbing, about this dehuman syndrome in the arts is not its candid realism in the portrayal of the female nude. Such naturalistic treatment in the American context goes back at least as far as Thomas Eakins and was fully developed by his successors among the urban realists of the early twentieth century (notably Robert Henri and John Sloan). What distinguishes the present-day vogue of self-styled "superrealism" is not then its open treatment of the human theme of sexuality but its point of view. Where the great American realists who were drawn to the female nude—their names include George Bellows, Edward Hopper, Isabel Bishop, Raphael Soyer and Moses Soyer, among others—were interested in their subjects as women, sentient as well as sensuous beings, fully alive and active, the attitude of contemporary realists is one of cold if not contemptuous detachment and disinterest— resulting in canvases replete with inert objects, anatomical curiosities, and an environment which falls somewhere between the laboratory and the crypt. This dehumanized perspective, as Norma Nichols has written, "is far removed from the warmth and sympathetic engagement of the main realist tradition. . . . It might also seem to be the denouement of that tradition. For a realism without heart, without the subjective involvement of the artist, is no longer an art of the real but of the unreal—of lifeless objects."[45] Nichols goes on to render a severe, but not unwarranted, judgment:

Such rigorous detachment and clinical observation, which gives the impression of an unintentional parody of the classical scientific pose, does not however escape from the disclosure of a moral point of view: it is a point of view not entirely unlike the scrupulous disengagement of the German doctors in the conduct of the final solution.[46]

If women have fared badly at the hands of various modern artists, men have not been treated much better. To be sure, there has been no such thoroughgoing dismemberment of the male body as that inflicted on the female anatomy; but the spirit of misogyny which we have traced among the high pornographers finds a close parallel in a widespread attitude of general misanthropy that focuses mordant attention as much upon men as upon women. A notorious case in point is that of the great pioneer of cubism, Marcel Duchamp, whose fractured *Nude Descending a Staircase* had been the sensation of the New York Armory Show in 1913. Ten years later he produced his curious construction, *Large Glass* or *The Bride Stripped Bare by Her Bachelors, Even*. The fact that Duchamp was himself a bachelor may or may not have had something to do with his symbolic portrayal of woman in this work as a kind of meta-machine, a mobile oven, not merely dehumanized but sniggered at. However, the Bride and her Bachelors alike are subjected to a joke that would be cruel if we were able to perceive any semblance of humanity in the mechanical subjects; the real theme of the work, as Robert Hughes has observed, appears to be the dismal fate of love in a robotomized age.

The imposing mechanism of the male sexual apparatus lends itself to symbolization by every sort of indescribably complicated machinery. But to Duchamp, who had every reason to know, the male mechanism of the Large Glass was not a bit imposing. The Bachelors are mere uniforms, like marionettes. According to Duchamp's notes, they try to indicate their desire to the Bride by concertedly making the chocolate grinder turn, so that it grinds out an imaginary milky stuff like semen. This squirts up through the rings, but cannot get into the Bride's half of the *Glass* because of the prophylactic bar that separates the panes. And so the Bride is condemned always to tease, while the Bachelor's fate is endless masturbation.[47]

The Glass is, in fact, as Hughes adds, a testament to indifference; and indifference is the affective posture of self-dehumanization, expressing withdrawal from life and feeling—an attitude that came to characterize Duchamp himself, who abandoned painting in favor of chess, a perfectly detached and cerebral exercise to which he became obsessively devoted. The dehumanization of art, in such cases, reflects the self-dehumanization of the artist.

Of course, art also reflects its time; and great art exposes the soul of its time. Modern art would be false to its age if it were not caught up in themes of victimage and alienation, in anguished responses to mechanism and conformity, in experimental forms and styles reflective of an actual world in wilder disarray and derangement than any artist (even Picasso) has yet been able to duplicate. In the age of the Dynamo, and of the Dynamo's murderous spawn, we should not expect romantic allegories and pastoral tableaux; and we should not believe Norman Rockwell. The artist paints what he sees; he paints what he must: he is not responsible for the state of the world, only responsive to it. Yet that is not the whole truth. The artist bears responsibility for his work; he is responsible, not for the world, but *to* the world. Any work of art is a statement, true or false, trivial or profound. Like ideas, art has consequences. As Erich Kahler has written: "Art, just as life itself, is not compartmentalized, and what happens to artistic form seriously affects the human form, the form of man."[48] And in the art of the modern age the human form, that of man and woman, has clearly suffered. The form and figure of the human has become for the artist, more and more, not merely an object but a disintegrated object, a broken mannequin destined for the garbage dump, where the bits and pieces of what was once the semblance of a whole human being will lie indifferently, as meaningless and repellent as the surrounding effluents and dreck of Man's own junkyard. Indeed, that is exactly the image presented by the American precisionist Hyman Bloom in his series of paintings of amputated limbs and rotting corpses, all of it meticulously observed, brightly illuminated, and undisguisedly the product of a necrophiliac imagination.[49] What appears to have happened in such morbid developments is the pathological extension and exacerbation of the honest purpose of the older realist tradition to strip away the cosmetics of romanticism and reveal the true face and figure of the human. But why then strip away the human as well?

One answer to that question—it is now the classical answer—was provided by Ortega y Gasset in his essay, referred to earlier, on "The Dehumanization of Art." Writing forty years ago, Ortega professed himself struck by two separate but related tendencies in modern art (by which he meant the characteristic art more or less abstract, of twentieth-century Europe): first, an impulse to abandon the "lived reality" of life, including the recognizable human form; and, second, an attitude of revulsion and "loathing" toward humanity itself. In order to create and furnish a new world of perception, in this view, the modern artist had first to dismantle the old, piece by piece; and among those pieces was the human subject, which in the previous century had become the dominant concern of art. Thus Ortega maintained that "the most general and the most characteristic feature of modern artistic production [has been] the tendency to dehumanize art." But this has not been accomplished by leaving the human being altogether, or by leaving him alone; rather, the artistic act of dehumanization has taken the form of attacking the human element head-on. The new artist "is brazenly set on deforming reality, shattering its human aspect, dehumanizing it." This art, said Ortega, is inhuman in its effect not because it is non-human in subject matter but because it is *anti*-human in temper.

> The question is not to paint something altogether different from a man, a house, a mountain, but to paint a man who resembles a man as little as possible; . . . For the modern artist, aesthetic pleasure derives from such a triumph over human matter. That is why he has to drive home the victory by presenting in each case the strangled victim.[50]

To Ortega, this rejection of the recognizably human in modern art was more than a repudiation of traditional realism; it expressed an aversion to humanity and to life itself: "It is not an exaggeration to assert that modern paintings and sculptures betray a real loathing of living forms or forms of living beings."[51] Underlying this abhorrence, Ortega believed, was a general withdrawal of sympathy on the part of modern artists, a denial of the pathetic element of life which had been so overworked in traditional art; and with that a note of ironic detachment, a "grimace of surfeit or disdain"—an emotional distancing not only of art from reality but also of the artist from his art ("the new art ridicules art itself"). In the modern idiom, he was saying, art has been not only dehumanized but debunked.

We need not endorse the whole of that unappreciative and possibly philistine critique in order to recognize its relevance to much of what has become fashionable in art in the decades since Ortega identified the dehuman syndrome of his own age and culture. The element of detachment and indifference, of emotional disengagement of the artist from the human world; the attitude of hostility, of derision and disdain for human sentiments and for life itself; the obsession with themes of decay, destruction, and death; the menacing sense of violence around, behind, and within the work of art; the ambivalent struggle of the artist with the spirit of the machine, sometimes painfully won but more often lost through self-surrender—these tendencies have become so prevalent in recent art as to seem almost its characteristic elements. Indeed they were so regarded by Matthew Lipman, in his perceptive survey in the sixties of the major recurring symbols and images of contemporary art. Beginning with the widespread absorption of mechanical elements and mechanistic principles into the art work—as in the giant metallic constructions of Lee Bontecou and Richard Stankiewicz—Lipman went on to describe the process in which mechanization finally takes command over its archfoe (freedom, spontaneity, creative expression) in the sanctuary of art itself. The takeover occurs at the stage when "the artist deliberately becomes himself as much of a machine as possible . . . [when] the medium and the technique scrupulously avoid the sense of the artist's participation in the creative act."[52]

Coinciding with the advent of this "deliberately impersonal quality" in recent art—which he observed particularly in the smooth mechanical veneers of the Pop Art school (the xerox reproductions of Andy Warhol, the comic-strip blowups of Roy Lichtenstein, etc.)—Lipman found a profusion of violent imagery, characteristically expressed in "the violent way in which physical forms . . . are distorted, abused, exaggerated, or coerced," and in the aggression displayed by abstract artists: "The explosive quality of shapes, the tearing and rending of mass, the consuming action of a highly aggressive kind of space, are frequently encountered."[53] One did not go to a modern museum or gallery, any more, to find tranquillity; art was not now a still point of the turning world—it was more like the eye of the hurricane. It was becoming, like the major elements of popular culture, an art of violence.

Yet that violence, as Lipman observed, was curiously impersonal, detached from the involvement or concern of the artist—like a bald statement of fact, a transmission of raw data, a candid snapshot untouched by human hands. Even with those matters traditionally regarded as of ultimate concern, there was a prevalence of description but an absence of response. "The imagery of the contemporary artist often evokes the idea of death, of decay, of destruction," wrote Sedgwick. ". . . And there is a death of the spirit as well as a death of the body, which also finds its expression in the art of our times."[54] But even in the portrayal of that final, private, utterly personal act of existence—the act of dying—the artist commonly gave the impression of removing himself from the proceedings, of being out to lunch. "More and more frequently the contemporary artist seems to be an instrument, a medium, a device for the transmission of forms and forces outside of himself, rather than the architect of self-established and self-selected themes."[55]

The peculiar absconding of the modern artist from his work is strangely paralleled, as Lipman has also made us aware, by the disappearing act of the human subject. "The individual in twentieth-century art," he writes, "is frequently hidden or disguised or masked"—so much so that "sometimes we feel that the contemporary artist is playing a guessing game with his spectators." The widespread use of the *mask*—suggesting illusion, deception, unreality—typifies this artistic game of hide-and-seek. Moreover, the mask has acquired a new prominence, a uniquely modern symbolism, that makes it a powerful metaphor for the age of alienation, the culture of mistaken identity, and the society of missing persons. Modern art, no less than modern thought, is largely the record of systematic flight from the self; it is no wonder that in our own age, for the first time in history, as Lipman believes, the mask has become "an independent art form," divorced from instrumental connections with performance or ritual. We shall have more to say about the contemporary importance of image, appearance, and deception later on (Chapter Four); but it is pertinent here to record the observation of the modern art historian that one of the most interesting and curious of recent developments has been "the emergence of works of art that are about human beings who aren't there." He goes on:

Sometimes we feel that certain recent works of art are like tracks in a forest; they let us know that something has passed by, and they may enable us to reconstruct exactly what this something was like, but we can never catch up with it, and we can consequently never precisely identify it. . . . All that it seems to say is: a human being was here. This is what he left behind.[56]

With that development the dehumanization of art would seem to be complete. We have witnessed the defacing and disfigurement of the human subject; the degradation and dismembering of the female form; the abstracted indifference and stealthy withdrawal of the artist; and, finally, the depopulation of the landscape and the total eclipse of the human presence.

Yet that is not quite all. There is a particular form of the human that has been willfully left behind, turned out of the picture—a human form as familiar to traditional art as to our ordinary lives, so familiar indeed that its disappearance from contemporary canvases has scarcely been remarked (or, at least, not thought remarkable). It is, of course, the *child*. Even after the turn of the modern century children were still abundantly in evidence in our paintings, joyously or tenderly or poignantly affirmed in their vital presence—not only by the exquisite Mary Cassatt but by urban realists like Robert Henri and George Luks. But then the children began to retreat from the scene, to lose the attention and interest of serious artists—banished, as it now appears, to the shallow lower depths of sentimental portraiture and greeting cards. There are powerful exceptions, of course (Philip Evergood's *Lily and the Sparrows* still haunts the imagination), but in the main we are met with a staggering neglect and indifference toward the child. Perhaps that should not surprise us, after all; it was Emerson who observed, over a century ago, that children are the true aliens in our society: strangers in a strange land, compelled to live among giants who talk only in riddles. But the measure of a civilization's heart (as of a person's) lies in the quality of its care and concern for children. On the testimony of our artists, then, contemporary civilization lacks a heart; for the main body of their work displays no element of compassion, no look of love, not even an awareness of the still sad music of humanity.

3

DEHUMAN ENGINEERING: THE SCIENCE OF GOOD BEHAVIOR

We have had religious revolutions, we have had political, industrial, economic, and nationalistic revolutions. All of them, as our
descendants will discover, were but ripples in an ocean of
conservatism—trivial by comparison with the psychological revolution toward which we are so rapidly moving. *That* will really
be a revolution. When it is over, the human race will give no
further trouble.—*Aldous Huxley*

I believe that the day has come when we can combine sensory
deprivation with drugs, hypnosis and astute manipulation of reward and punishment to gain absolute control over an individual's behavior.—*James McConnell*

THE ABSOLUTE CONTROL of human behavior has long been the dream
of tyrants. It has also been, for not quite so long a time, the
dream of scientists and pundits (as the above quotation from psychologist James McConnell illustrates).[1] More accurately, of course,
it has been the dream of *some* scientists and pundits while it has been
the nightmare of others. In fact, the extensive literature dealing with
behavior control in one form or another, from the time of Plato
onward, has been deeply and passionately divided on the issue. (The

57

Dialogues of Plato can be read in their entirety as a continuous debate on this question.)² That literature is today more divided than ever, for reasons that are both perennial and novel. The division is perennial in that, phrased in slightly altered terms, its subject may be seen to be the central issue of Western thought and civilization: the issue of freedom *vs.* power. And it is novel in that, for the first time in human history, the means of noncoercive control over individual and collective behavior, to a degree approaching the absolute, are presently at hand. They are real, they are known, and they are available. But that is not all: they are also being used.

Fifteen years after the publication of *Brave New World*, that futuristic fable of a totally pacified population of cheerful robots, its author wrote a new preface speculating on the plausibility of its prophecies. It was 1946; and Aldous Huxley could invoke the metaphors of the iron curtain, the cold war, and most pertinently of all the atomic age. From his immediate postwar perspective, he saw the remote fantasies of his novel—which had been placed in the year 600 A.F. (After Ford)—as becoming real and imminent possibilities to be realized within the next two or three generations. And those fantasies, of course, centered on the transformation of a whole society from independent, reflective and critical citizens into docile and willing slaves. "The theme of *Brave New World*," he wrote in retrospect, "is not the advancement of science as such; it is the advancement of science as it affects human individuals. . . . The only scientific advances to be specifically described are those involving the application to human beings of the results of future research in biology, physiology and psychology."³ The aim of the rulers in his faroff dystopia was not really destructive or even megalomaniac: ". . . they are not madmen, and their aim is not anarchy but social stability. It is in order to achieve stability that they carry out, by scientific means, the ultimate, personal, really revolutionary revolution."⁴

Huxley believed, in 1946, that that "final revolution" was about to move from the pages of his science fiction to the real world of the industrialized nations in the coming nuclear era. He predicted an increasing rapid centralization of power in these nations which would make them all essentially totalitarian; but, significantly, he did not envision that total power as manifesting itself in the traditional forms of overt oppression and terror but rather through the subtler devices of conditioning, persuasion, and distraction. "The most important

Manhattan Projects of the future," he anticipated, "will be vast government-sponsored enquiries into what the politicians and the participating scientists will call 'the problem of happiness'—in other words, the problem of making people love their servitude." There can be no doubt about what that would entail: "The love of servitude cannot be established except as a result of a deep, personal revolution in human minds and bodies."[5] This terminal revolution would be implemented, he thought, by means very like those outlined in the novel—among them improved techniques of suggestion and conditioning; the development of new drugs "less harmful and more pleasure-giving than gin or heroin" (the psychedelics?); "a foolproof system of eugenics, designed to standardize the human product and so to facilitate the task of the managers"; and, perhaps most interestingly, a vast increase of sexual freedom and experimentation, which a future dictator would do well to encourage since "[in] conjunction with the freedom to daydream under the influence of dope and movies and the radio, it will help to reconcile his subjects to the servitude which is their fate."[6]

There is little in Huxley's prescriptive formula for the painless subjugation of a people which has not since found its counterpart in the real world—whether it has occurred systematically or otherwise, consciously or not. (Indeed, when he returned to the same theme again in 1958, in *Brave New World Revisited*, Huxley observed that "the prophecies made in 1931 are coming true much sooner than I thought they would. . . . The nightmare of total organization . . . has emerged from the safe, remote future and is now awaiting us, just around the next corner.")[7] More particularly, his once-fanciful scenarios regarding the subversion of mind, the modification of behavior, and the distraction of consciousness read today for the most part like elementary textbook descriptions of standard procedures and accepted social conventions. In short there is not much in the organization and technology of his Brave New World that is any longer new—just as there was never anything in it that was truly brave.

But there is another aspect to this little novel of half a century ago that is worth recalling. While it came to be regarded as a prophetic vision of distant things to come, it does not appear to have been the author's intention to be taken literally in his broader depiction of the remote post-Fordian future. The treatment of the entire absurdist situation, let alone of the fantastic plot and its cast of caricatures, is too extreme and even comic to sustain so solemn a purpose; the book is not really a futuristic exposition in the Wellsian tradition nor an angry warning of the Stalinization of the world a la *Nineteen Eighty-Four*. Instead, written at the end of the twenties, it is a brilliant satire on its own age: the age of behaviorist psychology and scientific management, of the assembly line and the movie palace, of Henry Ford and John Broadus Watson. Huxley was doing, in a somewhat distinctive form, what he always did best (he had done it before in novels like *Antic Hay* and *Point Counterpoint,* and was to do it again in *After Many a Summer Dies the Swan*): i.e., mocking the mores and morals of his time, milking its sacred cows, and exposing its hypocrisies. He could not have wished us to believe that six centuries hence, "After Ford," people would walk around wearing religious pendants on which the cross was replaced by a (Model) T. The satirical point was not that such silliness might some day come to pass, but rather that it was happening *then,* under the thin guise of a religiousness turned materialistic. (It was the decade in which an advertising mogul, Bruce Barton, wrote a bestseller maintaining that the true greatness of Jesus lay in his superior powers of salesmanship.)[8] And the sharpest point of Huxley's satire was aimed directly at the growing cult of psychological behaviorism and its celebrated founder, John Broadus Watson.

Behaviorism: The Ministry of Fear

Toward the beginning of *Brave New World,* in the course of a guided tour of the Central London Hatchery and Conditioning Centre, the reader is introduced to the Neo-Pavlovian Conditioning Rooms, where a routine experiment is about to begin. It is, of course, the memorable scene in which the babies are conditioned by loud noises and electric shock to be terrified of flowers and coloring books. Following the experiment, which is reported in a truly harrowing manner, the Director of Hatcheries and Conditioning pronounces the moral: "They'll grow up with what the psychologists used to call an 'instinctive' hatred of books and flowers. Reflexes unalterably conditioned. They'll be safe from books and botany all their lives."[9]

The cruel scene of the mental and physical torture of infants, in the service of a degraded psychology (and politics) of mind control, has remained with many readers of *Brave New World* as the most dramatically compelling of the author's many imaginary instances of scientific man's potential inhumanity to man—and child. Disturbing as it was, however, the reader could be consoled by the knowledge that all this was merely futuristic fantasy—a remote possibility, to be sure, if mankind should ever become so thoroughly deranged, but barely conceivable even at that. Who could ever wish (the thought is outrageous) to so distort and cripple a child's very nature, his innocent and innately humane response to beauty?

Who indeed. It happens that this distressing episode of Huxley's novel, unlike the bulk of his fabulous fantasies, was not imaginary at all. It was based squarely on fact. Indeed, aside from a few theatrical details, it was almost a literal transcription of the fact. The actual event was reported in the scientific literature of the 1920s by the psychologist who conducted the experiment: none other than John B. Watson himself, the founding father who had given the name of Behaviorism to the science of human conditioning and control which he adapted in 1912 from the animal experiments of the Russian Ivan P. Pavlov at the turn of the century. (It is pertinent, in passing by Pavlov, to note that he himself never sought or wished to apply his own researches, which had to do with the salivary reflex and conditioning of dogs, to human psychology. It is also pertinent to observe that the Soviet government had no such compunctions; "reflexology," a bastardization of Pavlov's work, became the official psychology of the Soviet Union in the Stalin era; and *applied* reflexology became the quasi-official therapy, the corrective mental hygiene, of the vast institutional system for the "rehabilitation" of dissidents and nonconformists—all those who populated the Gulag Archipelago—a system which remains implacably in effect today in Mother Russia.)[10]

Watson achieved, in the second decade of the century, what might be called the Americanization of the conditioned reflex. He shared none of Pavlov's reservations concerning the distinction between animals and humans (although his own doctoral research had been confined to the behavior of rats).[11] He saw the human connection immediately, and he christened it Behaviorism. What he set out to accomplish, at least in theory—the transformation of America into a docile and contented nation of sheep—is well illustrated by the little experiment which was to furnish the inspiration for Huxley's fictive episode of the traumatized children and the fear of flowers.

The infant's name was Albert B., the eleven-month-old son (apparently illegitimate, since he was later adopted) of a local hospital nurse—an eminently available subject for experimentation. The infant was further qualified because, as Watson put it, "He was a wonderfully 'good' baby. In all the months we worked with him we never saw him cry until after our experiments were made!"[12] (That statement could hardly be improved on by Huxley himself.) The object of the experiment was "to attempt to build up fears in the infant and then later to study practical methods for removing them." The first step was to find an appropriate stimulus which would "call out the fear reaction quickly and easily." Although Watson had often used electric shock with excellent results, this time he decided upon a stimulus equally effective with babies: a sudden loud noise, produced by the striking of a steel bar with a carpenter's hammer just behind the baby's head, which was known to produce "the most marked kind of reaction." Watson's own laboratory notes contain a nicely objective account of the progress of his experiment in the manufacture of fear and the transformation of the baby who never cried:

> *Eleven months, 3 days old.* (1) White rat which he had played with for weeks was suddenly taken from the basket (the usual routine) and presented to Albert. He began to reach for rat with left hand. Just as his hand touched the animal the bar was struck immediately behind his head. The infant jumped violently and fell forward, burying his face in the mattress. He did not cry, however.
>
> (2) Just as his right hand touched the rat the bar was again struck. Again the infant jumped violently, fell forward and began to whimper.[13]

Watson adds that, due to Albert's "disturbed condition," the conditioners had to lay off for a week. Then, with all parties refreshed, they returned to their experiment—tirelessly presenting again and again the "combined stimulation" of rat and sound to the hapless infant, who sometimes cried and sometimes fell away in silent

terror—generally exhibiting a most interesting variety of fright responses and traumatic symptoms—until the climactic moment (the
eureka experience) when Albert reacted with the desired terror at the
sight of the rat alone, without the addition of the loud sound. One
can almost feel the triumphant satisfaction of the grand conditioner,
as he concluded his laboratory notes with this final italicized statement:

> (8) Rat alone. *The instant the rat was shown the baby
> began to cry. Almost instantly he turned sharply to the left,
> fell over, raised himself on all fours and began to crawl away
> so rapidly that he was caught with difficulty before he reached
> the edge of the mattress.*[14]

There is an epilogue to this story of little Albert and the friendly
scientist—or, more exactly, two epilogues. The first has to do with
the "spread or transfer" of the baby's conditioned fear response to
the white rat. For the experimenters were not quite finished with him;
curious about the possible spread effect of the specific terror they had
engendered, they next commenced a five-day series of experiments in
which they presented Albert in succession with "a *rabbit*, a *dog*, a
sealskin coat, cotton wool, human hair and a *false face*" (the italics
are Watson's). They must have been delighted with what they found:
the baby turned out to be afraid of every one (plus a Santa Claus
mask which was subsequently added)—but he was particularly terrified of the rabbit, which so intrigued the investigators that they
actually forced him into physical contact with the animal to test the
degree of his fright. Watson's description is some kind of classic: "He
leaned as far away from the animal as possible, whimpered, then
burst into tears. When the rabbit was placed in contact with him he
buried his face in the mattress, then got up on all fours and crawled
away, crying as he went. This was a most convincing test."[15]

The second epilogue to this narrative is contained in a terse statement by the conditioner, which is tossed off almost as an aside on a
later page of the same book: "No further tests could be made upon
Albert B., the youngster in whom the conditioned responses had been
built up, because he was shortly afterwards adopted by an out-of-
town family."[16] That announcement elicits mixed reactions from the
reader: first, a sense of relief that this "youngster" was spared further

torture in Watson's scientific Ministry of Fear through the providential appearance of his adoptive parents, and, secondly, a sense of outrage at Watson's indifference to the human havoc he had wrought in his coldblooded manipulation of a child's developing personality—his capacity for trust, his ability to love, his openness to the world, his human potentialities. Watson had taken a normal, healthy, happy infant—one that reached out to the world and its living forms with intelligent curiosity and delight—and he had traumatized that infant, shocking it again and again with strange and clamorous noise, introducing into its vulnerable life and mind a dimension of terror which (unidentified and unresolved) must surely have induced a profound and lasting state of neurotic anxiety—a lifetime of nightmares—if not a more critical derangement of mental faculties in the form of paranoid schizophrenia.

The "cry of the behaviorist," declared Watson, "is, 'Give me the baby and my world to bring it up in and I'll make it crawl and walk; I'll make it climb and use its hands in constructing buildings of stone or wood; I'll make it a thief, a gunman, or a dope fiend. The possibility of shaping in any direction is almost endless.'"[17] Aside from the sheer hubris of this desire to play God (or his ancient Adversary)— and ignoring the biological redundancy of *shaping* the behavior of a baby toward crawling and walking—the most curious feature of this behaviorist "cry" is its insistent emphasis, not on the constructive shaping of behavior, but on its negative and destructive *warping* ("I'll make it a thief, a gunman, or a dope fiend"). We have already observed the scientific sadism of the great behaviorist in the case of little Albert; other evidences of his inclination to go about creating fear and inflicting pain, as if in preference to their prevention and cure, turn up elsewhere in his published writings. Thus, in discussing the behaviorist's overriding urge to control human behavior, Watson put the question this way: "Can psychology ever get control? Can I make someone who is not afraid of snakes, afraid of them and how?"[18] This strange interest not merely in shaping or modifying behavior but in *distorting* it in unnatural ways, and in forcing the targeted individual to behave on command ("I'll *make* it crawl . . . I'll *make* it climb . . . I'll *make* it a thief"), exposes in graphic terms the barely hidden authoritarian impulse that underlies the psychology of behaviorism: it is, of course, the will to power, the secret wish to dominate. To "condition" behavior is to control it; and the meaning of control, in the real world as in the laboratory, is power. Watson himself, although he liked to talk of the "objectivity" of his science, made his practical intentions quite plain: "The interest of the behaviorist is more than that of a spectator," he wrote; "he wants to control man's reactions as physical scientists want to control and manipulate other [sic] natural phenomena."[19] Having defined man as no more nor less than "an assembled organic machine ready to run," the behaviorist defined himself as the engineer ready to run it.

In what direction? The explicit answer given by Watson to this irresistible question was: in the direction of *good behavior,* meaning simply that which conforms to established social norms and conventions. "The behaviorist," wrote Watson, ". . . would like to develop his world of people from birth on, so that their speech and their bodily behavior could equally well be exhibited freely everywhere without running afoul of group standards."[20] In other words, the behaviorist's world of people would always be on their good behavior, if not their very best; they could be counted on at all times to "behave themselves." Like the unflappable Mrs. Prothero in Dylan Thomas's reminiscence of a child's Christmas in Wales, they would do and say "the right thing, always." Moreover they would do so automatically, not to say cheerfully, having been so "developed" from birth on by the hovering Behaviorist—the ever-watchful Big Brother who would oversee their behavioral exhibition on the premise that they would or could make no waves. Least of all should they attempt to exercise free speech. The above-quoted passage occurs in the context of a remarkably candid footnote in which Watson expressed his contempt for the very notion of free speech:

Note: I am not arguing here for free anything—least of all free speech. I have always been very much amused by the advocates of free speech. In this harum-scarum world of ours, brought up as we are, the only person [sic] who ought to be allowed free speech is the parrot, because the parrot's words are not tied up with his bodily acts and do not stand as substitutes for his bodily acts. All true speech does stand substitutive for bodily acts, hence organized society has just as little right to allow free speech as it has to allow free action, which nobody advocates. When the agitator raises the roof because he hasn't free speech, he does it because he knows that he will be restrained if he attempts free action. He wants by his free speech to get some one else to do free acting—to do something he himself is afraid to do.[21]

Suffer, Little Children

Ideas have consequences—and some ideas have consequences that are immediate and lasting. Perhaps most consequential of all are those ideas propounded by professional experts (self-styled or otherwise) for the benefit of mothers seeking to know how best to raise their children. Such a practical work was Watson's 1928 volume, *The Psychological Care of Infant and Child,* solemnly "Dedicated to the First Mother Who Brings Up a Happy Child."[22] Watson's basic contention, here as elsewhere, was that only the objectively observable could constitute the data of science; that which could not be observed—*i.e.,* the child's wishes, needs, and feelings—must be excluded from scientific and professional interest and treated as if it did not exist. Children were to be handled much as mechanical objects that could be wound up and set to run in any direction. Sentimentality was to be avoided, since any show of love or close physical contact would only serve to make the child overly dependent upon its parents. One should not spoil children with affection; what one should aim for was the encouragement of self-reliance, self-sufficiency, and the avoidance of any dependence upon the affection of others. It was a prescription for the rearing of a race of rugged individualists turned heartless, whose entire philosophy of life might be summed up in the popular phrase of a later generation: "looking out for Number One."

In his views on infant and child care, Watson was compounding the egregious errors of the most prominent pediatrician of the age, Luther Emmett Holt, professor of pediatrics at Cornell University Medical School and author of the leading manual on child-rearing for more than half a century (1894 to 1984), *The Care and Feeding of Children*—a handbook read by millions of women, in which they were told among other things not to pick up their babies when they cried, to abolish the cradle, to feed them by the clock, and not to pamper them by too much handling.[23] In the opening sentence of his own book, Watson acknowledged his debt to Holt: "Ever since my first glimpse of Dr. Holt's [manual] I hoped some day to be able to write a book on the psychological care of the infant." The gist of Watson's advice to mothers was to keep their emotional distance from the child and especially to desist from kissing, coddling, or fondling it. They were not to respond too readily to their children's cries for food or attention. The child's capacities, said Watson, should be developed toward conquering the world; to meet this aggressive purpose children must be trained to master their feeding schedules, toilet training and other tasks according to a strict regimen. It was through techniques of problem-solving and absorption in strenuous activity that the child would be prepared to cope with the competitive demands of modern society. Such a child, wrote the supreme behaviorist, will be "as free as possible of sensitivities to people and one who, almost from birth, is relatively independent of the family situation." More specifically:

> There is a sensible way of treating children. . . . Never hug and kiss them, never let them sit in your lap. If you must, kiss them once on the forehead when they say good night. Shake hands with them in the morning. Give them a pat on the head if they have made an extraordinarily good job of a difficult task. Try it out. In a week's time you will find how easy it is to be perfectly objective with your child and at the same time kindly. You will be utterly ashamed of the mawkish, sentimental way you have been handling it.[24]

This mechanistic and thoroughly unsentimental approach to child-rearing greatly influenced psychology for a time and, more particularly, exercised a profound effect upon pediatric thinking and practice. Pediatricians advised parents to maintain a sophisticated aloofness from their children, keeping them at arm's length, and managing them on a schedule characterized alike by objectivity and regularity. Feedings were to be every four hours, no more and no less, and babies were not to be picked up during the interval, especially when they cried—for to yield to so maudlin an impulse would be to spoil the baby, and thereafter every time it wanted something it would cry. That would never do. And so millions of mothers sat and cried along with their babies, and—as genuinely loving parents obedient to the "best" thinking on the subject—bravely resisted the "animal impulse" to pick them up and comfort them in their arms.

There were countless mothers who felt in their hearts that this could not be right; but who were they to question the word of scientific authority?

With bottle-feeding being considered as good as breastfeeding—even better, since one didn't have to be there at all to feed the baby—the bottle rapidly displaced the breast, and until very recently some 96 percent of American women were bottle-feeding their infants. Even apart from any consideration of the damaging effects of cow's milk upon the human infant, the intimate experiences of the baby at the mother's breast are the earliest and most enduring of those events and relationships which contribute to the making of a humane, as well as human, being.[25] Therefore the triumph of the plastic bottle over the maternal breast is grimly symbolic of the broadly de-humanizing consequences of generations of pediatric folly, and of psychological nihilism, which have derived from the fallacy of mis-placed objectivity at the core of the behaviorist dogma.

The purpose here is not simply to expose the blatant philosophical naiveté (and ideological Babbitry) of the founder of behaviorism. If there were no more to it than that—if Watson's experiments and intentions, his formulas and fantasies, were only the idiosyncrasies of a crackpot of the laboratory, a psychological "Dr. Cyclops," as it were—then the entire dreary episode of Neo-Pavlovian Conditioning and dehuman engineering, of little Albert and the Ministry of Fear, of the putative manufacture of thieves and gunmen and dope fiends, might be regarded as no more than a quirky footnote to the real history of the twentieth-century science of behaviorist psychology. (And then we might only chuckle, rather than murmur amen, to the eleventh commandment of W. H. Auden: "Thou shalt not commit a social science.")

But the fact is that, while he had his idiosyncrasies, Watson was far from alone in his experimental efforts and purposes. He was not an eccentric but a prime mover in his field; the psychological school of behaviorism which he founded has been without doubt the most prominent and influential movement in American academic psychol-ogy (as distinct from clinical or therapeutic psychology) in the present century. His followers and disciples, among them B. F. Skinner, have modified and modernized his experimental methods but have not repudiated their thrust; indeed, as we shall see, they have carried the original program to new heights of ambition undreamed of in their founder's philosophy. Item: Watson had boasted that, given his own world and authority "from birth on," he could turn a baby into whatever monster he chose. Half a century later a post-Watsonian behaviorist, James McConnell, made a much better offer: "The time has come when if you give me any normal human being and *a couple of weeks* . . . I can change his behavior from what it is now to whatever you want it to be, if it's physically possible."[26]

There has always been a proviso to these grandiose claims of the behavior modifiers (or "people shapers," as Vance Packard has dubbed them). That proviso is usually implicit rather than avowed, but it is inescapable: it is that the psychologists themselves, those whom Skinner calls the "technologists of behavior," should set the goals and run the program. No one has ever been more forthright about this than Watson, who was given to expostulating about the irrational and unscientific character of existing social controls over citizen behavior. "Indeed if one were to characterize social experimentation in general during the past 2000 years," he wrote in a passage of almost Toynbeean sweep, "one would have to call it precipitous, infantile, unplanned, and say that when planned it is always in the interest of some nation, political group, sect or individual, *rather than under the guidance of social scientists*—assuming their existence."[27]

The notion of a technocracy, under the guidance of one or another version of the scientific expert, has a venerable history—not least of all in democratic America (where the elites supposedly never meet to eat). In the loosest sense the idea dates back at least as far as Plato's *Republic,* with its noble oligarchy of philosopher-kings. Since scientists and engineers have long since supplanted philosophers as the fountainheads of wisdom, it seems to many only a logical step from Plato's utopia to the efficient society envisioned by Thorstein Veblen, the American social theorist who first systematically broached the program of a technocratic government run by engineers. Veblen's plan gained particular currency in the twenties, alongside behaviorism, which for a time it rivalled in popular appeal (giving rise in fact to a devout social movement which spread across the country under the label of "Technocracy"). The coincidence in time of Veblen's and Watson's programs was explainable by their common denominator: the Engineer-King. For Veblen and his followers it was *social* engineering that was wanted; for Watson and his disciples it was (and is) *human* engineering. In practical terms these were, of course, interchangeable; the underlying principles were the same, and except for minor details so were the methods and the goals. The cry of the behaviorist was not merely "Give me this assembled organic machine, Man, and I will run it"; it was also "Give me this assembled inorganic machine, the State, and I will run it too."

The will to effectuate not only a technology of behavior but a technocracy of behaviorists was to become more pronounced in the next generation with Skinner's large-scale cultural designs; but it lurked as a possible dream (what René Dubos was to call the "dream of reason") in the minds of Watson and his colleagues. As a rational scientist, Watson was repelled by the "blind and haphazard" way in which American society was governed: "Our own country today is one of the worst offenders in history, ruled as it is by professional politicians, labor propagandists and religious persecutors."[28] As an experimental psychologist, a practitioner of human engineering on the individual scale, he evidently hankered for a wider social laboratory in which he could exercise his urge to control behavior and to "develop his world of people, from birth on," so that they might be freely exhibited everywhere without the slightest danger of running afoul of group standards.

The Engineering of Humans

The decade of the twenties, which was widely heralded as the Engineering Age, had more to show for its proclivities than Technocracy and Behaviorism. In particular, it had Scientific Management and Human Engineering. Although Frederick Winslow Taylor had introduced his managerial techniques (soon to be known as "Taylorism") as early as 1911, their large-scale application awaited the return of American industry to commercial production following the Great War—during which it had been the relative efficiency of the German *Wehrwirtschaft* directed by Walter Rathenau which made the world aware of the advantages of the scientific rationalization of production. The point of Taylorism was to rationalize not only the mechanical processes of the assembly line but its human components in particular; the "time and motion" studies of the twenties, striving to analyze in strictest detail what might be called the working state of the human organism, bore a curious resemblance to the contemporaneous researches of the subatomic quantum physicists—who were striving in their own minute way to describe the state of the electron by pinning down its exact position and movement. The resemblance of the two versions of scientific "management" went further than that: both of them foundered (or at least stumbled) on what came to be known in physics as the uncertainty principle. For the scientists of quantum mechanics this discovery of ultimate unpredictability, of a kind of quirkiness at the heart of matter which resisted (with no hope of correction) its precise description and (therefore) prediction and (therefore) *control*, took the form of the Heisenberg/Bohr equations of indeterminacy and complementarity. For the scientists of industrial management, the discovery of recalcitrance in the human unit took the form of a fuzzy compromise with rationality and precision—alternately labeled "human engineering" or "human relations."

The introduction of the human-relations approach into the factory and shop (and later the executive suite) resulted from the belated discovery of the scientific managers that individual efficiency and productivity were a function, not merely of incentives and rewards (Taylorism), but of something called "morale." If worker morale was low, no amount of carrots or sticks would turn it around; if morale was high, no additional incentive was needed. This was, of course, the proposition famously demonstrated by Elton Mayo (father of the human relations school) and his colleagues in the late twenties at a Western Electric plant in Hawthorne, Illinois. The management there had been applying conventional Taylorism to determine how incentives such as improved lighting might serve to increase production; but their findings had been strangely contradictory. When they separated out two groups of women employees for the test, one group to receive better lighting and the other not, they discovered that output went up in both groups. Entering the scene at this point, Mayo's team tried all sorts of incentive schemes with the experimental groups, but always with the same result: the selected workers pushed production up whether conditions were improved or not. After some years of this, the serendipitous discovery was made: the workers involved were putting out so well just because they were "involved"—i.e., selectively treated, noticed, made to feel important. The recognition of the morale factor was a victory for the new field of "industrial psychology," which sought to refute Marx by bringing the industrial worker back into adjustment with his work. The human relations approach was not a contradiction of scientific management but an extension of it; to the hard science of management was added the soft psychology of manipulation. The significance of this advance in human engineering has been well interpreted by Jacques Ellul in his formidable critique of "the technological society":

> When the worker feels that he is in a hostile environment and in an economic system opposed to his interests, he will not work (and this is involuntary) with the same ardor and skill. . . . Purely material transformations in the conditions of labor are insufficient. They are doubtless necessary to begin with, but physiological adaptation is not the only kind. Hygiene and safety must indeed be improved; the best location must be selected, and even music may have to be exploited to make labor more rhythmic and less disagreeable. But this is still not enough. The true problem is psychological. The worker is confronted by cut-and-dried procedures that must be carried out in unvarying sequence in order that work be systematic, rational, and efficient; he is bored, slowed down, and psychologically constrained. It is necessary to arouse in him reflective thought and to make him participate in the life of the entire plant. He must be made to feel a community of interest; the idea that his labor has social meaning must be instilled in him. In short, he must be integrated into the enterprise in which he is working.[29]

Elton Mayo himself showed the way to this whole-souled integration of the person into the system. On the basis of the Hawthorne experience, Mayo elaborated a social philosophy that closely paralleled and extended the cosmic vision of John B. Watson. Its aim was to activate the latent resources of spontaneous cooperativeness and sociability which Mayo believed to be the dominant drives of human nature ("Man's desire to be continuously associated in work with his fellows is a strong, if not the strongest, human characteristic")[30] and to enlist these in the service of the emerging "industrial civilization." The goal was the conscious creation of what Mayo called "an adaptive society"—i.e., one that would adapt the individual to social purposes and demands as fully as the primitive tribesman was absorbed within his group. When the process of adaptation was ultimately completed, Mayo was confident that the distinctions between the individual and society, between the private and the public realms, would vanish. It would be again as it once had been in that idyllic state of early man which Mayo looked upon as virtually a golden age. There

> The situation is not simply that the society exercises a forceful compulsion on the individual; on the contrary, the social code and the desire of the individual are, for all practical purposes, identical. Every member of the group participates in all social activities because it is his chief desire to do so.[31]

To bring about this new golden age Mayo proposed the establishment of an administrative elite—another version of the technocracy of human engineers—who would bring the individual uncoercively and almost unwittingly into harmony with the socioeconomic system. As William H. Whyte, Jr., has summarized the program: "They will adjust him. Through the scientific application of human relations, these neutralist technicians will guide him into satisfying solidarity with the group so skillfully and unobtrusively that he will scarcely realize how the benefaction has been accomplished."[32]

In practice, to be sure, Mayo was unable to gain for his coterie of technocrats the degree of power that would enable them to turn the entire society around. But he did gain general acceptance for his viewpoint within the industrial and business community through the rapid growth of the human relations approach and its psychological tools of soothing, shaping, and socializing. One of those tools found embodiment in the form of "nondirective counselors," either psychologists or pseudo-psychologists, whose function it was to provide a kind of silent therapeutic audience for the grievances and discontents of employees. In fact, the role of the counselor was remarkably like that of the priest in the confessional; in this secular version also the confessor was guaranteed confidentiality, as well as sympathy and a vague impression that the counselor was his ally if not his advocate. However (like some priests and unlike others), the industrial counselor only listened but did not respond; he offered neither practical solutions to the problems brought to him nor any real advice (which was doubtless just as well in view of his customary trained incapacity). The role of counselor was deliberately set up as a safety valve, a means of siphoning off hostility and frustration which might otherwise be directed against the company. In short, this counseling was not only nondirective; it was systematically unhelpful. Ellul has described the actual function of the counselors in trenchant terms:

> Employees may express their feelings to these "counselors" with the assurance that the counselors will say nothing to management. But the counselors never actually counsel anything. . . . Their sole duty is to encourage the voicing of complaints and to listen to them. It is well-known that suffering expressed is suffering relieved. It has been observed that certain psychological disturbances are provoked simply by being silent and that rebellions are nourished in secret. To let people talk does them good and quashes revolt. It is dangerous to allow the workers to talk over their problems among themselves. It is far more prudent to give them a safety valve in the form of a discreet company agent, a psychological technician, than to let them air their grievances in public.[33]

The immediate inspiration for the counseling idea had come from Mayo's Hawthorne experience, in which he found that his interviews with workers seemed to have a salutary psychological effect. The workers felt better for the chat; they went back and worked better because of it; perhaps they really *were* better for it. So he took the idea to the bosses and developed with their predictable approval what might have been called the Mayo Clinic (if there were not already another one in Kansas). Understandably, the industrial unions of the time were less enthusiastic; and largely through their opposition the Mayo counselors failed to catch on as a staple of management-labor relations. As it turned out, however, Mayo was ahead of his time; in the late fifties and sixties the human relations approach, replete with counseling (plus the whole paraphernalia of group dynamics, sensitivity training, encountering and transactionalizing), reappeared in force throughout the corporate system—not, this time, with respect to labor relations but with respect to the management of management.[34]

To return to Mayo, the underlying reason for his faith in the therapy of the counselor was his conviction that the source of "human problems" generally was not to be found in concrete issues of injustice, exploitation, discrimination and the like, but rather in the sphere of "communication"—of verbal misunderstandings, crossed signals and poor connections. At bottom he believed that most problems (if not quite all) were merely verbal; grievances were for the most part fancied rather than real; there was nothing like a good confidential talk, a letting off of steam and a letting down of hair, to make it all come right. This bland assumption of the absence of genuine conflict, of an underlying consensual framework and harmony of interests, was, of course, a version of the liberal-conservative American ideology which interpreted the nation's history in terms of consensus and continuity, described its society in terms of a unitary culture and a singular (not to say unique) national character, and was already beginning to apply to social concerns the engineering terminology of system and equilibrium. Apart from its consistency with the prevailing climate of opinion, Mayo's convenient theory of the verbal solution of social problems ("Come, let us reason together") was closely related to another school which gained such prominence in the thirties and forties as to take on the character of a social movement: i.e., semantics, and in particular its capitalized variation of General Semantics. At the hands of popular spokesmen like Stuart Chase and the young scholar S. I. Hayakawa, grounded in the arcane manuscripts of Count Alfred Korzybski, the school of semantics found a ready audience for its social gospel of the linguistic salvation of suffering humanity. The way to the frictionless society, the parliament of man and (ultimately) the federation of the world, lay through clear channels of communication. As with Mayo, this grand design would require an administrative elite of experts—i.e., the semanticists, later to be recycled into psycho- and sociolinguists—whose objective was the training or conditioning of the populace not just toward good behavior but toward good speech behavior.[35]

The Behavior Mod Squad

Peter Schrag, in his groundbreaking (and occasionally heartbreaking) report on the new scientific techniques of behavioral intervention, *Mind Control,* traces the origin of these efforts directly to the factory assembly line and the rationalized production system—

and more specifically to scientific management and its subsequent refinements. "Behavior modification," he points out, "is an attempt to apply the style and techniques of total institutions (and of factories) to the world outside."[36] In other words what is good for General Motors, as Charles E. Wilson once remarked, is good for America. That remark of an industrial manager turned defense secretary seemed impertinent to most Americans when it was uttered in the fifties; but it also seemed far-fetched. However, to a degree not yet sufficiently appreciated, the businessman's vision of an entire society governed (administered) on "sound management principles" has become political reality. It was no less a person than President Coolidge who said that the business of a democracy was business. It has been more than a century since the spoils system in public administration gave way to the civil service, animated by the lofty spirit of "meritocracy" (or the aristocracy of talent). During that time the burgeoning field of public administration, and in particular the federal bureaucracy, came to be pervaded by the style and philosophy of those whom historian Max Lerner has characterized as the Neutral Technicians—an administrative elite of scientific managers occupying positions in the public sector no less powerful than those they hold in the private sector. The "managerial revolution" in industry, which was first identified by Berle and Means in the thirties and systematically defined by James Burnham in the next decade, has long since spread to Washington.[37] Before David Stockman, even before Robert McNamara, the bureaucrat had become the technocrat, and the technocrat was becoming the autocrat. In the process the political state, once a more or less democratic affair of elected officials and a few reined-in clerks on the order of Dickens's Uriah Heep, has turned more and more into the Administrative State (in Dwight Waldo's term)—in effect, a hidden government of nonelective and irresponsible officials insensitive to "politics" and indifferent to any values other than their own technical imperative. The penetration of the neutral technicians into the corridors of political power—as well as in industry, much of science, and such professions as medicine—was viewed by Lerner as the most portentous development of the postwar period, largely because it carried with it a transvaluation of values in which democratic purposes, human needs, and public interests would become mere dependent variables of the overriding technical ethos of efficiency, organization, and social equilibrium. "The role of the

Neutral Technician," wrote Lerner, "thus casts its shadow over the whole present era. It becomes the Great Withdrawal, or—as Erich Kahler has put it—a kind of nihilism of values along with an exaltation of techniques."[38]

For social engineering on a large scale to become effective, and to be deemed acceptable, there had to be a conception of society and of the polity as itself a "system" amenable to the methods and manipulations of scientific managers. That model, which had been implicit in mechanistic images of society from Thomas Hobbes to F. H. Giddings,[39] was fully articulated in the forties and fifties by a succession of attuned social scientists—notably sociologist Talcott Parsons (*The Social System*) and political scientist David Easton (*The Political System*)—who provided the theoretical rationale for the mission of the social engineers and the technologists of behavior.[40] Their system model, drawn more or less consciously from engineering science, carried as its unstated major premise the notion of society as a kind of functional social-cybernetic mechanism governed by the principle of homeostatic equilibrium. Parsons in particular (like his Harvard colleagues Elton Mayo and B. F. Skinner) was drawn by his model to concentrate upon the issues of order, stability, social control, and survival of the System; for him also the ideal society was one in which the demands of the System would be internalized as "shared values" by all of its members, hence eliminating conflict and guaranteeing the frictionless operation of the great machine. In such a society, of course, to paraphrase Huxley, humankind would give no further trouble; it would be an unlonely crowd of organization men and women shaped by behavioral engineers into the happy consciousness of cheerful robots. The archaic issues of freedom, dissent, privacy, even of individuality itself, would be rendered meaningless by the complete integration of the person into the encompassing system. In the Parsonian utopia, as Wayne Hield has declared, "Man is a helpless creature to be adapted and adjusted to the *status quo* or what is called 'social control.'"[41] And another dissenting sociologist, Alvin W. Gouldner, has suggested that in such a brave new scientific world as Parsons's there would be little left of the human being to control:

> Man is a hollowed-out, empty being filled with substance only by society. Man thus is seen as an entirely *social* being, and the possibility of conflict between man and society is

thereby reduced. Man now has and is nothing of his own that need be counterposed to society.[42]

The engineering model which was agreeably constructed by social scientists like Parsons and Easton gave legitimacy to the passion of the technocrats for an engineered society. It helped to make respectable the spreading practices of scientific management and manipulation of the citizenry toward a new and better world. It not only affirmed that the social end justifies the psychological means; it made the means appear less *mean*. For it was not just social betterment that was sought; it was the betterment of man himself. The means of social adjustment and adaptation, of neo-Watsonian conditioning and behavior modification, in all their rich variety, were finally for the purpose of improving the breed. As B. F. Skinner was to declare: "A scientific view of man offers exciting possibilities. We have not yet seen what man can make of man."[43]

Well, we had seen—even before Skinner—what some men might make of other men, and even what a few men would make of all men if they could. But it is certainly true that with the arrival of Skinner we have seen more: possibly, as some of his readers would say, more than we cared to see or wished to know. For Skinner has done more than carry on the work of Watson and the line of human engineers; he has proposed a grand design for the total reconstruction of society and the transformation of modern culture. He is at once the father of contemporary behaviorist theory and the godfather of behavior-modification practices. With the sole exception of Freud, Skinner is doubtless the most influential and the most controversial psychologist of the twentieth century (at least in America). His influence alone warrants critical attention; his controversiality positively reinforces it.

As a prologue to Skinner, it should be recalled that the psychology of behaviorism has from its inception concentrated attention exclusively upon observable (objective) behavior and has ignored subjective experience entirely. But it has not only disregarded the internal states of mind and feeling, of cognition and conation—in the way that physiologists, for example, have quite properly disregarded them as lying outside their scientific competence. Behaviorists have not been so modest; believing that nothing human is alien to them, they

have simply excluded the life and qualities of mind from their definition of humanity. (There is an apparent, but not real, exception in the
case of Skinnerian theory, which acknowledges the existence of what
is called "private stimulation" but then proceeds to reduce it to the
same functional analysis within the same stimulus-response framework which is used for "public stimulation"; as Skinner himself
maintains, "The skin is not that important as a boundary. Private and
public events have the same kind of physical dimensions.")[44] Not
much has changed since the original manifesto of the grand conditioner. The behaviorist began, declared Watson, "by sweeping aside
all mediaeval conceptions. He dropped from his scientific vocabulary
all subjective terms such as sensation, perception, image, desire, purpose, and even thinking and emotion as they were subjectively
defined."[45] Such primitive ideas interfered with the construction of a
rigorously objective science of behavior; they contradicted its fundamental premise—namely, that man is a *machine*, no more and no
less. Watson was only the first of his school to sweep away the
medieval notions of purpose and meaning. One of his prominent
disciples, Z. Y. Kuo, for example, repeated the declamation with
equal fervor: "The concept of purpose is a lazy substitute for . . .
careful and detailed analysis. . . . The duty of a behaviorist is to
describe behavior in exactly the same way as the physicist describes
the movement of a machine."[46] And Clark L. Hull, a dominant figure
of the following generation, became so exercised over the stubborn
persistence of the ghost in the machine—he labeled it "subjective
anthropomorphism"—that he devised an elaborate "prophylaxis" to
ward off its sinister effects in the laboratory. In order to avoid the sin
of studying humans in humane terms (i.e. as sentient and sensual
beings), Hull proposed that the experimental researcher should discipline himself to regard them as "subhuman organisms" or, better yet,
as robots:

> One aid to the attainment of behavioral objectivity is to think
> in terms of the behavior of subhuman organisms, such as
> chimpanzees, monkeys, dogs, cats, and albino rats. Unfortu-
> nately this form of prophylaxis against subjectivism all too
> often breaks down when the theorist begins thinking what he
> would do if he were a rat, a cat, or a chimpanzee . . .

> A device much employed by the author has proved itself to be
> a far more effective prophylaxis. This is to regard, from time
> to time, the behaving organism as a completely self-
> maintaining robot, constructed of materials as unlike our-
> selves as may be.[47]

In practice, of course, the convinced behaviorist did not regard his
human subjects as mechanical robots only "from time to time": he
thought of them that way all the time. From Watson's organic machine ready to run, through Hull's completely self-maintaining robot,
to the ultimate dispossession of "Autonomous Man" by Skinner's
technology of behavior, the commitment of the behaviorist to a mechanical model of human nature has been faithful and unyielding. To
be sure, it is not only behaviorists who hold this belief. The mechanistic view of man has an ancient history, an archive of theoretical and
documentary materials, and (especially in our own cybernetic age) a
widening circle of true believers. It is the outgrowth of the conceptual
revolution which began with Newtonian mechanics, Cartesian philosophy, and Hobbesian psychology in the seventeenth century and
which peaked in the next century with the advent of the Enlightenment school of mechanistic philosophers led by the French Ency-
clopedists La Mettrie, D'Holbach, Condorcet and Cabanis. La Mettrie
made the point succinctly: "Let us conclude boldly then that man is a
machine, and that there is only one substance, differently modified,
in the whole world. What will all the weak reeds of divinity,
metaphysic, and nonsense of the schools, avail against this firm and
solid oak?"[48] And D'Holbach drew the psychological conclusion: "If
man believes himself free, he is merely exhibiting a dangerous delu-
sion and an intellectual weakness. It is the structure of the atoms that
forms him, and their motion propels him forward; conditions not
dependent on him determine his nature and direct his fate."[49]

Not even the rhetoric has changed that much in the intervening
centuries; and the underlying assumptions have not changed at all.
Indeed, for the present-day mechanist of behavior, they have hardened. Thus Skinner has reinforced the thesis of D'Holbach:

> The hypothesis that man is not free is essential to the applica-
> tion of scientific method to the study of human behavior. The
> free inner man who is held responsible for the behavior of the

external biological organism is only a prescientific substitute for the kinds of causes which are discovered in the course of a scientific analysis. All these alternative causes lie *outside* the individual.[50]

Skinner's unrelenting antipathy to the very ideas of human freedom, dignity and responsibility has become notorious since the publication in 1971 of his bestselling testament, *Beyond Freedom and Dignity*. It would seem to be a singular characteristic of the man. But we have observed, in reviewing the writings of his predecessors and mentors, that this hostility is no mere idiosyncracy of Skinner's; it goes with the territory. The denial of the reality of freedom (and *a fortiori* of choice, purpose, resourcefulness, creativity, will, and the like) is regarded by behaviorists as something like a formal prerequisite to admission into their fellowship—a kind of scientific loyalty oath. This commitment to the principle of total determinism in the field of human conduct is, as Skinner wrote in *Science and Human Behavior* (1953), "a working assumption which must be adopted at the very start. We cannot apply the methods of science to a subject matter which is assumed to move about capriciously."[51] That image of personal freedom as a sort of puckish conceit or wild impulse, a form of mis-behavior, does appear to have a peculiar prominence in Skinner's view of things; the identical idiom was employed by his fictional alter ego, Frazier, in the utopian novel *Walden Two* (1948): "I deny that freedom exists at all. I must deny it—or my program would be absurd. You can't have a science about a subject matter which hops capriciously about."[52] It is clear that freedom, to Skinner, is in a literal sense *disorderly conduct*. His view of reality is that of a proper schoolmaster: there *will* be no hopping about in his cosmic classroom; students *will* do as they are programed; otherwise we *cannot* proceed with our science experiment. In short, we must all behave. The science of behavior is really the domestic science of good behavior.

There is another revealing passage in *Walden Two,* in which the founder of that tranquil and orderly community momentarily bares his soul:

"I have only one important characteristic, Burris: I'm stubborn. I've had only one idea in my life—a true *ideé fixe* . . .

to put it as bluntly as possible, the idea of having my own way. Control expresses it, I think. The control of human behavior, Burris. In my early experimental days it was a frenzied, selfish desire to dominate. I remember the rage I used to feel when a prediction went awry. I could have shouted at the subjects of my experiments: '*Behave*, damn you, *behave* as you ought.' "[53]

There seems no reason not to take this confession seriously. Virtually everything Skinner has written, and almost everything that has been spun off from his experiments, has been directed to controlling behavior—initially the behavior of pigeons and rodents, next the behavior of humans. He has never made any bones about it: the science of behavior generates a technology of control. That technology is in place; it is there to be used, on every stage of human action and in every arena of power—from the prison and the kindergarten to the total culture of a nation. "Control" is easily the most resonant and recurrent term in Skinner's vocabulary; it appears in every context, at the end of every chain of reasoning. There is not only "control" but "counter-control"; there are controlled environments and controlling measures; "we all control and we are all controlled." Even apart from the confession of Frazier, the inference is irresistible that the vision of control, of power over others, is for Skinner an *ideé fixe*: an obsession.

"Behave, Damn You"

Skinner has also made plain where his own "controlling interests" lie; it is wherever the technology can be effectively enforced and where human beings are most controllable—i.e., most vulnerable and powerless. "The things that impress me," he once said in an interview, "are not so much the laboratory experiments with human subjects but the success of the technological applications to humans. This is most easily done under controlled environments, such as institutions for the care of psychotics or the retarded, or with juvenile delinquents, or small children. There you have more control than in the world at large."[54] He might have added prisons to his list, because (as we shall see) it is in these most total of institutions that behavior mod has had its greatest "successes"—if that is the term for its unde-niably potent results. But his own roster of preferred environments, as it stands, is significant for its one common denominator: the rela-tive defenselessness and manipulability of those to be controlled. In truth the asylum and the detention center (whatever may be said for the elementary school) are *ipso facto* agencies of social control—of the management of deviance and the maintenance of order—a func-tion which they hold in common with the prison. They are in simple fact the primordial modifiers of behavior; they exist for the purpose of shaping the conduct of their wards, and "good behavior" is the officially desired and rewarded outcome. (The time-honored expres-sion for the shaping they undertake—one that is shared with the military and other authoritarian institutions—is "shaping up.")

That institutional objective should not be confused with healing, or even helping. "Cures" do, of course, occur in asylums, at a fairly stable rate, no matter what therapies or aversive reinforcements are applied to patients; and rehabilitation does occasionally transpire, for one or another reason, in detention centers of all kinds. But these happy outcomes (which are mainly remarkable for their infrequency) are a byproduct of the basic managerial assignment of such custodial institutions—which might well be labeled "Mission Control." The test of success with any of their programs is the elimination of resis-tance, passive or active, and the shaping up of the inmate population. Long before the emergence of the modern behavior modifiers, these institutions were already systematically modifying behavior, both aversively and nonaversively. Now that Behavior Modification (BM) is upon us, with its impressive arsenal of reinforcers and extinguishers, its awesome technology, the age-old mission of control has not been supplanted or transcended but rather has been scientifically validated and technically perfected. The one undeniable accomplishment of BM after nearly three decades of application has been its massive augmentation of the resources of power in the hands of custodians and managers; to the old armory of conventional weapons, so to speak, it has added a whole new line of superweapons. Against these efficient technologies there is little or no defense. Among them are: psychosurgery; electrical stimulation of the brain (ESB); psycho-pharmacology (mind-altering drugs); electroconvulsive therapy (ECT); prefrontal sonic treatment (PST), and a battery of aversive conditioning techniques directly descended from Watson's primitive ministry of fear. As one observer of the scene, generally sympathetic to Skinner's work, has concluded: "Behavior mod seems to appeal to the worst in us all. It is a power trip that allows us to dominate other human beings. In setting after setting, behavior mod has been introduced and implemented essentially to control other people."[55]

As Skinner has himself indicated, the preferred arenas for the practice of behavior modification are those "controlled environments" in which the controller can have his way and perform his operations without restriction or resistance. In the setting of the asylum, for example, circumstances are almost ideal for the behaviorist since the patients are already "preconditioned" to a manipulated milieu replete with rewards and punishments, surveillance and obedience, in which there are no rights but only uncertain privileges. As sociologist Erving Goffman has put it, "punishments and privileges are themselves modes of organization peculiar to total institutions. Whatever their severity, punishments are largely known in the inmate's home world as something applied to animals and children; this conditioning, behavioristic model is not widely applied to adults."[56] But those who enter here must abandon hope of such standard civilian safeguards of the self as privacy, responsibility, voluntary choice, mobility, and the like. They are beyond freedom and dignity: fair game for the controller.

It was in the mental hospital that Skinnerians first developed the special technique of reward and punishment—the "token economy"—that was to become popularly associated with behavior modification and to find wide application in other institutions such as prisons and schools. Tokens are credits, rewards for good conduct (or appropriate responses), which are given to or taken away from inmates and which can be turned in like gold stamps for whatever objects (candy bars, cigarettes) or valued events (access to a TV program) are set forth in the "contract" presented to the patient-subject. In the simplest form of the token economy the inmate accumulates tokens for such actions as making his bed, washing his hands before a meal, or simply obeying orders. That is the basic program of positive reinforcements; in practice it has often been supplemented by aversive (punishment) procedures as well, in the form of "fines" against the patient of so many tokens for such and such an infraction of the house rules. Just how significant this mock-capitalist ethic can be to an inmate of the asylum is indicated by one study cited by Geiser, in which the release of patients from the hospital itself—the very evidence of cure or rehabilitation—was made contingent upon the garnering of one thousand tokens.[57] In other programs the ordinary perquisites of full meals and personal articles, above the level of bare subsistence, have had to be "earned" by patients in token form by demonstrations of cooperative behavior. In one program, a certain number of tokens was required to obtain permission to go to bed; in another a token-poor patient was permitted to go five days without meals.[58] The punitive and coercive character of these instances of behavior mod is illustrated by this description of one not untypical program:

> The token economy is designed so that patients can exist comfortably only by participating actively in the program. Unless they work at a job, earn tokens and spend the tokens, they are not able to live at more than a subsistence level. None have been content for more than a few days with a free mattress on the floor and every fourth meal provided.[59]

These stringent measures, be it noted, were carried out not in prisons—where the coercive containment of inmates has at least some legal justification—but in mental hospitals where the inmates are officially defined as patients (injured persons) rather than as prisoners (injuring persons). It is difficult for a nonbehaviorist to comprehend how these procedures differ either in substance or effect from the time-dishonored devices of "correction" enforced by old-fashioned custodians and overseers without benefit of behavioral science—e.g., the withholding of meals, denial of yard privileges, solitary confinement, demerits, and good-conduct medals. There is no need to dwell at length on the dubious ethics of the microcosmic "acquisitive society" fostered by the token system of exchange—with its economics and psychology of greed, hoarding, fawning and faking which has given it the appearance of a Marxist parody of hard-hearted capitalism (one female schizophrenic reportedly accumulated tokens from male patients in return for sexual favors, thereby reinventing the oldest commercial profession).[60] More significant is the universal disposition of behavior modifiers in the setting of the hospital to regard their programs as management tools, technologies of control, in the service of the institution rather than of the patient.

Thus Geiser concludes that "By and large, token economies have been management control techniques, making patient care easier for the caretakers . . . . In most institutions contingencies are arranged for the comfort and convenience of staff rather than for the benefit of the inmate population."[61]

It could scarcely be otherwise. Behavior modification never promised patients a rose garden; it only promised administrators a clean well-lighted place. It offered an alternative vision to the old image of the asylum as a snake pit and a cuckoo's nest; in its stead there would be a peaceable kingdom, an orderly social system in which everyone (of the subject class) worked and no one shirked, a system based on a money economy and a stratified structure of social ranks designed to appeal to the upwardly mobile—as in the following summary of numerous hospital programs:

> Sometimes the entire institution is organized into successive levels, called steps or tiers, and progress from one level to another is tied into a token economy. The levels provide different degrees of physical comfort and privileges for patients. Step one might be to live in a dormitory with a mattress on the floor to sleep on. The next step might allow you to earn a bed for the mattress. The next level might be to a semiprivate or private room. Other comforts and privileges are also distributed over the levels, such as the quality of the food, visiting and grounds privileges, choice of recreational activities, better work assignments, and so forth. Discharge from the hospital may or may not be made contingent upon reaching the highest level.[62]

"From each according to his ability, to each according to his work." It would be hard to say whether this little token society more resembles the capitalist or the socialist model of a well-regulated and smoothly running social order; but there is no doubt that it thoroughly embodies and articulates the behaviorist model. It looks like nothing so much as a miniature Walden Three.

From a different standpoint it may seem to fall short of perfection. Just as BM invariably reflects the interests and goals of the managers rather than of the patients, so it is inclined to regard all resistance or recalcitrance as willful, destructive, and punishable. Deviant behavior, in sum, is not allowable. But here a cruel paradox asserts itself: the institution involved is after all a mental hospital, a community of deviants. To require the mentally ill, the disturbed and confused, the traumatized and brain-damaged, to "shape up" instantly as mentally healthy or face the aversive consequences is to produce a version of "Catch-22." The only way for the seriously disturbed individual to perform normally is to fake it: to manage a passable impression of compliance long enough and well enough to escape punishment and acquire a modicum of tokens. He must therefore keep his fantasies to himself, confine his mutterings to his private space, and let no one (least of all the modifiers) know his inner terrors and distress. Hence he may, if he is fortunate, succeed in the institutional game and rise in its pecking order *at the price of receiving no help at all in the resolution if his troubles.* He may even be "graduated" at the top of his class; but then, unaided and untreated, trained to cope only with the peculiar rituals of the custodial institution, he is naked to the world—and will almost certainly be recommitted. Much has been done to him, but little has been done for him.

The cruel irony of suppressing deviance—and oppressing the deviant—in a community made up of involuntary deviants points to an additional paradox of BM. According to the Skinnerian dogma, the individual human being, normal as well as abnormal, is never responsible for his own behavior. All of the real causes of behavior, as Skinner has repeatedly insisted, "lie *outside* the individual . . . . These are the things which make the individual behave as he does. For them he is not responsible, and for them it is useless to praise or blame him."[63] But in the practical contexts of BM, in the asylum or the prison or the school, praise and blame are the indispensable reinforcers. If the individual is not responsible for his conduct, why is he rewarded when he does the "right thing" and punished when he does the "wrong thing"? Surely the assumption can only be that he must take responsibility for his actions, his little conformities and derelictions, and that his responsibility becomes more complete (more rational and more substantial) as his performance becomes more successful. This conflict between behaviorist theory and BM practice is a graphic evidence of the movement's intellectual confusion. The behaviorist bible, in both its Old Testament (Watson) and its New Testament (Skinner), tells of the Fall of Man—the dispossession of "Autonomous Man" and his replacement by the divine forces of

Natural Law. It is a compelling drama; and the rhetoric of its narrative has an almost King Jamesian quality:

> What is being abolished is autonomous man—the inner man, the homunculus, the possessing demon, the man defended by the literatures of freedom and dignity.
>
> His abolition has long been overdue. Autonomous man is a device used to explain what we cannot explain in any other way. He has been constructed from our ignorance, and as our understanding increases, the very stuff of which he is composed vanishes. Science does not dehumanize man, it de-homunculizes him, and it must do so if it is to prevent the abolition of the human species. To man *qua* man we readily say good riddance. Only by dispossessing him can we turn to the real causes of human behavior. Only then can we turn from the inferred to the observed, from the miraculous to the natural, from the inaccessible to the manipulable.[64]

That is the holy writ. But the moving finger of Skinner, having writ, moves on to manipulate—and what it manipulates is not the external causes, the determining forces out there, but the Old Adam himself, the homunculus, the responding organism. And he is manipulated *as if* he has a choice, as if he is capable of taking responsibility for his actions, of learning from the sanctions imposed upon him and correcting his "mistakes." If BM is to work at all, the BM'er must put aside the Book and revive the ghost in the machine. The left hand of God does not know what the right hand is doing. The imputation of a degree of responsibility, however latent or incomplete, is most clearly evident in the institutional use of "deprivations" (punishments), which have tended to become the rule rather than the exception in BM programs designed for the correction of deviant behavior. An especially lurid example of "aversive reinforcement" was uncovered by an investigating committee in 1974 in a Florida school for the retarded, where a token system of rewards was counterbalanced by a regimen of "programmed abuse" (the committee's term) which embraced such measure as

> forced public masturbation and forced public homosexual acts for engaging in proscribed sexual behavior; beating with

a wooden panel for running away; and washing the mouth with soap for lying, for abusive or vulgar language, or sometimes for speaking at all. Further, food, sleep and visitation privileges were withheld as punishment, incontinence was punished by requiring residents to lie in soiled sheets and to hold soiled underwear to their noses . . . and one boy was required to walk around publicly clothed only in female underpants.[65]

How much more responsibility for his behavior or misbehavior can a human being, let alone a retarded and confused youth, be asked to bear?

The Invasion of the Brain Snatchers

The case of the Florida school (which might well be labeled the "Jacksonville Horror") is no doubt extreme; but neither its philosophy nor its practices are at all exceptional in the annals of behavior modification. The punishments it enforced upon its hapless students were cruel but not unusual. Many of the more blatant BM exercises in mass dehumanization disguised as therapy ("aversion therapy" and "negative reinforcement therapy" are among the favored designations) have surfaced in the last decade as a result of legal actions and legislative investigations—notably that of a Senate committee chaired by the redoubtable Sam Irvin.[66] Among them were cases in which prisoners entering a BM program were immediately placed in solitary confinement, not for infractions committed but simply because all the succeeding steps in the token system would appear that much more desirable. And there were many more cases in which prisoners discovered that the possibility of parole itself was made contingent upon their "volunteering" for a BM program. That contingency presented a novel version of "Prisoner's Dilemma" (a strategic game-theory conundrum in which the player may find himself "doomed if he does and doomed if he doesn't").[67] If the prisoner should decline the invitation to submit to the program, he would be denied parole and often subjected to other punishment. In one case, for example, a particularly resistant convict was held in solitary confinement for a period of eight years, although his total sentence was only for five years! On the other hand, if the prisoner should join the program, he would be subjected to its (often undisclosed) battery of interventions and experiments—typically including, along with all the tokens, some version of electric shock or "electroconvulsive therapy." In numerous cases, the entrapped prisoners have found themselves transformed into guinea pigs for any of a host of novel (i.e., potentially lethal) drugs or devices previously tried out only on rodents. From some of these "treatments"—notably the various operations grouped together under the heading of psychosurgery, or what someone has called "laundered lobotomy"—the prisoner may never return as a whole human being.

Psychosurgery in its several forms is the sophisticated contemporary version of an ancient medical practice—that of drilling holes in the head, or removing portions of the skull, of an individual exhibiting (the vocabulary depends on the culture) evil or malignant or crazy or deviant behavior. The assumption behind the practice is always the same: the source of the bad conduct is in the body, more specifically in the head, and (most recently) in the brain. The prognosis: pinpoint the area of trouble, then either cut it out or blast it with a dose of electric shock. (The latter treatment long predates the lightning-induced birth of the Frankenstein monster and the demonstration of Ben Franklin's kite; according to Peter Schrag, electric shock therapy goes back at least to Roman times when an early technologist of behavior named Scribonious Largus sought to cure the emperor's headaches with an electric eel.)[68] The method of lobotomy, which involves the removal of the guilty part of the brain, was apparently practiced by various primitive tribes; in modern times it was probably approximated by numbers of physicians treating the insane with therapies of violence before one Gottlieb Burckhardt, a Swiss asylum director in the eighteen nineties, performed the first recorded operations to remove brain segments from several frenzied patients. But it was in the nineteen thirties that both the method of lobotomy and that of electroshock gained sudden and widespread acceptance as legitimate means of behavior modification in cases beyond the simpler reinforcements of the carrot and the stick. The father of modern lobotomy was a Portuguese doctor, Egas Moniz, who was inspired by the surgical pacification of neurotic monkeys through excision of the frontal lobes; with what may have been undue haste he performed the same operation on several psychotic patients and achieved such apparently dramatic results that he was awarded the Nobel Prize for his discoveries. (That was the good news for Dr. Moniz; the bad news was that one of his "successfully" lobotomized patients went berserk, obtained a gun, and shot the doctor in the spine, leaving him partially paralyzed for life.)

The Americanization of the lobotomy occurred in the same decade at the hands, so to speak, of two pioneer psychosurgeons, Walter Freeman and James W. Watts, whose yankee ingenuity soon streamlined and simplified the operation so that it could be performed quickly and efficiently by any trained neurosurgeon in his own office without the mess and bother of hospitalization. The Freeman technique, which soon became famous as the "icepick" method, involved the insertion of a sharp-pointed instrument through the skull into the prefrontal lobes and then maneuvering it so as to sever the lower sections of the lobes. However, as Samuel Chavkin points out, ". . . the surgeon was operating blindly and destroying not only the presumed targeted area but also a good deal of the surrounding tissue."[69] No one appears to have been deterred by the crudeness and destructiveness of the operation, least of all Dr. Freeman—who is said to have racked up a total of four thousand icepick lobotomies before he was induced to cease and desist in the fifties. In all there may have been fifty thousand such operations across the country in the decade and a half after its discovery—assisted significantly by the enthusiastic support of the Veterans Administration and the military services, which were quick to perceive the economy as well as the efficiency of icepick therapy in the solution of the vast wave of "battle fatigue" problems associated with World War II. Conventional psychology and psychiatry were not only slow but suspiciously soft in their treatment of "shell-shocked" GIs; more than a few army medics favored the sterner approach of General George Patton, for whom neurotic behavior in a soldier was a form of malingering. In those cases that did not respond to a slap in the face, or alternatively to electroconvulsive therapy (ECT), lobotomy appeared as the ideal and virtually irresistible answer. It was soon extended to a broad range of mental and emotional difficulties; as Schrag observes, as early as 1943 the VA urged special training in lobotomy procedures for its staff neurosurgeons who were advised to seek out as likely candidates those soldiers who exhibited symptoms of "apprehension, anxiety, and depression . . . also cases with compulsions and obsessions, with marked emotional tension."[70] By the late forties lobotomy had become virtually "standard operating procedure," a kind of surgical chic, applicable to any poor soul who displayed erratic behavior or mental confusion and who lacked the capacity to resist the medical nemesis. Some surgeons reportedly performed as many as fifty lobotomies in a day.[71]

The early wave of lobotomy operations—the first invasion of the brain snatchers—receded in the fifties mainly due to the emergence of the new tranquilizing drugs in the treatment of psychiatric disorders. It was also becoming clearer by then, to those who bothered to check, that the icepick operations had produced a population akin to T.S. Eliot's "hollow men . . . stuffed men / Leaning together / Headpiece filled with straw." The method had modified behavior in all cases, to be sure; but for the vast majority (probably for all without exception) the cure was demonstrably worse than the disease. Far from eliminating confusion and distress, the lobotomies generally left their victims more confused and disturbed than ever, frequently unable to function in the most elementary ways, and often (the supreme irony) more frustrated, angry and hostile than before. The lobotomizers had not only failed to cure whatever it was that troubled their patients; they had scrambled their brains and opened a Pandora's Box of bizarre behaviors and unforeseen afflictions. Nearly a third of the cases fell subject to epileptic seizures; others succumbed to cerebral hemorrhage; many were incapacitated for any but the simplest tasks. The notorious Dr. Freeman, the Henry Ford of brain engineering, while he remained enthusiastic about his panacea, was obliged to concede the widespread occurrence of destructive consequences among those he still held to be "cured." His laconic admissions are themselves almost as shocking as the facts. For example: "On the whole," he once remarked, "psychosurgery [i.e., lobotomy] reduces creativity, sometimes to the vanishing point."[72] Again, with a nice touch of levity, he observed that the negative behavior engendered in many victims of the operation represented "all the Boy Scout virtues in reverse"—by which he meant that the victims had become surly, apathetic, and indifferent to others. But whatever became of the lobotomized person after his release as "cured" was, of course, not the doctor's responsibility; it was up to the victim's family to pick up the mutilated pieces. "The function of the family," said Dr. Freeman, "is to help the patient grow up from this surgically induced child-hood."[73]

The general result of the mass assault on the brain conducted by the first generation of psychosurgeons is graphically conveyed by Chavkin's statement that it left behind "a 'lobotomy wasteland' littered with some 50,000 human 'retreads,' many of whom had slid into a vegetablelike state."[74] During the next decade or so, as the classical operation fell into disrepute and apparent disuse, not much was heard about lobotomy; indeed it became apparent that an embarrassed medical profession was beginning to wish it had never happened and that it would now go away. Of course, that is not what occurred; the principle of mind control through brain manipulation had been established, however uncertain the results, and more particularly a formidable technology of behavior had been devised, however crude the process. In obedience to the technological imperative the devotees of psychosurgery set about to retool the line and upgrade the procedure; specifically, they traded in the obsolete icepick for an array of electronic precision instruments and opened up shop under new management. The bankruptcy of the old enterprise had merely cleared the way for the new entrepreneurs of psychotechnology. The extent to which they had recovered and regrouped was divulged by psychiatrist Peter R. Breggin in 1972 in a meticulously documented report, "The Return of Lobotomy and Psychosurgery," which provided the basic support for critical testimony before a Congressional committee.[75] The gist of the Breggin report has been summarized by Ivan Illich in deliberately blunt terms:

> New methods are available to destroy parts of the brain by ultrasonic waves, electric coagulation, and implantation of radium seeds. The technique is promoted for the sedation of the elderly, to render their institutionalization less expensive; for the control of hyperactive children; and to reduce erotic fantasies and the tendency to gamble.[76]

That summation of the motives and methods of the new psychosurgeons was accurate enough; but it was incomplete on both counts. Not only were there many more methods in operation, but there was one additional compelling motive which helps to explain their strong appeal to various government agencies in the sixties and early seventies. That motive, simply stated, was the promising potential of these drastic measures of behavior mod to control and extirpate the new eruptions of deviance and dissidence (particularly by antiwar activists and hippie nonactivists, by militant blacks and other mobilized minorities) which were seen to represent sinister forces threatening the foundations of American society. For there was a peculiar virtue to the BM devices of electroshock, ultrasonic shock, mind-zapping drugs (Anectine, Prolixin, etc.), and the like: they not only promised to eliminate bad behavior but they were also a powerful form of punishment in themselves. Since they were "therapeutic," however, the punitive purposes need not be admitted; no reasonable person could maintain that their exercise reflected motives of sadistic retaliation and revenge against those who dared disturb the universe. That was the great merit of these weapons of psychological warfare upon the mind; they effectively cloaked, behind a facade of scientific and medical rhetoric, the hidden agenda of violent reprisal against violent disobedience. That such an agenda existed was demonstrated by the shootings at Kent State (and more particularly by their subsequent public endorsement) as well as by the Rockefeller-ordered massacre at Attica prison; but it was also revealed over and over again in the vengeful and sometimes bloodthirsty remarks of public officials ranging from Chicago Mayor Richard Daley (who commanded his police to "shoot to maim" the youthful demonstrators of the 1968 Democratic Convention) to Vice President Spiro Agnew and President Richard Nixon. The artillery of psychosurgical intervention provided an irreproachable outlet for the impulse to vengeance; it was rage masquerading as rehabilitation. And the scientific theories were there, of course, to make the punishment fit the crime. Thus, following the Detroit riots of 1967, three eminent proponents of psychosurgery announced that "brain dysfunction" was a probable cause of the rioters' misbehavior; [77] and a Berkeley psychiatrist, speaking from the epicenter of the youthquake, issued a summons to his profession:

> We have a grave responsibility to protect society, the so-called normal people, from the social disturbers, violent agitators,

multiple murderers and drug addicts responsible for our increasing violence, crime rate and deterioration in respect for law and moral and social standards.[78]

The point is worth dwelling on. Our ordinary language habits afford revealing clues to the associations we tend to make, casually and for the most part unconsciously, between individual aberrations and social problems. There is, for example, the suggestive parallelism of the term "disorder" as used alike for mental difficulty and for social strife; it denotes simply a lack or absence of order, which seems neutral enough, but its connotation is shown by the adjective "disorderly"—as in "disorderly conduct" or (more pointedly) a "disorderly house." Dis-order means more to us than un-order; it also means, as Webster's New World Dictionary verifies, "jumble" and "confusion."[79] It is a red-flag word, conveying ominous overtones of imminent riot and potential anarchy. With the suggestive encouragement of language, the connection of civil disorder and emotional disorder appears altogether "natural" and almost irresistible. What could be more plausible than to suppose that the roots of disorder "out there" are to be traced to the germs of disorder "in here"? Much the same subtle and invidious associations are attached to other words commonly applied to mental aberration; thus persons who are described as "disturbed" would seem, by definition, to be likely to cause "disturbances"—and someone who is mentally or emotionally "troubled" is potentially a "troublemaker."

There is more to it, of course, than the tyranny of words. The ascription of malevolence to the "deviant" and powerless is an ancient custom which civilization and science have done little to render obsolete; what they have accomplished is mainly to invent new mythologies (such as behaviorism) and to devise new mystifications (such as behavior mod) with the effect of obfuscating the issue, perpetuating the problem in the guise of addressing it, and thoroughly fudging the bald realities of power, prejudice, and persecution. The story of Behavior Modification in America warrants barely a footnote in the history of education, or even in that of psychotherapy; but it constitutes an important chapter (indeed a continuing saga) in the history of custodial correction, population management, and social control.

Shocking Behavior

Among the most effective instruments in the toolbox of behavior mod, and possibly its most characteristic, is that of electric shock or Electroconvulsive Therapy (ECT). It is characteristic of what is "mod" in behaviorism not because of its potency but because of its imagery: it conveys the contemporary chic of electronic technology, as well as the older magical aura of electricity, which ordinary men have never quite understood but have held in special reverence. Something of the awe with which the invisible power was regarded in the mid-nineteenth century is suggested by the exclamation of Nathaniel Hawthorne (in *The House of the Seven Gables*): "Then there is electricity, the demon, the angel, the mighty physical power, the all-pervading intelligence!" As an instrument of punishment and terror, electricity has long had a special fascination; the lightning-bolts of Zeus (and before him of Buddha) symbolized a primordial fear of the lethal force of electrical storms, and of the terrible vengeance of the gods. The appropriate modern symbol of the avenging thunderbolt is the electric chair—the "civilized" successor of the executioner's block and the hangman's noose, a clean and faultlessly efficient engine of death, cousin to Henry Adams's deified dynamo and forefather of the ultimate triumph of dehuman engineering: the nuclear bomb.

The principle of electroshock was well known to the pioneer behaviorists, who devised any number of ingenious methods for bringing about desired responses through the inflicting of pain. Thus Watson reported that "One of the simplest ways to bring about an unconditioned response by an unconditioned stimulus is to use a cutting, bruising stimulus. The electric shock is a convenient one."[80] He also divulged an untried plan for the electrical conditioning of children which might well have inspired Huxley's horror story of the zapping of the infants by the "Director of Hatcheries and Conditioning."

> I hope some time [wrote Watson] to try out the experiment of having a table top electrically wired in such a way that if a child reaches for a glass or a delicate vase it will be punished, whereas if it reaches for its toys or other things it is allowed to play with, it can get them without being electrically shocked.[81]

By contemporary standards such procedures were primitive in their understanding of the aversive uses of electroshock—on a par, perhaps, with the electric cattle prods utilized against civil rights demonstrators by Southern police in the fifties and the equally unrefined Gestapo method of extracting confessions by electrically shocking a prisoner's genitals. The sophisticated modern technique of ECT was first developed in the thirties by an Italian specialist, Ugo Cerletti, who applied to his patients a procedure previously limited to animal experiments. The nature of that process, still the one most widely used, has been summarized by Schrag:

> It is a relatively simple procedure: the electrodes are attached to the subject's head, either at the temples (bilateral) or at the front and back of one side of the head (unilateral), and the current turned on for a half-second or a second, generally at a strength of 70 to 150 volts at 500 to 900 milliamperes— roughly the power required to light a 100-watt bulb. The consequence is a convulsive grand mal seizure, an artificially induced epileptic fit.[82]

Another description of the process, more colorful but not less accurate, has been provided by novelist Ken Kesey in *One Flew Over the Cuckoo's Nest*:

> "That's the Shock Shop I was telling you about. . . . The EST, Electro-Shock Therapy. . . ."
> "What they do is"—McMurphy listens a moment—"take some bird in there and shoot *electricity* through his skull?"
> "That's a concise way of putting it."
> "What the hell *for*?"
> "Why, the patient's good, of course. Everything done here is for the patient's good." . . .
> "What a life," Sefelt moans, "give some of us pills to stop a fit, give the rest shock to start one."
> Harding leans forward to explain it to McMurphy. "Here's how it came about: two psychiatrists were visiting a slaughterhouse . . . and were watching cattle being killed by a blow between the eyes with a sledgehammer. They noticed that not all of the cattle were killed, that some would fall to

the floor in a state that greatly resembled an epileptic convulsion. 'Ah, *zo*,' the first doctor says. 'Ziz is exactly vot ve need for our patients—zee induced *fit!*' . . . If they were going to knock a man in the head, they needed to use something surer and more accurate than a hammer; they finally settled on electricity."

"Jesus, didn't they think it might do some damage? Didn't the public raise Cain about it?"

"I don't think you fully understand the public, my friend; in this country, when something is out of order, then the quickest way to get it fixed is the best way."[83]

The explanation for the shocking effects of ECT remains as much a mystery today as the lightning-bolt was to the primitive mind or the phenomenon of electricity to the Victorians. As Schrag points out, "Neither Cerletti . . . nor his contemporaries ever learned how ECT worked, nor do any of their successors understand it today." Indeed the treatment would seem to be less a matter of science than of mystification: an unexplained device of unproven value but of "powerful magic" which has captured the fancy of thousands of physicians whose unflagging faith in the ritual defies all evidence and reason. What little scientific evidence does exist on the efficacy of ECT is either inconclusive or resoundingly negative; and one clinical case cited by Schrag—a case which had been held up by proponents as clear proof—demonstrates as vividly as anything could the persuasive power of blind faith on the part of scientific true believers. That case involved "an ECT machine in a British hospital which was used 'successfully' on hundreds of patients over a two-year period in the early seventies before a nurse and a doctor accidentally discovered that it had never worked at all."[84]

Despite such revelations—reinforced by mounting opposition and criticism from within the medical profession as well as from damaged ex-patients—ECT remains the popular treatment of choice on the part of several thousand physicians for a grab-bag of ailments ranging from depression to alcoholism (one doctor reportedly prescribes it for "migraine, hay fever, asthma, eczema, allergic rhinitis, and conjunctivitis").[85] One particularly devout believer has boasted of hitting his patients with this version of electroshock no fewer than 50,000 times over thirty years; and it is estimated that something over a million treatments per year are being administered to perhaps 200,000 Americans.[86] Much of this mass electrification has taken place, not surprisingly, in prisons and mental institutions where the objective is more or less openly that of producing docile behavior rather than therapeutic help. Those in the business of controlling behavior were especially encouraged by the enthusiastic report of a California physician, Lloyd H. Cotter, who had carried out a model experiment in the late sixties upon the bodies and brains of several hundred Vietnamese mental patients (not enemy prisoners but South Vietnam allies). Dr. Cotter's objective was, in the spirit of Scrooge, to solve the problem of excess population in his hospital by rousting the schizophrenic patients (all of whom incidentally suffered from other disabilities such as TB, dysentery, malaria and malnutrition) out of their beds and into the fields where they could also alleviate the chronic problem of food shortages affecting the war effort. The method, beautiful in its simplicity, was to continue administering "unmodified electric shock" (meaning that the usual anesthetics were dispensed with) to these uncomprehending indigenous personnel until they agreed to shape up and get to work. The doctor was quite frank about his purpose: "It can be seen," he wrote, "that the ECT served as a negative reinforcement for the response of work for those patients who chose to work rather than to continue receiving ECT."[87] There was also positive reinforcement of a sort: those who agreed to work were paid the equivalent of one cent a day for their labor. (This generous incentive was surely called for; it turned out that the patients were to be put to work in fields well within the range of active enemy guns.)

Cotter's program of work-or-be-shocked was, in his view, so successful with Vietnamese patients that he later became something of a missionary, traveling to mental hospitals throughout Asia, Europe and the Middle East to convey his message. He summed it up this way:

The novelty of operant conditioning techniques as applied in this area lies in the possibility or probability of its being utilized effectively with all patients not totally physically incapacitated. If the less effective, but more usually relied on, reinforcements of productive behavior do not work, then a more effective reinforcement, such as food for hungry patients, will produce the desired results. . . . The use of effective reinforcements should not be neglected due to a misguided idea of what constitutes kindness.[88]

The Cotter method of operant conditioning, with its combination of work and restraint, is remarkably similar to the treatment proposed for criminals nearly half a century earlier by Watson himself. Defining criminals as either insane or "socially untrained," the founder of behaviorism had a simple solution for the former group: "The question as to whether the hopelessly insane should be etherized has of course been raised time and again. There can be no reasons against it except exaggerated sentiment and mediaeval religious mandates."[89] As for the latter group, they should be trained if possible, "made to put on culture, made to become social." But if that is not possible:

Failing to put on the training necessary to fit them to enter society again, they should be restrained always, and made to earn their daily bread, in vast manufacturing and agricultural institutions, escape from which is impossible. . . . strenuous work twelve hours per day will hurt no one. Individuals put aside thus for additional training should of course be kept in the hands of the behaviorists.[90]

Not everyone, however, has agreed with Watson and his heirs that criminals and mental patients should be kept in the hands of the behaviorists. As a result of the disastrous "modifications" of mentality and personality wrought by the behavioral technologies of psychosurgery and ECT, resistance to their use has been mounting in recent years and has found expression in what Skinner might describe as "countercontrol" measures. A few programs have been terminated by judicial edict, following lawsuits on behalf of injured patients or prisoners; other programs have been disallowed by legislative action, and still others have been affected by the judgments of congressional committees that such practices violate constitutional protections relating to "cruel and unusual punishments" and to the principle of "informed consent."[91] Organizations like the Network Against Psychiatric Assault (NAPA), made up of former patients and concerned psychiatrists, have sought to alert the public by regularly publishing the names of "shock doctors" and others engaged in aversive (and abusive) BM practices. Unfortunately these efforts to stop the shock troops have had the general appearance of delaying actions in a losing struggle against the medical nemesis—voices of conscience crying in the wilderness. The interests of the patient, the "consumer" of psychosurgical services, have for the most part been far outweighed by the vested interests of the producers: not only the medical profession and its psychiatric cadre but the farflung network of agencies and institutions, both public and private, which execute the mandates of the Administrative State. Psychosurgery and other assaultive forms of behavior modification have been stoutly championed and richly funded by the Veterans Administration, the National Science Foundation, the Department of Defense, the Law Enforcement Assistance Administration, the Department of Labor, the National Institute of Mental Health, the Federal Bureau of Prisons, and more. Despite the accumulating evidence of inhumane treatment and disastrous effects, despite the continuing horror stories of permanently traumatized or vegetablized victims, despite the formidable negative testimony of antiestablishment psychiatrists and doctors—despite reason and despite conscience—the psychosurgical beat goes on.[91A] In fact, the technology of brain and behavior manipulation, having found a "captive market," has developed in novel and innovative directions, spinning off a host of electronic devices which make ever more plausible the Huxleyan prophecy that his Brave New World now awaits us just around the next corner. To the "thousand natural shocks that flesh is heir to" the scientists of good behavior have added another thousand unnatural shocks. Like latterday Prometheans, having stolen the fire of the gods, they are turning it against their own race of humans.

ESB: The Terminal Man Redivivus

In a bestselling novel of 1973, *The Terminal Man*, author Michael Crichton told a harrowing tale of science fiction in which a group of neurosurgeons with power on their minds contrived to wire an individual to a computer (for dramatic purposes the protagonist was a paranoiac with homicidal tendencies) in order to correct and command his behavior by remote control. The rationale for the electrical hookup, and for its potential extension to millions of other troubled and troubling souls, was explained by one of the fictional doctors in terms of the supposed physical causation of violent behavior. "You cannot correct physical brain damage with social remedies," he says at one point, maintaining that his solution "shoots down a lot of theories about poverty and discrimination and social injustice and social disorganization."[92] It is not clear whether the irony of the surgeon's violent figure of speech ("shoots down") was intentional; but it is apparent that Crichton drew heavily for his evidence and argument upon a scientific treatise published three years earlier, *Violence and the Brain,* by Vernon H. Mark (a neurosurgeon) and Frank R. Ervin (a psychiatrist who had been Crichton's teacher at Harvard). For it was the thesis of Mark and Ervin—writing at the crest of the wave of 60s riots, protests and demonstrations—that the real cause of these eruptions was in the damaged brains of the culprits rather than in the overpublicized area of so-called social problems. Not only that: their researches had convinced these psychosurgeons that there were at large in the land about ten million Americans suffering from "obvious brain disease" and another five million with more "subtle" brain damage—all of whom were prone to sudden outbreaks of rage, assault, and general violence. Given that dire mass diagnosis, the prognosis seemed to them as obvious as it was urgent: namely, the administration of a mass screening program to weed out those Americans with a "potential for violence" and apply to them the necessary psychosurgical preventive measures. In a manner reminiscent of the nineteenth-century pseudoscience of phrenology, Mark and Ervin and company would examine the heads of their suspect population for physical signs of future criminality. "Our greatest danger," they wrote, "no longer comes from famine or communicable diseases. Our greatest danger lies in ourselves and in our fellow humans . . . we need to develop an 'early warning test' of limbic brain function to detect those humans who have a low threshold for impulsive violence."[93]

Given their own estimate of ten to fifteen million violence-prone candidates for surgery out there on the streets, it would be quite an operation. Fortunately the doctors had at their disposal a new and improved psychotechnology which could solve the problem at a stroke, so to speak. It involved the implantation of electrodes in the brain, specifically in the so-called limbic system thought to regulate emotionality—thereby enabling the surgeon either to control mood and behavior through stimulating the guilty cells with a weak alternating current or to destroy them altogether with a stronger direct current. The first of these alternatives is the procedure known as ESB (electrical stimulation of the brain); the second is a now conventional form of psychosurgery. Mark and Ervin were adept at both procedures; their book is a compendium of case studies offered in proof of their thesis of the physical cause and the surgical cure of violence. (One chapter is rather ominously entitled "The Surgery of Violence"; but the double entendre is probably unintentional.) A case in point is that of a woman patient who underwent two of their psychosurgical operations and then angrily refused to undergo another. Her anger (which would seem quite reasonable and even appropriate in the circumstances) was dismissed by the doctors as "paranoid"; but they did permit her to leave the hospital on a shopping trip. Once outside the woman promptly made a farewell phone call to her mother and committed suicide by swallowing poison. Remarkably, the doctors interpreted that action as a "gratifying" sign that the patient was well on the way to recovery—thus giving literal and sober meaning to the old comic line, "The operation was a success; the patient died."[93]

Another case presented by Mark and Ervin as equally supportive of their claims was that of Thomas R., whom they described as "a brilliant, 34-year-old engineer, with several important patents to his credit."[95] Hospitalized by his psychiatrist for periodic attacks of rage and alleged assaultive behavior, Thomas came under the tender loving care of Mark and Ervin, who first subjected him to a ten-week brain-scan by implanted electrodes in order to "pinpoint" the exact source of the trouble. Next they sought Thomas's consent to their surgery, but were surprised to discover that (in their words) "the suggestion that the medial portion of his temporal lobe was to be destroyed . . . would provoke wild, disordered thinking."[96] The doctors countered this unseemly resistance by the judicious application of ESB: "Under the effects of lateral amygdala stimulation, [Thomas] showed bland acquiescence to the suggestion." Unfortunately, when the effects of the soothing probe wore off, the patient again "turned wild and unmanageable," the doctors reported. "The idea of any-one's making a destructive lesion in his brain enraged him. He absolutely refused any further therapy, and it took many weeks of patient explanation before he accepted the idea of bilateral lesions being made in his medial amygdala." The doctors' persuasive stimulation having finally prevailed, they performed the psychosurgery. Later, looking back with pride, Mark and Ervin reported on their apparent success: "Four years have passed since the operation, during which time Thomas has not had a single episode of rage. He continues, however, to have an occasional epileptic seizure with periods of confusion and disordered thinking."[97]

That terse summing up of the case of Thomas R., with its bland implication of general success, turns out to have been misleading at best. The real truth emerged as the result of an independent follow-up investigation carried out at the request of Thomas's family by Dr. Peter Breggin (the psychiatrist who authored the report on the return of psychosurgery and lobotomy). Breggin's report made two crucial points: first, the drastic operation was almost certainly uncalled-for on the basis of Thomas's actual behavior and diagnosed condition (for one thing, the only occurrences of violence recorded in the hospital files were those that had been provoked by the actions of Mark and Ervin); second, as a result of the treatment Thomas lost his job and his engineering career, was divorced by his wife, became unable to cope with ordinary social reality, was several times hospitalized where he was at last diagnosed as a "schizophrenic, paranoid type," and became (in his mother's words) "almost a vegetable." Breggin summarized the outcome rather differently from Mark and Ervin: "Thomas is chronically deluded and hallucinates frequently: lives in constant terror that surgeons will again control his mind."[98]

His apprehension was not unjustified. More than a few psychosurgeons, among them the ubiquitous Mark and Ervin, have proposed programs of mass surveillance and behavioral control of various suspect elements of the population through the surgical implantation of electrodes or other monitoring devices—two-way pacemakers for the mind—some of which would permit electrical stimulation of the brain on command. It is a dream of power and a fantasy of crowd control born of the riots and rebellions of the sixties, when, as noted earlier, the forces of law and order began to cast about for effective and unobtrusive means of pacification of the urban villagers. Among the most attractive of those new means was the promising technology of ESB, which had the advantages of being relatively painless, apparently nonpermanent in its impact upon brain tissue, and—best of all—conferring the godlike power of electronic remote control and fine-tuning of deviant behavior through the implanted electrodes which could be activated at a distance of many miles. Supported by the increasingly popular theory of "brain dysfunction" or abnormality as the root cause of most social problems, the psychiatric Electric Company drew up various plans for the permanent tracking and manipulating of both the outer behavior and the inner desires of selected target groups. One of the most impressive of these surveillance scenarios, as reported by Chavkin in *The Mind Stealers,* was the "Crime Deterrent Transponder System," an elaborate scheme devised by a Defense Department computer expert named J. A. Meyer. His plan, which was projected ultimately to embrace some hundreds of thousands of wired human subjects, involved the attachment of tiny radio transceivers to the persons of "criminal recidivists, parolees and bailees to identify them and detect their whereabouts." The cost of this human radio network would be partially defrayed by charging the involuntary "subscribers" (Meyer's term) five dollars a week for the purchase and maintenance of the high-tech equipment with which they would be literally stuck. Thus, for example, Meyer proposed that the "high crime area" of New York's Harlem, a 400-block region, could be effectively monitored on a street-by-street basis by "a system of about 250 transceivers" strung about the region and sending off signals—like little electric parasites feeding off the human hosts. By this ingenious network of bugs, the activities not only of subscribers but of all whom they might contact could be checked out; the unfortunate parolees would in effect become stoolpigeons for the system. Meanwhile Big Brother and a legion of little brothers would be able to follow every move of the trapped victims: "At their place of work, a human surveillance system will operate. Low-power transceivers in their domiciles can monitor them indoors. Alarm transceivers in banks, stores, and other buildings would warn security personnel of their approach."[99] And the bugged subscribers, deprived not only of freedom of movement but of effective self-direction and self-control, would become nothing more nor less than inmates of the first electronic prison without walls.

Proposals such as this—alternately described in the literature as "telemetric surveillance" and "electronic rehabilitation"—have been advanced by imaginative behavioral technologists over the last decade and a half to meet a variety of regulatory demands. Ralph K. Schwitzgebel, a psychologist and inventor with a number of experimental applications of group ESB to his credit, has recognized how far such electronic buggery could be carried by less scrupulous persons than himself: "some administrators may wish, for example, to control certain behaviors by high-risk probationers, suspects in gang war activity, Communist Party members, or government employees." Targeted individuals might in fact be "committed on minor violations for the purpose of later releasing them under surveillance."[100] With the availability of such secret antipersonal weapons and "stealth" devices as these, and with the advent of a social climate of opinion in which their use against the citizenry can be seriously contemplated, we find ourselves no longer dealing with the possible futures of science fiction but with the present options of science fact. It is not only the technology that is in place, it is also the state of mind. Given the recent history of governmental tracking, bugging and spooking of disfavored citizens by J. Edgar Hoover and Richard M. Nixon—and given the equally ominous authorization by Ronald Reagan of a domestic CIA, doing unto us at home what it has clandestinely done to enemies abroad—no one can comfortably dismiss the dramatistic visions of a clockwork-orange society and a city full of terminal men as mere flights of fevered creative fancy. Already the two-way television screen of Orwell's *Nineteen Eighty-Four* begins to look old-fashioned and unimaginative beside the radio-controlled subscribers of the Crime Deterrent Transponder System: the living walkie-talkies of an all-too-Electric Age. And "Dr. Strangelove," that once-ludicrous caricature of cinematic black comedy, seems no longer quite so ridiculous but plausible and even recognizable, perhaps a bit eccentric but otherwise drawn straight from life. It is not so much that he resembles a clone of Henry Kissinger (the self-styled "lone ranger" of power politics) or of General Al Haig ("I am in charge here at the White House")—nor of the Prussian Guards Haldeman and Ehrlichman, nor even of J. Edgar and G. Gordon, the twin masters of conceit. "Dr. Strangelove" comes rather to look like a composite portrait of the new wave of mass-behavior modifiers, the would-be architects of a visionary society of short-circuited people, all wired for sound, tuned in to the police channel, ears collectively cocked for the master's voice.

It should be emphasized that the various proposals for mass menticide (or what the prisoners in one victimized institution called "psychogenocide")[101]—the brainstorms of the brain doctors—have been widely criticized in medical and psychiatric circles where they have not been thoroughly repudiated. Their underlying theory of what might be called the cranial causation of human behavior (of personal distress and social disorder) is generally regarded as scientifically untenable if not outrageously prejudiced.[102] More specifically, the very principle of psychosurgery and ESB—that the exact locations of brain dysfunction or abnormality can be identified and thereupon electrified without damage to surrounding tissue—is so broadly disputed among neurosurgeons and neuropsychiatrists as to be effectively nullified as a scientific proposition. Most professional criticism of psychosurgery in all its forms centers around what might be termed its lacks and losses: i.e., the existing lack of knowledge about the intricate processes and interwoven workings of the human brain, on one hand, and the human losses sustained potentially or actually by the subjects of psychosurgery on the other hand.[103] The undeniable fact is that the brain, while not quite a *terra incognita*, is still largely unknown, unexplained, and inaccessible; the last thing that anyone should suppose is that an exact science of the human brain has been perfected. But if the state of the science is tentative and inconclusive, the state of the *art* (of psychosurgery) is primitive to the point of folly. Even the fraternity of psychosurgeons, as revealed by Eliot Valenstein in a careful survey, disagree strongly and widely on virtually every aspect of the practice. Each psychosurgeon evidently has his own favorite "target" in the brain and his own definition of the problem and procedure. "It seems clear," concludes Valenstein, "that with strong and significant disagreement among those who practice psychosurgery, it cannot be convincingly argued that our understanding of the physiological basis of psychosurgery has advanced very far."[104] Who shall decide, when doctors disagree?

In light of the blatant controversiality of the practice, as well as the extravagant visions of its major practitioners, it may seem remarkable that the electronic plugs and probes have not been pulled from the skulls of all the hospitalized and imprisoned subjects in the land—on the grounds both of scientific prudence and ethical concern, not to mention the constitutional protections of personal liberty and privacy. But while a large and increasing body of informed opinion— medical, legal, sociological, and psychiatric—has been demanding at least a moratorium on the experimental and therapeutic bugging, shocking and mutilating of humans in the service of behavioral control, the dubious interventions and manipulations flourish almost un-

abated; while the Pavlovian-Orwellian proposals for the mass transformation of the deviant, the difficult and the defenseless continue to
be disseminated and reviewed for policy implementation in the corridors of technocratic power. From the perspectives of pure science,
pure reason, or pure humanitarianism this situation might appear
intolerable and inexplicable. But from a different standpoint—that of
political and social reality—it makes perfect sense. For the crucial
issues surrounding psychosurgery and behavior modification, the de-
cisions governing their enforcement, and the very definitions of their
function, are not objective matters to be settled by medical evidence
and empirical test. They never have been. They are matters of social
philosophy, political ideology, and cultural mythology; they hinge on
tacit assumptions (rarely made explicit) concerning the nature of
man, the norms of conduct, the maintenance of order, the mystique
of science. These assumptions lurk in the grand designs of the
prophets of psychotechnology and psychocivilization, from Watson
through Mayo to Skinner and Schwitzgebel; they are visible through
the murky camouflage of what Valenstein calls the rhetoric of
"neurologizing" in "pseudo-physiological phrases" which "create
the illusion of an explanatory power that does not in fact exist at
all";[105] and, most insidiously, they hide behind the walls of corrective, custodial and therapeutic institutions in the form of a "hidden
agenda" (as Judge David Bazelon has termed it) of power relations
and managerial motives.[106]

Behavior modification, with its brute offspring of electroshock and
psychosurgery, is the creature of an apprehensive society in full retreat from the ancestral values of the Bill of Rights and its accumulated legacy of constitutional law focused upon the *person*—
manifesting a concern for his liberty and a respect for his privacy,
extending around him a blanket of immunities and protections, and
furnishing a framework for the free exercise of self-expression and
self-determination. That democratic spirit, with its generous faith in
the potentiality of human nature (what used to be called its "indefin-
ite perfectibility"), has represented the mainstream of American
thought and belief up to the present day—when it has been abruptly
and formidably challenged by forces of reaction whose hour, it is
supposed, has come round at last. These are the same dark forces that
have always lurked in the shadows and waited in the wings, and more
than once have had their brief hour upon the stage—but each time

have been undone by their inherent ruthlessness and "paranoid style" of politics, as Richard Hofstadter termed it. Both the original un-adorned McCarthyism and the white-collar version of it worn by Richard Nixon became repellent in their naked grabs for power. But since then public relations and public imagery have vastly improved. Today the forces of reaction wear a face described by Bertram Gross as that of "friendly fascism": they appear not so much repressive as redemptive, not machiavellian but moralistic, not even authoritarian but only avuncular. Their deepest wish is to save us, the fallen race of humans, from ourselves—from our violent natures and destructive impulses. They are like the faceless oligarchs of Huxley's dystopian society, of whom he wrote: ". . . they are not madmen, and their aim is not anarchy but social stability. It is in order to achieve stability that they [would] carry out, by scientific means, the ultimate, personal, really revolutionary revolution."

For that they have their professional class of psychotechnocrats. The prophets of behaviorism and its engineering applications have always been in the vanguard of those who would, if they could, repeal the entire Bill of Rights and return the disposition of human lives to a star chamber of expert authority. Watson, as we know, was openly scornful of free speech or "free anything"; Skinner has gone even farther in his wholesale repudiation of the "literatures of freedom and dignity" (of which the Bill of Rights is the distilled essence), which he correctly perceives to stand in the way of a technology of behavior and a technocracy of behavior control. And the zealous designers of Future Shock have been equally clear on the issues of freedom and equality: they are pleasant illusions but contrary to human nature, and the only way to make them "real" is to produce them artificially (as we would a robot) by the electrical stimulation of the brain. But it is not the will or purpose of the mind controllers to enhance individual freedom and dignity, even if they knew the way; for that would only compound the problem of a society already too diverse and disputatious, too riddled with dissenters and trouble-makers. What they offer instead is a scientific method—laboratory-tested and asylum-proven—for the total elimination of mental and social disorder and the mass production of good behavior. If they should have their way, as Huxley prophesied, theirs would be the final revolution—after which the human race would give no further trouble.

4

THE SEDUCTION OF THE MIND: PERSUASION, ILLUSION, AND DISTRACTION

The power to dominate a culture's symbol-producing apparatus is the power to create the ambience that forms human consciousness. . . . The unanticipated outcome is that the United States enjoys the dubious distinction of having allowed the television business to score a first in human history: the first undertaking in mass behavior modification by coast-to-coast and intercontinental electronic hookup.—*Rose K. Goldsen*

MORE THAN at any time in history since the garrulous days of Pericles and Socrates—when oratory was the highest of arts and rhetoric the grandest of sciences—we Americans live today in a persuasive society. In fact, we far surpass the classical Athenians at their own specialty, due to two modern developments of which the ancients were necessarily unaware. The first is the technology of persuasion, which has immeasurably amplified the human voice and multiplied its messages. The second is the psychology of persuasion, which has transformed the process of communication and vastly augmented the power of the persuader. The combination of the new technology and the new psychology has produced an unprecedented, and potentially lethal, threat to the essential faculties of the human mind: the ability to reason, the capacity to choose, and the will to act upon that choice.

There are instructive parallels, as well as obvious differences, between our own persuasive society and that of the Athenians of the fifth century B.C. Theirs was still very much an oral society, characterized by the chatter of voices and the spectacle of speechmakers, with the citizenry nearly always engaged in conversation when they were not embroiled in argument. Athens was not only the center of the Mediterranean world for the exchange of goods but also, as Stringfellow Barr has remarked, for the "exchange of words." As a result there developed a highly sophisticated science of persuasion, known as rhetoric, and a flourishing profession of teachers and practitioners of the supreme art of oratory. (There was also a prominent minority of dissenters from the conventional orthodoxy, led by Socrates, who perceived the dangers to mind and freedom implicit in the artful science of persuasion; but that is another matter to which we shall return.)

So it is again in our own time. Persuasion as art and science (or pseudo-science) has never been more central to the affairs of society and the lives of its members—never more powerful, more pervasive, and more beguiling—than it is today. The communications revolution of the mid-twentieth century may not yet have retribalized mankind within the "global village" of Marshall McLuhan's vision, but it has substantially revived the oral tradition of discourse which characterized the civilizations of Greece and Rome and was eventually overtaken and absorbed within the written tradition—culminating in the print culture of the modern world which McLuhan dubbed the "Gutenberg Galaxy." The return to prominence of the *spoken word,* broadcast and magnified by the new technologies, has thrust us into a social environment reminiscent in important ways of the oral cultures of the ancient world. Once again it is the human voice—rather than the printed page—that is the prime source of authority and relevance, of enlightenment and agitation, of wisdom and of folly.

To be sure, it is not only the amplified voice that resonates around us and within us in the audio-visual age: it is a kaleidoscope of sound and sight, of color and motion, an orchestrated concert of sensory cues directed less at the autonomous mental system than at the autonomic nervous system. It is in this sense that the message of the media becomes a "massage"; we are not only consciously persuaded but unconsciously swayed, not just sensibly engaged in the process but sensorily assaulted. It might well be argued that the characteristic syndrome of contemporary culture is not "future shock" or "eco-spasm" (as Alvin Toffler keeps telling us) but *persuasion overload*—giving rise to symptoms of massive cognitive dissonance. It has become clear at any rate that the paramount challenge to human liberty in the post-literate era is no longer that of resisting coercion—the primordial threat of force—but of withstanding persuasion. The traditional hardware of torture and intimidation, with its archaic psychology of negative reinforcement and "aversive control," has given way throughout the nontotalitarian world to the new software of motivation research and subliminal seduction—the positive reinforcements of psychotechnology. The newer mechanisms of cultural control are aimed not at the pain reflex but at the pleasure bond; their appropriate symbols are no longer the dungeon and the rack but *TV Guide* and the thirty-second commercial.

The Management of Persuasion

The critical role of persuasion in contemporary society cannot be explained solely in terms of the "information explosion" or the communications revolution. More fundamentally it is related to a profound change of phase, or shift in direction, on the part of the industrial system of manufacture, marketing and management. Having "won" the battle against nature and solved the problem of material production, the basic thrust of economic society has moved subtly from the manipulation of *things* to the manipulation of *minds*—from the engineering of goods to the engineering of consent. As George Lichtheim has observed: "There is a change in emphasis in the industrial system from force to persuasion, a growth of public relations, managerial counseling, and mass advertising; in short, an extensive shift from production to consumption and from overt authority to covert ideological inducement."[1] And John Kenneth Galbraith, in his classic primer on the New Industrial State, points to the same phenomenon: ". . . there has been a further massive growth in the apparatus of persuasion and exhortation that is associated with the sale of goods. In its cost and in the talent it commands this activity is coming increasingly to rival the effort devoted to the production of goods."[2]

The transition from coercive to persuasive modes of business management, as well as marketing, reflects a long-term trend away from the aggressively competitive individualism associated with past industrial society toward the cooler and apparently more cooperative style of post-industrial society—a change symbolized a generation ago by David Riesman in the successive images of "inner-direction" and "other-direction," and by William H. Whyte, Jr., as the transition from the ancestral Protestant Ethic to the more congenial "Social Ethic." One aspect of this ethical sea-change is evident in the ascendancy of the human-relations approach to industrial management; where once there were unilateral commands and directives from the top, with no back-talk allowed, the newer managerial style embraces modish forms of involvement, interaction, and informality—with back-talk reintroduced as "feedback." The widespread adoption by management of the pop psychologies of self-actualization and mutual stroking—such as Transactional Analysis ("I'm OK, You're OK"), encounter groups, and sensitivity workshops—illustrates how far the business society has moved in its internal as well as its public relations since the authoritarian age of the Rugged Individualists. But the surface appearance of congeniality and sociability in the executive suite, as Christopher Lasch and Michael Maccoby have made us aware, masks an underlying power struggle in which intimidation and manipulation are as real as ever but have become more subtle, seductive, and "scientific." As Lasch rather bluntly puts it, "The happy hooker stands in place of Horatio Alger as the prototype of personal success."[3] The cajolery of clients and the courting of superiors requires a mastery of the arts of impression management and self-presentation—in short, the arts of persuasion.

The essential reason for the new prominence of persuasion in the industrial process, which Galbraith in particular has emphasized, is that the "management of consumer demand"—that is, the manipulation of public needs and tastes—has become as central a feature of industrial planning as the control of prices, and for the same reason: to minimize risk and stabilize the market. In reality, the modern corporation is engaged as prominently in the business of mass persuasion as it is in that of mass production.

The control or management of demand is, in fact, a vast and rapidly growing industry in itself. It embraces a huge network of communications, a great array of merchandising and selling organizations, nearly the entire advertising industry, numerous ancillary research, training and other related services and much more. In everyday parlance this great machine, and the demanding and varied talents that it employs, are said to be engaged in selling goods. In less ambiguous language it means that it is engaged in the management of those who buy goods.[4]

The principal means of the management of consumer demand is the manufacture of need and the engineering of taste. As Galbraith observes, the proportion of goods devoted to the satisfaction of physical and material wants is already small and rapidly dwindling; most of what is produced in the affluent society meets "wants which are psychological in origin and hence admirably subject to management by appeal to the psyche." These subjective desires, being less definite and palpable than the demands of hunger or pain, are all the more vulnerable to persuasive manipulation. It is not the starving man and the desperate character, after all, who are the easiest targets for the commercial seducers. "The further a man is removed from physical need the more open he is to persuasion—or management—as to what he buys. This is, perhaps, the most important consequence for the economics of increasing affluence."[5]

Galbraith's famous analysis of a score of years ago shed light upon the economics of persuasion as it functions in our post-industrial society; his emphasis was entirely upon the management of demand, the control of taste and appetite, for commercial purposes—for selling a product. And his conclusion was that this manipulative massage of the consumer has become steadily more essential to the economy, more pervasive in its application, and more powerful in its effect. The heavy artillery of corporate enterprise—its battalions of scientific researchers, its public-relations armadas, its high-priced satellites of Madison Avenue, and its foot soldiers of sales—have been brought to bear in a synchronized campaign to reduce the individual as consumer from a responsible being capable of free will and reasoned choice to a passive organism of conditioned reflexes, artificial appetites, and controlled desires.

The Politics of Persuasion

But that is not, of course, the only form of persuasive management to which the contemporary citizen is subject. Accompanying the economics of persuasion there is a politics of persuasion, which is at least as threatening in its implications for the freedom of mind. Here the danger is compounded, and confounded, by the fact that an element of persuasion is also intrinsic to the political process and indispensable in a democracy. Political persuasion in actuality takes place on two different levels of consciousness: that of overt argument and appeal surrounding particular policies or candidates, and that of covert suggestion—the infiltration of messages beneath the threshold of awareness—which operates to ratify some viewpoints and values while it discounts or disparages others. In a free society, the persuasive politics of competing claims and charges at the overt level—the rhetoric of propaganda and counter-propaganda—is not by itself a cause for alarm; on the contrary, like the adversary system of forensic debate, it serves to expose the strengths and weaknesses of opposing alternatives and thereby to enhance the capacity of the citizen to choose, vote, and act responsibly. The principle of "free trade in ideas" is as valid now as it was when Justice Oliver Wendell Holmes proclaimed it in 1919: ". . . that the best test of truth is the power of the thought to get itself accepted in the competition of the market." But the difficulty is, of course, that free trade presupposes an open market—or, in this case, an open forum—with reasonable access, if not "equal time," for all who seek to enter. Few would maintain that those optimal conditions of political dialogue exist today, if in fact they ever did; in an age of electronic communications and fast-fed culture, when invisible audiences (summoned instantaneously in their millions and tens of millions) become "media markets," and when messages alternate indistinguishably between the commercial and the noncommercial (when an ad becomes an "important announcement" and a real announcement imitates an ad), it is not surprising that the economics and politics of persuasion should combine to pre-empt the field and divide the spoils. In our time the "marketplace of ideas" has ceased to be a metaphor; the public forum has literally become a merchandise mart where politicians are packaged, issues are showcased, and presidents are sold—by the same wonderful folks who brought you Ring Around the Collar.

A fair sample of the prevailing Madison Avenue approach to politics may be found in the notes of a Nixon campaign consultant, Harry Treleaven, as quoted in Joe McGinnis's case study, *The Selling of the President 1968*:

> A few thoughts:
> The more informally he is presented the better.
> He looks good in motion.
> He should be presented in some kind of "situation" rather than cold in a studio. The situation should look unstaged, even if it's not. A newsreel-type on location interview technique, for example, could be effective. The more visually interesting and local the situation the better.
> Avoid closeups. A medium waist shot is about as tight as the camera should get. He looks good when he faces the camera head-on.
> Still photographs can be effectively used on TV. Interesting cropping, artful editing and juxtaposition of scenes, an arresting sound track, can all combine to make an unusual presentation. Added advantages: there's a wide range of material to choose from, and we'd be free to select only the most flattering pictures.[6]

That strategic manipulation of images, which by now has become so routinely exercised as to seem not only legitimate but admirable, is only the frosting on the cake of political illusioneering. Beneath the cosmetic surface of this show-biz politics is a murkier level of mass persuasion—that of "covert ideological inducement," in Lichtheim's phrase—which, far from promoting an open competition of ideas and issues, fixes boundaries to the permissible universe of discourse and shrinks the parameters of choice and opinion. It is at this lower depth of psychic penetration that "culture heroes" are created—as well as culture villains and culture clowns who embody all that is regarded as illegitimate, outrageous, and contemptible. The scenarios of this shadow morality play, acted out for the most part below the threshold of consciousness, are not only contained in the sales pitches and staged appearances of candidates but are ritually repeated, over and over, in the melodramas of the mass media—the recycled myths and fairy tales of popular fiction, movies, comic strips, and "situation comedies." The role of popular culture as an agency of social control, a vehicle of acculturation and a transmission-belt for the "idols of the tribe," is only now beginning to be appreciated. As distinguished from the elite arts of sophisticated (high) culture, which serve a critical and questioning purpose, the popular arts constitute the folklore and "fake-lore" (in Richard Dorson's term) of modern society; their function is not to challenge but to reaffirm and reinforce what Durkheim called the "collective representations" of a people—its master metaphors of virtue and vice, courage and cowardice, authority and anarchy. Thus for a politician (or a celebrity) to obtain mastery of these symbols—to possess Excalibur—is to acquire the *mana* or magic power of the race which accrues to charismatic leaders. There was more than sentimentality to the mystique of Camelot that clung to the Kennedy administration (and was passed on, with slightly diminished magnetism, from brother to brother); and there is more than nostalgia for the lost frontier involved in the western-marshall image so meticulously cultivated, meanwhile, back at the Reagan Ranch. Nor is it by accident that well-counseled candidates contrive to be photographed whenever possible before a cozy fireplace (symbol of the Domestic Hearth), with a half-furled flag (symbol of Country) visible in the background; preferably seated behind a desk (the Work Ethic), against a book-lined wall (Learning), and so on. As Jacques Ellul has emphasized in his study of propaganda, persuasion in its direct and open form can be effective only against a background of preconditioned and generalized indoctrination.

> Direct propaganda, aimed at modifying opinions and attitudes, must be preceded by propaganda that is sociological in character, slow, general, seeking to create a climate, an atmosphere of favorable preliminary attitudes. No direct propaganda can be effective without pre-propaganda, which, without direct or noticeable aggression, is limited to creating ambiguities, reducing prejudices, and spreading images, apparently without purpose.[7]

It is this tacit form of ideological insinuation which was identified by Herbert Marcuse, in a notable work of the nineteen-sixties, as the principal factor nudging us unwittingly toward a "one-dimensional society" by virtue of its surreptitious and gradual "closing of the

political universe of discourse." To the extent that this mental enclo-
sure movement succeeds it generates a world in which, as a wag has
put it, the bland lead the bland: a homogenized society from which
not only passion and conflict, but all serious dispute and critical
inquiry, are effectively shut out. The dominant forces of American
culture, according to Marcuse, have shown themselves capable of
subtly co-opting and containing social change through the elaboration
of a rhetoric of consensus—variously disguised as bipartisanship,
unity, national purpose, and so on—which creates a spurious impression of reconciling conflicts, resolving issues, and embracing all viewpoints. In particular, this consensual rhetoric purports to eliminate
significant differences over *ends* (that is, fundamental issues) by reducing them to mere technical quibbles over *means* (that is, administrative measures). "As the project unfolds," wrote Marcuse, "it
shapes the entire universe of discourse and action, intellectual and
material culture. In the medium of technology culture, politics, and
the economy merge into an omnipresent system which swallows up
or repulses all alternatives."[8]

It may be debated, of course, whether this radical critique represents an accurate portrayal or a simplistic distortion of political and
cultural reality; but it is enough for our purposes to take note of the
growing apprehension on the part of numerous observers—both on
the left and the right—that a virulent form of "hidden persuasion" is
being practiced upon the American people by influential elites in
control of the media (Kevin Phillips's "mediacracy"), toward the end
of seducing the public into a mindless acceptance of political pieties.
This vision of an organized cabal of powerful forces dominating the
agencies of communication is a familiar one, to be sure; but it has
never before enjoyed such widespread support. While to critics on the
left the power elite is a troika of military-industrial-governmental
cadres, to those on the right (like Phillips, Michael Novak and Spiro
Agnew) the conspirators are the "liberal network" of mass-media
commentators and editors who allegedly control both the presses and
the airwaves, and so enjoy privileged access to the hearts and minds
of the national audience. Novak, for instance, argues that television is
pervaded by a liberal "class bias" imparted by an intellectual elite of
the highly educated who seek to shape the medium in their own
ideological interest. "In harmony with the images of progress built
into both liberalism and capitalism," he writes, "television seems,

however gently, to undercut traditional institutions and to promote a restless, questioning attitude. The main product—and attitude—it has to sell is the new. This attachment to the new insures that television will be a vaguely leftist medium, no matter who its personnel might be."[9] (Compare the view of a prominent liberal student of TV, Harry Skornia: "In many of the most advanced countries in the world, the leadership of broadcasting is in the hands of intellectuals, educators, philosophers, religious leaders, and the like. . . . Not so in the U.S. Here broadcasting is a business, in the hands of advertisers and salesmen, with the other groups treated as outsiders.")[10]

Since these two critical theories appear to be mutually contradictory, it might seem that neither need be taken seriously. But underlying their ideological difference is the shared intuition of a powerless public systematically converted into a captive market—a common interpretation which conveys the frustrated sense of dispossession and defeat felt by those who find themselves at the end of the receiving line in the mass-communication network. The apprehension of conspiracy, whether intentional or institutional, plotted by a few or intrinsic to the system, is at the heart of both critiques; and the dominant impression given by each is of the progressive attrition of the powers of resistance, independence, and volitional choice on the part of the public audience. The essential point has been well-summarized by Rose K. Goldsen in *The Show and Tell Machine*:

> Wittingly and unwittingly this business and its client industries set the stage for a never-ending performance stripping away emotional associations that centuries of cultural experiences have linked to patterns of behavior, institutional forms, attitudes and values that many cultures and subcultures revere and need to keep vigorous if they are to survive. . . . The scale is so vast, the images and sounds so insistent, the support system so interpenetrating, that few families can pit their own authority against the authority of the show and tell machine. They are drowned out by this emissary in every home of powerful communications empires that span the globe.[11]

To be sure, there is another countervailing opinion of the relationship between the media and the masses which maintains that the audience is never quite so powerless or passive as the monolithic structure of the system, and the jeremiads of its critics, would make it seem; on the contrary, the power of public opinion over the content of programming is so formidable as to pose a different kind of threat: that which de Tocqueville described a century and a half ago as the "tyranny of the majority." In this view it is not the media moguls but the great audience out there which decides the fate of sitcoms and celebrities, rather like the plebs of the Roman Colosseum who held in their thumbs the power of life and death over the gladiators. In a strictly technical sense this may be true; network programs do generally live or die by the thumb of the "Nielsen family." But if the collective opinion of the multitude of viewers is not the deliberative response of a thinking public but the knee-jerk reaction of a captive mass audience—if it is reflexive rather than reflective—then its semblance of power is neither rational nor real but only the preconditioned feedback of its master's voice.

This distinction between an opinion which is genuinely "public" and an opinion which has the character of a "mass" was sharply drawn by C. Wright Mills during the fifties in his influential analysis of the emerging power elite (the military-industrial-government complex) and the complementary mass society in which all of culture—politics, art, even education—becomes a commodity to be compulsively consumed. According to Mills, the classic liberal concept of the public as a body of independent citizens deliberating on high policy possessed some relevance in the preindustrial America of earthbound yeomen, town meetings and simple print media, but has been rendered totally anachronistic by the facts of life in a postindustrial megalopolitan society characterized by computer technology, lonely crowding, and instant gratification. The myth of Rational Man, which once sustained the idea of the public, has in this view given way to the spectral image of Mass Man, a creature of appetites and impulses, easily inflamed and as easily pacified: Archie Bunker as Narcissus, gazing at his reflection in the tube. Under the conditions of mass society, according to Mills, it was inevitable that

> there should arise a conception of public opinion as a mere reaction—we cannot say "response"—to the content of the mass media. In this view, the public is merely the collectivity

of individuals each rather passively exposed to the mass media and rather helplessly opened up to the suggestions and manipulations that flow from these media.[12]

More recently, in his provocative study of *The Fall of Public Man*, sociologist Richard Sennett has extended this thesis by documenting the end of that impersonal order of public life which flourished in the eighteenth and nineteenth centuries as a counterpoise to the private realm of family and friendship—the intimate world of primary relations where spontaneity and self-expression could be allowed free reign. Public life, in Sennett's account, was characterized not by open self-disclosure and "authenticity" but by prudent social distance and calculated role-playing under formal rules in the service of self-interest; in effect, it was the marketplace writ large, where men knew their own interests and judiciously appraised the claims of others—notably of those whose claims were to public authority. The very impersonality of the public realm, and the rationality which governed its exchanges, provided a check against the intrusion of nonrational sentiments appropriate to private life—such as the feelings of intimacy and liking, the appeals of personality and "character." But in the latter half of the last century, largely through the advent of modern mass communications, the protective civilities and restraints that had marked public life began to be eroded by the attractive images of charismatic personality and the illusion of intimacy fostered by the new media and their corollary industries of publicity and public relations.

> For instance, it became logical for people to think of those who could actively display their emotions in public, whether as artists or politicians, as being men of special and superior personality. These men were to control, rather than interact with, the audience in front of whom they appeared. Gradually the audience lost faith in itself to judge them; it became a spectator rather than a witness. The audience thus lost a sense of itself as an active force, as a "public."[13]

Moreover, as the citizenry became more passive in its political role, hence more powerless, the politician who adapted to the new oppor-

tunities became more active and powerful in his projection of himself
and his command of the audience. At the same time, significantly, he
was liberated from the difficulties of having to deal with the substan-
tive issues of policy and program. "In politics," Sennett observes,
". . . the presence of personality 'subtracts' political content." As the
rationality of the public realm was replaced by the emotionality of the
"intimate society," deliberation on issues gave way to presentations
(and ratifications) of personality—as demonstrated in public displays
of sincerity, openness, friendliness, and the like. In other words, as
politicians abandoned content in favor of style ("image"), so audiences could forsake rational thought and judgment in favor of sentimental appraisals of character and virtue—appraisals which were
unconsciously conditioned by role-models drawn both from personal
life and from the fake-lore of mass culture.

Whether or not American public opinion has deteriorated generally
to the level of primitive emotional responses may be argued, of
course; but it is undeniable that both the economics and the politics
of mass persuasion have grown rapidly in power and reach as a result
of the revolution in communications technology. Moreover, the big
media have something else going for them; there has always been an
oracular quality, an aura of omniscience and infallibility, surrounding the major institutions of journalism: "If you read it in *The Sun,* it
must be true." The mere fact of the publication or broadcast of an
utterance—any utterance—constitutes a kind of validation of its
claim to truth, a psychological reinforcement of a kind understood all
too well by demagogues and advertisers. Television, with its multi-
pronged assault upon our senses and sensibilities, appears to have
carried this power of reinforcement so far as virtually to reverse the
natural order of perceived events; now the second-hand reproduction
of an occurrence has come to seem more *real,* more believable and
significant, than the actual event itself. This is the ominous development anticipated by Daniel J. Boorstin in his pioneering study of the
early sixties, *The Image,* which proclaimed the age of the "pseudo-
event": an Orwellian world of mirrors wherein the fabricated fac-
similes of the media have overtaken and superseded the mundane
reality of unmediated, unedited and undramatized events. The disturbing implications of this hypothesis, for the independent mind and
the free society, warrant a deeper examination.

Graven Images: The New Magic Theater

The ascendancy of the image (simulation, imitation, illusion) was attributed by Boorstin to a cultural sea-change of the past century which he termed the "Graphic Revolution": that is, the extraordinary growth of "man's ability to make, preserve, transmit, and disseminate precise images—images of print, of men and landscape and events, of the voices of men and mobs."[14] Most revolutionary of all were the new techniques of photography which had led us "by a giant leap . . . from the daguerrotype to color television in less than a century." The rapid development and sophistication of photography brought with it an unanticipated consequence of immense significance; as Susan Sontag has more recently demonstrated, it made "ever more literal the senses in which a photograph gives control over the thing photographed." Sontag summarizes this transformation in a single complex sentence:

> The technology that has already minimized the extent to which the distance separating photographer from subject affects the precision and magnitude of the image; provided ways to photograph things which are unimaginably small as well as those, like stars, which are unimaginably far; rendered picture-taking independent of light itself (infrared photography) and freed the picture-object from its confinement to two dimensions (holography); shrunk the interval between sighting the picture and holding it in one's hands (from the first Kodak, when it took weeks for a developed roll of film to be returned to the amateur photographer, to the Polaroid, which ejects the image in a few seconds); not only got images to move (cinema) but achieved their simultaneous recording and transmission (video)—this technology has made photography an incomparable tool for deciphering behavior, predicting it, and interfering with it.[15]

The meaning of the graphic revolution was misinterpreted from the outset, and remains largely unrecognized today. What appeared to be taking place was a vast increase in our perception of reality: the acquisition of new sights and sounds, the ability to travel with

Fitzpatrick and Lowell Thomas to remote lands and exotic cultures, to accompany *Life* to war and NASA into outer space. But what was actually taking place was a steady weakening of our hold on reality and an equivalent strengthening of the illusionary power of the replica—which eventually came to be more evocative, more colorful, and more "alive" than the original. "Vivid images," as Boorstin put it, "came to overshadow pale reality." By the time network television had completed its penetration of the American home, reality *was* as reality appeared on the tube; and when Walter Cronkite intoned "That's the way it is" on the evening news, there were few out there in the nationwide audience who believed it could be otherwise.

Daniel Schorr, the former network news reporter who lost his job with CBS in the mid-seventies after "leaking" a secret government report, immediately found himself regarded as having lost his identity if not his actual existence. "In my first months out of CBS," he wrote, "many asked how it felt to be off television, as though they feared that I was suffering some kind of cosmic withdrawal symptoms. I finally grasped that underlying their questions was the concern that since I had derived my identity from being on the air, I might now, in some existential scheme, be in danger of vanishing altogether." Schorr came to interpret his experience as symptomatic of a "great American malady" in which the televised image not only over-shadows reality but has virtually extinguished it. "The illness had progressed beyond the previous stages of image-making and image-manipulation employed in the selling of products and politicians. The perceived world was beginning to crowd out the real world, with consequences often odd and sometimes ominous."[16]

All of this might be fairly innocuous if the images conveyed by the media were no more than vivid copies, however retouched, of the real world out there. That is sometimes the case, no doubt; but the "pseudo-event" of which Boorstin wrote, the illegitimate offspring of the graphic revolution, is neither a carbon copy nor reasonable fac-simile but a conscious distortion of reality—a visual forgery or impos-ture intended to deceive the audience and, by deceiving, to manipu-late its responses and modify its behavior. The pseudo-event is any manufactured occasion, staged performance, or contrived occurrence that seeks to pass as the real thing. Boorstin cited as classic examples the arranged interview and the press conference—e.g., the carefully designed "Checkers" speech of Richard Nixon and the melodramatic convocations, typically empty of content, summoned by Senator Joseph McCarthy in the early fifties. Those classic pseudo-events seem nowadays almost innocent compared to the sophisticated engineering of episodes and opportunities by a wide variety of public figures ranging from presidents and popes to media-smart demonstrators enacting guerilla theater at the "siege of Chicago" in 1968 and the "siege of Teheran" in 1980. Media management, as Christopher Lasch observes, has turned into "spectacle manipulation"; today it is not only the media and the audience which are managed and choreographed but the very swirl of life itself. Given a videotape and a movieola, any filmmaker now can reconstruct an event to make it "happen" differently, for those (nearly all of us) who view it only in replay. In recent years we have been witness, for the most part unknowingly, to piecemeal revisions of history routinely carried out by the camera crews of candidates seeking to make political-commercial capital out of every recorded timestrip of interview, encounter, arrival, departure, public appearance, and private soliloquy.

This is the truly sinister characteristic of the new Magic Theater of tele-revision, where it is no longer mere illusion that is presented but *illusion compounded by deception*. To illustrate: when an actor (say, Robert Young) plays the part of a doctor ("Marcus Welby, M.D.") in a TV drama series, that is a simple illusion without the element of deception; but when the same actor, now identified implicitly as "Dr. Welby," endorses the benefits of a decaffeinated coffee in a TV commercial, that is a compound illusion—and an act of deception. The old-time magician in his live theater actually depended on the audience's ability (not its inability) to distinguish illusion from reality; no one supposed for a minute that the girl was really being sawed in half, and so everyone delighted in the trickery. The new magician of the electronic theater relies instead upon our *confusion* of reality and appearance; if "Marcus Welby" says this brew is good for us, we do not applaud his acting—we believe him. (Check the sales charts.)

The pseudonymous realm of the image and imposture, as this example suggests, is largely the creation of commercial advertisers, originally in the print media and ultimately in the multidimensional medium of television. Boorstin's pseudo-event has its almost exact counterpart in the "pseudo-truth" which anthropologist Jules Henry, writing in the mid-sixties, found to characterize what he called the philosophical world of advertising.

No sane American would think that literally everybody is "talking about the new Starfire," or that Alpine cigarettes literally "put the men in menthol smoking" or that a woman wearing a *Distinction* foundation garment becomes so beautiful that her sisters literally want to kill her. Since he will not take these burblings literally, he will not call them lies, even though they are all manifestly untrue. Ergo, a new kind of truth has emerged—*pecuniary pseudo-truth*—which may be defined as a false statement made as if it were true, but not intended to be believed. No proof is offered for a pecuniary pseudo-truth, and no one looks for it. Its proof is that it sells merchandise; if it does not, it is false.[17]

Henry went on to point out that acceptance by the audience of the "pecuniary logic" behind the advertiser's pseudotruth involves something like a willing suspension of rational disbelief and so tends to paralyze the capacity for judgment and decision. His argument was that this assault upon the mind had become an economic necessity in an industrial society dependent upon an ever-rising rate of consumption which becomes not only conspicuous but compulsive. "From this it follows that in order for our economy to continue in its present form people must learn to be fuzzy-minded and impulsive. . . . If we were all logicians the economy could not survive, and herein lies a terrifying paradox, for in order to exist economically as we are we must try by might and main to remain stupid."[18] To this it might be added that if we were all logicians the politics of personality also could not survive, for in order to exist politically as we are, we must try no less strenuously to remain mindless.

It is at least arguable that we are well on the way to succeeding in that regressive effort—that we have exchanged our birthright of critical intelligence for both a mess of pottage (consumption) and a pot of message (persuasion). But there is still more to our dilemma than that. For the essentially dehumanizing potential of the mediacracy, apart from the profit motives of its merchandisers and the power drives of its manipulators, lies in its irresistible impulse to simplify reality and trivialize content—and in so doing to diminish public awareness and deaden private sensibility. To be sure, this desensitizing factor did not originate with television; as far back as the forties sociologists were drawing attention to the "narcotizing dysfunction" of the prevalent media, due to their overload of information on the one hand and their leitmotif of distraction on the other.[19] Nor would it be accurate to attribute the contemporary culture of narcissism and of "consciousness lowering" solely to the mechanical genie of the TV tube; as other chapters in this book undertake to demonstrate, the responsibility for the dehuman syndrome runs much wider and deeper. But it remains a fact that the most compelling evidence of cultural deterioration today is the quality of experience manufactured, mediated, and inflicted by commercial television. As a mass industry catering to consumers of culture, television resembles nothing so much as its sister mass industry of fast food; its product is "fast culture," junk food for the mind. As critic Richard Schickel has put it, "Our mental diets consist very largely of cultural junk food. We eat it up regularly, because we are under the misapprehension that it is actually health food."[20] (To which Jim Hougan adds: "The most popular American poem does not begin with 'April is the cruellest month . . .' but 'You deserve a break today . . .'")[21]

The analogy with junk food points not only to the trivializing function of mass culture but to its debilitating effects; a diet of Twinkies and Big Macs is not just lacking in culinary appeal but in solid nutrition. It is not improbable that, in the same way as the human body may be starved and stunted to the point of deformity by a glut of chemical additives and artificial substitutes in the food chain, so the human mind must in time be softened and addled by the continuous spoonfeeding of synthetic imitations of life: pseudo-truths in place of information, pseudo-events in place of reality. Today it is not only the adult movie that is routinely "edited for television," but the adult occurrence as well—the naked truth and the unpleasant fact. (On more than one occasion it has been seriously proposed that presidential news conferences should, like the network talk shows, be taped in advance for later broadcast in order to permit judicious editing and even retakes for a smoother performance. No one, apparently, has yet suggested the obvious next step: the insertion of a laugh track.)

The web of illusion spun by the new Magic Theater—its alchemical conversion of shadow into substance and of hyperbole into truth—has often been analyzed by scholarly critics of the electronic media. But no one yet has more sharply exposed its power of deception and potential for dehumanization than the playwright Paddy Chayevsky, himself a veteran of television writing, in the 1976 movie *Network*. The next voice you hear will be that of Howard Beale, the Mad Prophet of the Airwaves, reporting on the Network News Hour of the (fictional) UBS Television Network. Howard:

> You people and 62 million other Americans are listening to me right now. Because less than three percent of you read books. Because less than 15 percent of you read newspapers. Because the only truth you know is what you get over this tube. . . .
>
> We deal in illusions, man. None of it is true. But you people sit there day after day. Night after night. All ages, colors, creeds. We're all you know. You're beginning to believe the illusions we're spinning here. You're beginning to think that the tube is reality and that your own lives are unreal. You do whatever the tube tells you. You dress like the tube. You eat like the tube. You raise your children like the tube. You even think like the tube. This is mass madness! You maniacs!
>
> In God's name, you people are the real thing. We are the illusion. So turn off your television sets. Turn them off right now. Turn them off and leave them off. Turn them off in the middle of the sentence I'm speaking to you now. Turn them off![22]

5

COUNTER-COUNTERCULTURE: THE GANGRENING OF AMERICA

To shoot a genocidal robot policeman in the defense of life is a sacred act.—*Timothy Leary*

Hitler was a tuned-in guy who leveled the karma of the Jews.—*Charles Manson*

Offing those rich pigs with their own forks and knives, and then eating a meal in the same room, far out! The Weathermen dig Charles Manson.—*Bernardine Dohrn*

THE FABLED YOUTH COUNTERCULTURE of the 1960s, in the brash confidence of its insurgent years, projected a luminous vision of the "greening of America"—an elevation of consciousness, an awakening of the senses, and a new birth of freedom for all. In Charles Reich's widely hailed book of prophecy, as in a host of others on the same theme,[1] the Young American Dream envisaged a revolutionary transformation not only of capitalist society but of human nature itself: nothing less than the spontaneous creation of a New Man and New Woman, pure in heart and at one with nature—authentic, androgynous, and Aquarian.

There is a revolution coming [wrote Reich]. It will not be like revolutions of the past. It will originate with the individual and with culture, and it will change the political structure only as its final act. . . . It promises a higher reason, a more human community, and a new and liberated individual . . .[2]

This greenhouse fantasy of the flower generation was largely sustained, if not originally inspired, by the rich buffet of psychedelic drugs (LSD, marijuana, hashish, STP, peyote, mescaline, psilocybin, etc.) which became readily available during the sixties and soon acquired a kind of spiritual validation as ritual tokens of membership in the underground society of A.S.C. (Altered States of Consciousness). At its high noon the countercultural imagination presented an electric kaleidoscope of rock and rebellion, of the revolution of Self and the levitation of the Pentagon, of vanilla fudge and tangerine skies and strawberry fields forever. The theme was Love and the message was Peace; and the Mecca of it all was indubitably San Francisco, by the dock of the bay. "If you go to San Francisco," sang Scott McKenzie, "be sure to wear some flowers in your hair . . ."

At least that was how it felt and looked while the vibes were still strong and all the acts were together—as they were, for perhaps the last time, at the famous Woodstock Festival of 1969. It was the Age of Aquarius, the era of Be-Ins and Love-Ins, of the making of a counterculture and the plotting of an alternative society. We remember it well and for the most part fondly; indeed it has all been reverently recorded and recycled in every major medium of popular culture (most notably in the rock-grand operas "Hair," "Godspell," and "Jesus Christ Superstar"). What is not so well remembered, however, is that the "youthquake" of the sixties was not in reality an endless summer of magical mystery tours through the tunnel of love and the festival of life; there were also, particularly toward the end of the cycle, recurrent bad trips that stumbled off the garden path into jungles of brutality, degradation, and terror. The flip side of the young American anthem presented a deadly parody which mocked the romantic ethos of the counterculture and turned its happy dream into a hideous nightmare. This "counter-counterculture" replaced the image of a brave new world with the specter of a primordial underworld—an inferno of the spirit characterized by depleted consciousness, ravaged sensibility, "polymorphous perversity," instant self-gratification, and explosive outbreaks of violence and depravity on a scale never before encountered or imagined in middle-class America.

None of this was on the agenda of the counterculture, of course. All that the young were seeking was a genuine alternative to the perceived duplicity and boredom of conventional adult society: a liberated lifestyle in which the tedious "mindfucking" of rational thought and material consumption would give way to the spontaneous expression of feeling and the release of natural impulse. "If it feels good, do it." What they got, as it turned out, was more than they had bargained for; the wish of the youth for a distinctive culture of their own was swiftly granted, but at a cost unanticipated and undesired. Item (1967):

> Pretty little 16-year-old middle-class chick comes to the Haight to see what it's all about and gets picked up by a 17-year-old street dealer who spends all day shooting her full of speed again and again, then feeds her 3000 mikes and raffles her temporarily unemployed body to the biggest Haight Street gang bang since the night before last.[3]

The making of a counterculture, heralded by Theodore Roszak in his metaphysical essay of 1969, reached its apotheosis at Woodstock in the summer of that year—and met its apocalypse at Altamont in the following winter. The Woodstock Festival, nearly half a million bodies strong, was all flowers, fellowship, and frolic; it was truly as it saw itself to be, the "Woodstock Nation," a rhythmic community and convivial society held together by a common language (rock music) and a common ritual (grass or LSD). Woodstock was a joyous tribal celebration, unprecedented in scope and duration, which flourished through several days of rain, overcrowding, and successive mechanical failures without a single major incident of violence or disorder—surely a peak experience of the counterculture and a vindication of its virtue.

Altamont was something else, something unimaginable: a shocking debacle of chaos, mayhem, and murder. It dramatized, in gruesomely literal terms, the death of the counterculture and the degradation of its dogma. The full story of what took place on that improbable killing ground came to light after the event in a detailed report by

Rolling Stone (the leading magazine in the field of rock music). Coincidentally, it was the Rolling Stones, a British rock group whose popularity was surpassed only by the Beatles, who conceived and organized the festival as a free concert climaxing their American tour. The Stones were also responsible for the strategy behind the occasion (they sought to duplicate the media success of Woodstock by marketing a film of their own) and the shrewd tactic of saving money on security arrangements by hiring a band of "Hell's Angels," the notorious motorcycle gang, to maintain order—for an outlay of $500 worth of beer.

The result might have been anticipated; in the words of historian William L. O'Neill, "The Stones did their thing and the Angels did theirs." Faithful to their name and code, the Hell's Angels interpreted the assignment as a license to persecute hippies and other degenerates. By the time the macabre festival was over, a young black man had been beaten to death onstage (to the accompaniment of the Stones' whimsical theme song, "Sympathy for the Devil"), many had been clubbed or mauled, and at least three others lay dead (more or less accidentally). The audience generally was left in a state of shock—except for those too stoned to notice that anything unusual had happened. But the bloody holiday was not a total loss. The Stones got their movie (with most of the violence edited out) and their profits; the Hell's Angels got their beer and their kicks. And the youth counterculture, though few were aware of it then, got its epitaph. The rock composer Don McLean wrote the appropriate words for that epitaph a short time after; it was, he said, "the day the music died." McLean's extraordinary requiem for the golden age of rock and roll ("American Pie") also contained this refrain:

> Bye, bye, Miss American Pie,
> Drove my Chevy to the levee but the levee was dry;
> All those good old boys were drinking whisky and rye,
> Singing "This will be the day that I die,
> This will be the day that I die."

"Haight is Love"

If the Altamont Death Festival (as it was dubbed by *Rolling Stone*) symbolized the end of the counterculture, the beginning of the end had been clearly signaled more than two years before, at the conclusion of what was advertised by San Francisco's hippie community, the Haight-Ashbury district (and publicized nationally by the media), as the "Summer of Love." Earlier that year the city had played host to the First Human Be-In—a "gathering of the tribes" of hippiedom, some 10,000 strong, representing every wing of The Movement from the campus radicals of Berkeley to the flower children of the "Hashbury." Remarkably, the Be-In had come off without incident—even though, among other happenings, "A dazed Santa Claus liberally threw LSD capsules and marijuana to the winds." An astonished *Time* Magazine reported that "The huge crowd was peaceful . . . an amazing tribute to Haight-Ashbury." A counterculture spokesman, Richard Neville, added: "More accurately, it was a tribute to LSD which had begun to suppress local aggression on an ever-increasing scale."[4]

That pleasant illusion was not to survive the summer of love— when the Hashbury was abruptly overwhelmed by an invasion of thousands of youths (perhaps 50,000 in all) seeking to join the action. Almost overnight the district was transformed from a peaceful haven for flower children into what someone called Hell's Kitchen West. Well before the long hot summer came to an end, an underground publication (*The Communication Company*) issued a broadside describing the change of atmosphere in the district:

> Rape is as common as bullshit on Haight Street. . . .
> Kids are starving on The Street. Minds and bodies are being maimed as we watch, a scale model of Vietnam. There are people—our people—dying hideous deaths among us and the Council is planning alternative activities. Haight Street is ugly shitdeath and Alan Watts suggests more elegant attire. . . .
> Tune in, turn on, drop dead? One wonders. Are Leary and Alpert and the [San Francisco] Oracle all in the same greedy place? Does acid still have to be sold as hard as Madison Avenue still sells sex? What do these nice people mean by "Love"?
> Are you aware that Haight Street is just as bad as the squares say it is? Have you heard of the killings we've had on Haight Street? Have you seen dozens of hippies watching

passively while some burly square beats another hippy to a
psychedelic red pulp? Have you walked down Haight Street
at dawn and seen and talked with the survivors?

The trouble is probably that the hip shopkeepers have believed their own bullshit lies. They believe that acid is the
answer and neither know nor care what the question is. They
think that dope is the easy road to God. . . .

They would never believe that they are guilty of monstrous
crimes against humanity. They won't believe it this summer,
when the Street reeks of human agony, despair and death
death death.[5]

The image of death took on deeper dimensions in the fall of 1967
with the almost simultaneous occurrence of two parallel events at
opposite ends of the country. The first was a mock-ceremonial funeral in the Hashbury proclaiming the "Death of Hippie," complete
with mourners, a coffin filled with beads and beard clippings, and
black-bordered funeral notices reading "HIPPIE. In the Haight-
Ashbury district of this city, Hippie, devoted son of Mass Media.
Friends are invited to attend services beginning at sunrise, October 6,
1967, at Buena Vista Park." The symbolism may have been over-
strained, but the message was plain: it related the killing of the
dream. The symbolic swiftly became the real. Two days after the
funeral of hippie, the nude bodies of two New York flower
children—Linda Rea Fitzpatrick, 18, and James Leroy "Groovy"
Hutchinson, 21—were discovered in the boiler room of an East Village building; they had been murdered while high on acid. It was not
the commonplace fact of the murders that drew front-page attention,
however, but the identities of the victims and the peculiarly vicious
manner of the killings. As a writer in the *Village Voice* put it: "A man
and his woman are hauled or lured down to the boiler room, where
amid rags and ratsmell she is banged senseless, and both are stomped
dead." The stark reality of this slaughter of the innocents brought a
shock of recognition to the underground community East and West,
as the *Village Voice* observed in its obituary for the Movement:

That fear is all over the East Village today. The murders
were too plausible to be ignored, the suspects too real to be
dismissed. . . . Everyone knows that Groovy died in a man-

dala of his own blood. And suddenly, everyone remembers why. Other killings come to mind; not the publicized ones—like the fatal stabbing of Walter Coey on his stoop on East 11th, or the bizarre ones—like the Central Park mugging of Bruce Mantel, "the poet," and the rape of his 15-year-old "flower bride." They remember the casual murders (five or six since the early summer, some claim). Accounts of unreported rape abound, and hallway muggings seem to be a rite-de-passage east of Tompkins Square.

It is a slum; Groovy's death seems to have awakened that realization. And hippies, they mutter, are the new niggers. "The odds are incredibly stacked," they say. "Flower power was a summer vacation," they hiss. "In San Francisco, they staged the death of the hippie. Here, we got the real thing."[6]

But San Francisco too was getting the real thing. A particularly lurid episode was the murder of a celebrated Hashbury character, a black dealer in dope nicknamed "Superspade"; he was stabbed, shot, trussed in a sleeping bag, and left hanging from a cliff top. Another West Coast pusher was found stabbed to death with his right forearm cut off. More pervasive, if not more menacing, than the threat of violent death was the atmosphere of degradation and despair that now hung over the Hashbury. A visiting reporter from the *Village Voice* recorded the mood in an article entitled "Autumn in the Haight: Where Has Love Gone?":

There's not much reason now to go to Haight Street unless it's to cop. . . . It is not a pleasant place to sit, yet hundreds do, huddled in doorways or stretched out on the sidewalk, in torn blankets and bare feet, bored voices begging for spare change, selling two-bit psychedelic newspapers that were current in the spring, and dealing, dealing, dealing. The dealing is my strongest impression of Haight Street. . . .

The pace of dealing picks up at night, when the dark provides some protection. Walking down Haight Street at night, the offers are whispers in the shadows or in the crowds. Mostly it's acid. But street acid is usually a combination of a taste of acid fortified with anything from methedrine to strychnine. There have been a lot of bad trips here lately, because there has been a lot of bad acid.[7]

The Politics of Ecstasy

The use and abuse of LSD was a crucial factor, though not the only one, in the swift decline and fall of the Hashbury—as it had been in the ecstatic birth of the hippie headquarters a few years before. The two visionary prophets who had provided the original inspiration for the Haight community, Timothy Leary and Ken Kesey, grounded their respective philosophies squarely on the magical-mystical properties of LSD. For Leary, the ex-Harvard instructor who coined the motto "Turn on, tune in, drop out," the act of dropping acid was the sacrament of a new religion and the harbinger of a new era. In books like *The Psychedelic Experience* and *The Politics of Ecstasy,* and through his League for Spiritual Discovery (LSD), Leary preached a gospel of Holy Acid with irresistible appeal to the alienated youth of the sixties. "There are," he proclaimed, "three groups who are bringing about the great evolution of the new age that we are going through now. They are the *dope dealers,* the *rock musicians* and the Underground *artists and writers.*"[8] However opportunitistic it may have been, there was nothing petty about Leary's vision; among other things he proposed a series of Be-Ins across the continent of Europe, "perhaps retracing the steps of the Crusades. We could call it a Crusade of Penitence or . . . Yeah, the Children's Crusade . . . and that we start moving through Europe to the East so that we would, on September 21st, be on the door between India and China, with as many Indians or Westerners or people that we've picked up on the way . . . I think that's the quickest way to end racial prejudice and the war in Vietnam."[9]

Leary's own sustained experience with Holy Acid did not, as it turned out, convert him into a man of peace capable of charity toward all. In 1970, following his conviction on charges of drug possession and his subsequent escape from prison with the help of the Weathermen, Leary issued a public letter from underground which contained the following sentiments:

Brothers and Sisters, this is a war for survival. Ask Huey and Angela. They dig it.

Ask the wild free animals. They know it. . . .

I declare that World War III is now being waged by short-haired robots whose deliberate aim is to destroy the complex web of free wild life by the imposition of mechanical order.

Listen. There is no choice left but to defend life by all and every means possible against the genocidal machine.

Listen. There are no neutrals in genetic war. There are no non-combatants at Buchenwald, My Lai or Soledad. . . .

Listen Americans. Your government is an instrument of total lethal evil.

Remember the buffalo and the Iroquois!

Remember Kennedy, King, Malcolm, Lenny!

. . . Resist spiritually, stay high . . . praise god . . . love life . . . blow the mechanical mind with Holy Acid . . . dose them . . . dose them.

. . . Resist physically, robot agents who threaten life must be disarmed, disabled, disconnected by force . . . Arm yourself and shoot to live . . . Life is never violent. To shoot a genocidal robot policeman in the defense of life is a sacred act.[10]

The other principal spokesman of the LSD revolution, novelist Ken Kesey, maintained a markedly lighter, if not soberer, note through his brief career as a prophet and role model. Kesey and his Merry Pranksters, touring the United States and Mexico in a converted schoolbus and introducing thousands to the "Electric Kool-Aid Acid Test," made little pretense of religious wisdom but went in for mixed-media "psychedelic-stroboscopic" extravaganzas centered upon a driving version of "acid rock" which became known as the San Francisco Sound (and brought fame to groups like the Grateful Dead and the Jefferson Airplane, besides influencing the subsequent course of rock music in general). Kesey's message was that anyone who dared could fly over the cuckoo's nest, with a little help from his friends; and that sometimes a great notion, like the acid truth, came along to prod the human race out of the ruts of routine into a higher realm of pure play power. "The Pranksters," wrote Tom Wolfe, "thought of themselves and Leary's group as two extraordinary arcane societies, and the only ones in the world, engaged in the most fantastic experiment in human consciousness ever devised. The thing was totally new."[11]

For a short time the dream of turning everybody on, of dosing the civilized world with psychedelic chemicals, seemed plausible not only to the handful of Pranksters but to many thousands of rootless young people in search of a purpose. In Wolfe's idiosyncratic imagery:

> Like, I mean,
> You know,
> Can't you *see it coming*:
> Ten thousand children of the flowers and grass and acid,
> speed and poppers, yellow jackets, amyl nitrate,
> Ten thousand heads, freaks, beats, hippy-dippies, teeny-
> boppers descending from the crest of Haight Street
> Tinkling, temple bells, rattling, donkey heads, reeking,
> grass, shuffling, elf boots, swarming prostrate
> Before the returning Prophet in the bowels of Winterland.
> All of psychedelphia moaning to the polyphonic droning of
> the Merry Prankster band![12]

The dream died almost as quickly as it had arisen; and the merriment soon went out of the Pranksters. One cause of the collapse was the eventual dissatisfaction of Kesey himself with the miracle of the drugs; by the fall of 1967 he was proposing an "Acid Test Graduation," a vague scheme of post-LSD enlightenment or at least mystification which was all but universally rejected. Another and more fundamental reason for the Pranksters' decline was the highly volatile mixture both of people and of drugs which fueled the movement. Although acid remained the basic ingredient, the whole panoply of psychedelic and psychotropic agents came into use. As Wolfe described a day in the life: "Nobody can sleep so they keep taking more speed to keep going, psychic energizers like Ritalin, anything, and then smoke more grass to take the goddamn tachycardiac edge off the speed, and acid to make the whole thing turn into something else." A somber episode in Wolfe's mostly enraptured chronicle of the Pranksters recounts the breakdown of a young woman who joined the tour, took increasingly heavy doses of acid (dissolved in orange juice), became wildly agitated and miserable, but was left strictly alone on the principle that it was her private trip and that everyone must "go with the flow." Before long she became completely withdrawn, huddled naked in a corner (and hence was humorously re-christened "Stark Naked"). The end was reached in a sudden display of total derangement. "And there," as Wolfe concludes the episode, "amid the peaceful Houston elms on Quenby Road, it dawned on them all that this woman—which one of us even knows her?—had completed her trip. She had gone with the flow. She had gone stark, raving mad."[13]

There were a few, a rare few, among the heroes and gurus of the counterculture who challenged the gospel of Holy Acid. One conspicuous dissenter was the author William Burroughs, himself an ex-addict, who spoke out in the underground press against the potentially lethal effects of what he termed the "destructive drugs" (embracing the strong hallucinogens along with heroin and amphetamines like speed).[14] But such warnings were unwelcome and unacknowledged—as a letter writer to Rolling Stone complained in pointing to "the hushing up and blatant sidestepping by heads of a frank discussion of all the terrifying aspects of dropping acid . . . [although there are] thousands of us who have experienced the profoundest anxieties, loneliness, and fear while tripping."[15] When the bad trips grew too common and conspicuous to be denied, they were rationalized or shrugged off; the holy chemical was not to be questioned.

Nevertheless new doubts were emerging. For one thing, it began to be noticed that even a good trip, for all its brief euphoria, was no guarantee of virtuous behavior; feeling good was not the same as doing good. Witness the testimony of a Hell's Angel, recalling a particularly memorable street fight: "Those Hippies say that if you fight or something like that on acid you'll freak out. They don't know what they're talking about. It was the best fight I was ever in, that fight when I was on acid. Beautiful. Just beautiful."[16] In short, to get high on acid was not necessarily to get religion; it might also beget sympathy for the devil—or for (in another Rolling Stones' lyric) the "Street-Fighting Man."

For many users much of the time, however, LSD seems to have performed its advertised function all too well. To them the acid trip was not merely pleasurable but transcendent, not just an altered state but a profound mystical experience. "In this state the user feels a sense of unity, transcendence of space and time, positive moods of joy, peace and love, awe and reverence, philosophical insight, and ineffability."[17] For these devotees the problem was not one of getting religion but of keeping it—sustaining the sense of illumination and, more practically, making it work in their lives. To sustain the experience meant, on the one hand, repeating the trip more and more often, mixing or reinforcing it with other drugs—and on the other hand seeking out others (especially gurus) who could define and validate the spiritual character of the event. The need for confirmation and reassurance became more urgent as doubts began to circulate even among the initiated as to the authenticity of the drug experience and the reality of spiritual change. A former graduate student of Leary's, Allan Y. Cohen, spoke for many in describing his disenchantment:

> . . . one of the phantasies we used to have is now demonstrably false. This is the belief that if you take enough psychedelic drugs, you will become holy, spiritually sophisticated, wise, expanded consciousness, love will flow from you. It doesn't happen to work. Haight-Ashbury in San Francisco in the last six years has turned from a reserve of flower children to a jungle where even the police aren't safe. The use of psychedelic chemicals in that culture did not lead to a social utopia.[18]

Drug Left and Drug Right

If the psychedelic experience failed to produce either the social utopia or personal salvation promised by its prophets, however, it did powerfully affect the consciousness of the multitudes who made it a regular part of their lifestyle. Whether or not (as numerous studies have claimed) LSD damaged the brains of users, it did "blow their minds" and turn their heads—not merely away from the conventional values of adult society but, increasingly, *against* them. What had begun as a passive retreat turned more and more into a revolt—a "Great Refusal" which soon split off in two extreme directions, one to the Left (toward the political sects) and the other to the Right (toward the spiritual cults). The apparent opposition of these two extremist movements, viewed in political or ideological terms, masked their psychological affinity and the striking similarity of their consequences: both were to give way to unparalleled eruptions of violence, cruelty, and dehumanization. Their common source was a sullen mood of implacable hostility toward the mainstream society of elders and straights; and their common modus operandi was a charismatic and authoritarian leadership commanding submission and self-abasement on the part of members.

The manipulative pathology underlying the post-hippie cults, whether ostensibly of the Left or Right, led a perceptive observer of the scene (David Felton, then an editor of *Rolling Stone*) to coin the term "acid fascism" as a definition of their common character. The phrase conveyed two implications:

> First, as a kind of historical label, it refers to the host of rigid, teacher-oriented communities—both Jesus and non-Jesus—that have sprouted across the land with the drug revolution of the sixties. . . . . This new personal fascism is unique, occurring as it does during the greatest period of moral and personal liberation in the nation's history. It has split young self-realizers into two camps—a kind of Drug Left and Drug Right. . . .
>
> But the term "acid fascism" has a second implication, the notion that for some people psychedelics create or deepen a spiritual hunger. Does acid lead to harder stuff—like Manson or Lyman?
>
> The young Americans who grew up in the sixties were the first to experience psychedelics, the first to experience a euphoric—if temporary—heaven on earth unknown to any previous generation. We're not talking about a few freaks and losers, now, we're talking about a huge portion of people—millions. For this reason alone they are a different breed. Television, the war, might have affected them more deeply, but the drugs affected them *differently,* in ways we may not see for some time, let alone understand.[19]

The left turn of the post-hippie counterculture, spurred by the unpopular war and its attendant draft, proceeded through student radicalism (e.g., the Free Speech Movement and Students for a Democratic Society) to the guerilla theater of the Yippies and, finally, to the revolutionary violence of the Weather Underground and splinters like the Symbionese Liberation Army. Meanwhile the right turn proceeded from the zen/yoga ashrams and Jesus temples through such

authoritarian cults as Mel Lyman's Fort Hill Commune, Charles De-
derich's Synanon, Mo Berg's Children of God and Robert Wood's
Process Church of the Final Judgment, onward to the ritual murders
by Charlie Manson's Family and the terminal "Kool-Aid acid test" of
the Reverend Jim Jones.

Taken together, these dehumanizing movements represent the
counter-counterculture which came to maturity during the seventies:
the dark underside of the hippie counterculture which had flourished
and expired in the sixties. For it was predominantly the hippies—the
self-styled freaks, dropouts, street people, acid heads, flower
children—who were to fill the ranks of these antisocial movements.
Strung out on drugs, unable to cope with the real world, desperate for
love and leadership, they were pathetically susceptible to new
prophets preaching heady gospels of revelation and redemption. As
one of them wrote, referring to the psychopathic leader of the Fort
Hill Commune:

> Many of Lyman's followers are like thousands of us who
> have experienced the profoundest anxieties, loneliness, and
> fear while tripping. But when searching around for someone
> with whom to communicate the gripping paranoia of those
> fears, found only silence, smugness, and pretended ignorance.
> So they found Mel, who did speak the truth about it, but who
> took that truth and those fears, and twisted them and used
> them to humiliate and control.[20]

Charlie's Angels: One Man's Family

It is difficult in retrospect to avoid the conclusion that, despite
the aura of sweetness and light which surrounded it, the hippie counterculture was an intrinsically schizoid movement that nurtured
within itself the seeds of its own destruction. As Felton prophesied in
his 1970 report on acid fascism, ". . . something dark may indeed
lurk beyond the Aquarian Age." Other observers after him have
discerned a strong undercurrent of aggression and hostility lying beneath the placid surface of the hippie lifestyle—a repressed force of
destructive energy which, being inadmissible, was projected outward
onto bourgeois society until the time when—having created its own

fearsome *Doppelgänger*—it could emerge self-righteously in acts of retaliatory terrorism and gestures of conspiratorial bravado. Thus Michael Selzer has suggested "that the hippie diagnosis of bourgeois America may actually have been a covert, unconscious expression of the destructiveness the hippies themselves sought to express."[21] And William O'Neill, describing the hippie origins of the Manson family, has diagnosed the hidden flaw which brought about the denouement of the counterculture:

> Of course hippies were not murderers usually. But the re-pressed hostility, authoritarian perversity, and mindless paranoia that underlay much of the hippie ethic were never displayed more clearly. The folkways of the flower children tended toward extremes. At one end they were natural victims; at the other, natural victimizers. The Manson family were both at once.[22]

In truth the extended Manson "family" was a grotesque caricature, a distorted but recognizable mirror-image, of the hippie counterculture in virtually all of its prominent features: in its critical dependence on drugs (principally LSD), its insistently polymorphous sexuality, its devotion to the themes and postures of acid rock, its elaborate fantasies of religious inspiration, its communal-familial lifestyle, its seething rage against society, its renegade and runaway constituency. The Manson girls (Squeaky, Gypsy, Sadie, Sandy, and the rest) were mostly homeless kids plucked off the streets; the Manson boys (Bobby, Tex, Danny, Clem, and the rest) were typically dropouts or outlaws drawn from motorcycle gangs. Charlie Manson himself affected, at one time or another, most of the faddist and cultist vogues of the sixties scene—ranging from Scientology (in which he attained the high status of a "beta clear") and The Process Church (from which he derived his Jesus-and-Satan theology), to apparent imitation of the Merry Pranksters and, most significant of all, enraptured veneration of the Beatles.[23] Manson's ghoulish interpretations of the "messages" hidden in Beatles' lyrics—especially those collected in the "White Album" of late 1968—have been made familiar through Vincent Bugliosi's chronicle of the family and its bloody career, *Helter Skelter*. We know that Manson took as his major text the album track entitled "Revolution 9" (a curious montage of nonmusical and strangely ominous sounds)—which pointed irresistibly to the ninth chapter of the Book of Revelation (Revelation 9) prophesying the Battle of Armageddon and the advent of doomsday. The weird abstractionism of "Revolution 9" might have been enough by itself to galvanize and focus the destructive paranoia of the Manson mind, but there was much more to the White Album than that: an entire panoply of clues and cues, insinuated in song after song, creating a powerful cycle of mutual reinforcement and revelation, urging the paterfamilias on to his fateful mission as the catalyst of Armageddon and the dark horseman of the Apocalypse. Nearly every one of the thirty "songs" in the double album held a secret meaning for Manson—many of them appeals direct to Charlie from the Beatles, who had surely become aware that he was the reincarnated Christ they were searching for (the Maharishi having failed them). In the early weeks of 1969, replaying and decoding the album obsessively, Manson and the girls not only wrote letters to the Beatles but sent telegrams and even sought, unsuccessfully, to reach them by telephone. Meanwhile the grand design of "Helter Skelter" was becoming clearer and more urgent. Manson had long believed that the final conflict, Armageddon, would be a race war pitting whites against blacks; now it was obvious from songs like "Blackbird," "Rocky Raccoon," and "Piggies" that the Beatles were a step ahead, pointing the way. It was all there in the lyrics: the "blackbird" was only waiting for this moment to arise; the "piggies," who dined out in their finery, eating bacon with their forks and knives, deserved a damned good whacking (Leno LaBianca was to be found dead with multiple knife wounds and with a carving fork stuck in his stomach); Helter Skelter was "coming down fast"; and "Rocky Raccoon," the black man, was due for a revival—you could check it out in the Bible ("Gideon checked out").[24]

And so Manson (a.k.a. Man's Son, a.k.a. JC, a.k.a. Satan) set it violently in motion; the Tate/LaBianca slaughters were intended as the precipitating act, the Sarajevo incident, of the ultimate war of extermination. With that preliminary mission accomplished, the family settled in on their remote desert ranch, marked their foreheads with the sign of the cross, and prepared to increase their flock to the ordained number of the saving remnant (144,000), according to the prophecy of Revelation 9. The prologue of "Helter Skelter" had come down, but the main event never came off. The ritual murders, with their bloody graffiti ("Death to Pigs," "Helter Skelter," "Rise") were not blamed on rampaging black hordes, up from Watts to off the pigs; and so there were no vigilante reprisals to trigger the interracial holocaust. All that happened was that Charlie and his angels got caught, red-handed; the grand design turned out to be only a madman's dream. It was not Armageddon, after all, but just another Hollywood spectacular.

If the adventures of the Manson family represent a clearcut case of "acid fascism"—complete with racism, sexual chauvinism, and the *Fuehrer-prinzip*—it is noteworthy that they were loudly celebrated by many at the opposite end of the ideological spectrum: specifically, by the proponents of what might be called "acid anarchism." The Weatherman leader Bernardine Dohrn, shortly before going underground in 1970, reportedly had this to say to a convention of Students for a Democratic Society: "Offing those rich pigs with their own forks and knives, and then eating a meal in the same room, far out! The Weathermen dig Charles Manson."[25] (The Weathermen also promoted a bumper sticker bearing the legend: MANSON— THE YEAR OF THE FORK.)

Equal adulation was given Manson by the Yippies (Youth International Party), the mock-revolutionary faction organized by Jerry Rubin and Abbie Hoffman whose guerilla-theater antics had stolen the show at the 1968 Democratic Convention. "I fell in love with Charlie Manson the first time I saw his cherub face and sparkling eyes on TV," declared Rubin, who also wrote: "His words and courage inspired us. Manson's soul is easy to touch because it lays [sic] quite bare on the surface."[26] The *Los Angeles Free Press* featured interviews with Charlie, and for a time ran a rambling column under his byline. Another L. A. underground paper, *Tuesday's Child*, which described itself as the Voice of the Yippies, heralded Manson in one issue as "Man of the Year" and in another issue pictured him hanging from a cross above the simple caption: "Hippie." On the basis of this sympathetic publicity, psychedelic "head" shops in major cities began to stock Manson posters, T-shirts, and buttons (reading "Free Manson").

"Sirhan Sirhan Is a Yippie"

Manson was not the only cold-blooded killer to become the object of the Yippies' affections. The two Kennedy assassins, Lee Harvey Oswald and Sirhan Sirhan, also made the honor roll. The reasoning was the same in all cases: they were simple men of the people, agents of the oppressed, who dared to assault the rich and powerful and thereby strike a blow for freedom. In his book *Do It,* Rubin poured forth his sympathy and admiration for Oswald:

> I thought to myself: "Kennedy—the jewel of Amerika: one bullet and the beauty, money, fame, power, a family dynasty are all gone." *Far out!*
>
> The next day, the papers carried a full-page picture of the accused, Lee Harvey Oswald. I couldn't take my eyes off his bitter face. I had seen that scowl so many times in the streets of Amerika. . . .
>
> Who is Lee Oswald? With a rifle Lee forced the world to see. He found he could participate in the dream of Kennedy greatness only by killing a Kennedy.
>
> Who knows what divine madness boiled beneath that bitter scowl?[27]

A few sentences later on, Rubin turned his adoring gaze upon the countenance of the other Kennedy assassin: "When he assassinated Robert Kennedy, Sirhan Sirhan consciously saw himself as an Arab patriot, representing oppressed peoples as he fired a pistol bullet, shattering the myth of rich, white, Amerikan power. . . . What dedication and fanatacism is inspired by Amerikan greed!"[28] Elsewhere in the book appears the subtitle: *"Sirhan Sirhan Is a Yippie."*

The special affection displayed by Rubin and the Yippies for these "political" murderers was entirely consistent with the philosophy and program of the movement. From their birth in 1967, the Yippies combined the vaudeville turns of the Merry Pranksters with the violent tactics of the New Left; they were, as they dubbed themselves, "politicized acid freaks" whose theatrics concealed a deep and angry sense of outrage and an avowed intent to destroy the system of bourgeois institutions (the favored slogan was "Fuck the System"). The Yippies may have been, in Abbie Hoffman's phrase, "revolutionists for the hell of it"—but they were revolutionists all the same. Their talent for political street-theater, and their instinctual mastery of the media, became apparent to the nation at large during the "siege of Chicago" which highlighted the 1968 Democratic Convention. Something of the viciousness which underlay the fun-and-games facade of the Yippies may be gleaned from their announced "program"—a mixture of fantasy and reality—intended to disrupt the Chicago Convention:

> Among the fantasy-realities the yippies predicted for their Festival of Life: . . . the disruption of traffic by staging a mass stall-in of vintage cars on the express ways; the shanghai-ing of delegates in cars disguised as cabs in order to dump them in Wisconsin or other places far from the Convention; the use of yippie call-girls who would seduce delegates and dose their drinks with LSD; the insinuation of agents into the kitchens of Convention hotels to drug the food; . . . the capture of all petrol stations in order to flood the sewers and set the city alight; . . . the bombardment of the Convention Amphitheatre with mortar fire; the recruitment of sexually athletic yippie males to rape the wives and daughters of Convention delegates.[29]

A favorite theme of Rubin's, reiterated in numerous campus lectures across the country (which took him as far as the University of Hawaii), was his playful advice to youth: "Kill your parents!" Another more earnest proposition advanced by Rubin and Hoffman was that stealing, looting, and otherwise "ripping off" the shops and businesses of straight society was a wholly legitimate, morally correct, and psychologically liberating activity. "All money represents theft," declared Rubin. "To steal from the rich is a sacred and religious act. To take what you need is an act of self-love, self-liberation. While looting, a man to his own self is true."[30] (A London rock group named the Deviants, at about this time, recorded a song entitled "Let's Loot the Supermarket.") For all their parade of political rationalizations, Rubin and Hoffman were clearly appealing to a debased level of narcissistic impulse—the uninhibited urge to total self-gratification, sensual abandonment, and the joyous shattering of taboos—which was calculated to have a special resonance for their alienated and still-adolescent constituency. All ambiguities, moral or intellectual, were swept aside as bourgeois hangups; regression to the wishful self-indulgence of the spoiled child was the way of wisdom and the path to freedom—to the Revolution of Self. The Yippie movement, like the acid revolution of Tim Leary before it, was an undisguised children's crusade—but one devoid of innocence and conceived with malice aforethought:

Liberation comes when we stop doing it for the bread and do what we always wanted to do as children. . . . (Shoplifting gets you high. Don't buy. Steal. If you act like it's yours, no one will ask you to pay for it.) . . . (Kids should steal money from their parents, because that is true liberation from the money ethic: true family.) . . .

Representative democracy is the enemy. The goal is each-man-his-own-revolution. . . .

When in doubt, burn. Fire is the revolutionary's god. Fire is instant theater. No words can match fire. . . .

Burn the flag. Burn churches.

Burn, burn, burn.[31]

The advent of the Yippie ethic signaled a crucial turn in the history of the youth counterculture. Where the philosophy of the hippies had been symbolized by the act of *giving* (flowers, love, food, sanctuary), the philosophy of the Yippies was symbolized by the act of *taking*— stealthily if necessary, violently if called for, freely in any case. The old ethic had emphasized economic self-sufficiency, tolerance, generosity, and respect for others (notably in the free services provided by the Diggers); the new ethic depended on the artful dodges of guile, deceit, and thievery—and came more and more to look like an unconscious parody of the greedy acquisitive society it professed to despise. As Nigel Young, in a cogent analysis of the failure of the New Left, has observed:

The change from the Diggers to Abbie Hoffman and the Yippies is not just from "giving" to "taking"; it is the translation of "freedom" into theft—as against "cashlessness," production, and cooperation. If it is not given, then it must be seized; the post-scarcity ethic has become more aggressive and individualistic, less antagonistic to commodity, and it marks an important cultural watershed.[32]

The shift from hippie altruism to Yippie grab—from hands-off to rip-off—not only compromised the claim of the counterculture to a higher morality and a gentler lifestyle; it opened the ranks of the movement to elements from the criminal subclass who were untroubled by philosophical hangups and who introduced a dimension of violence and paranoia that middle-class revolutionists-for-the-hell-of-it found irresistibly fascinating. In fact, the *frisson* had always been there; the romance of the Acid Left with the Criminal Right began with the nervous wooing of the Hell's Angels by rock bands like the Rolling Stones and by antic groups like the Merry Pranksters. Tom Wolfe has given us a vivid impression of that uneasy alliance:

> One way or another, the Hell's Angels came to symbolize the side of the Kesey adventure that panicked the hip world. The Angels were too freaking real. *Outlaws?* they were outlaws by choice, from the word go, all the way out in Edge City. Further! . . . In their heart of hearts, the heads of Haight-Ashbury could never stretch their fantasy as far out as the Hell's Angels. Overtly, publicly, they included them in— suddenly, they were the Raw Vital Proles of this thing, the favorite minority, replacing the spades. Privately, the heads remained true to their class, and to its visceral panics.[33]

There had also existed, in the heyday of San Francisco's Haight-Ashbury and New York's East Village, an inflammatory mixture of subcultures which was as dangerous and frequently lethal as the mixture of drugs on the street. When the flower children first went down into the ghettos and tenderloins to inaugurate their alternative society, they found themselves confronting the permanent residents—the original street people—whose resentment of the long-haired white youths crowding their tenements was expressed in regular and routine muggings, beatings, and killings. As a matter of survival, the early hippie ethic of love and joy soon gave way to the counter-ethic of the urban jungle. There emerged what one writer of the time called "a new slum-hippie [who] lives in the ghetto and acts like it. . . . The word has gotten around that some Diggers in New York and San Francisco carry guns—and intend to use them. The flower child, now a veteran of violence, is toughening up."[34]

The admixture of hardcore criminality which increasingly infiltrated the counterculture was the result, at bottom, of the ubiquitous activity which was its most common denominator: the illegal trafficking in drugs. Apart from the organized crime associations of many of the "pushers" (dealers), the simple acts of buying, imbibing, or possessing psychedelic drugs such as marijuana or LSD (after 1966) were defined as criminal—thus at once reinforcing the estrangement of the "heads" from normal society and blurring the distinctions between the so-called "underground" and the real underworld. The Weathermen in particular sought to make capital, and gain recruits to the cause of revolutionary violence, out of this confusion of identities and roles. "We fight in many ways," declared Bernardine Dohrn in the first communique from the Weathermen Underground. "Dope is one of our weapons. The laws against marijuana mean that millions of us are outlaws long before we actually split. Guns and grass are united in the youth underground."[35] And the Jefferson Airplane, perhaps the most radicalized of the rock bands, set the same theme to music:

> We are all outlaws in the eyes of America . . .
> We are obscene lawless hideous dangerous dirty violent and
>   young . . .
> We are forces of chaos and anarchy
> Everything they say we are we are
> And we are very
> Proud of ourselves.[36]

Basking in the self-glorification of their outlaw status, the new Drug Left found it only natural to make common cause with others who were in defiance of the law—the more flagrant and violent their crimes the better. In a Yippie manifesto issued on the eve of the 1968 election, signed by Rubin and Hoffman, the doors of the movement were opened to the good, the bad, and the ugly: "Come all you rebels, youth spirits, rock minstrels, bomb throwers, bank robbers, peacock freaks, toe worshippers, poets, street folk, liberated women, professors and body snatchers . . ."[37] In addition to these strange bedfellows, the Yippie broadside also extended the invitation to "snipers." Clearly, if anyone on the wild side was omitted from this sweeping call to arms, it was an oversight. The counter-ethic of the Yippies proposed, and sought to carry out, a complete inversion of conventional moral codes: violence became virtue, murder was heroism, theft was a sacred act, looting was liberation, and all of it was therapeutic. Of course, these lurid scenarios were heavily theatrical—a sort of real-life "Rocky Horror Picture Show"—and the bark of the Yippies (Yip! Yip!) was generally worse than their bite. But they did bite; some of their bloodiest scripts were acted out in the streets, both by the Yippies themselves and (still more viciously) by their official allies the Black Panthers and their unofficial heirs of the Weather Underground. However, their most enduring contribution

lay in their encouragement of the systematic transformation of liberation into license and of nonviolent protest into what has been called
the "politics of atrocity."[38] The Yippies gave positive reinforcement,
not to say inspiration, to the most deranged and depraved per-
sonalities within reach of their rhetoric; and their improvised gospel
of revolutionary nihilism, of total rebellion without a cause, conveyed
the promise of absolution for any crime, however cruel or senseless,
directed against people or property. "Bonnie Parker and Clyde Barrow," exclaimed Rubin, "are the leaders of the New Youth."[39]

The phenomenon of the Youth International Party held the stage
for only a few years in the late sixties. There was more, and worse, yet
to come than was dreamt of in their puerile philosophy. But the
strategy of confrontation, the tactics of terrorism, and the underlying
theme of what might be described as revolutionary narcissism ("revolution for the hell of it") were thoroughly articulated by Rubin,
Hoffman, and the self-styled freaks and street people who joined
them on their picaresque adventures. The corrupted model of the
counterculture which the Yippies embodied came to exert a dispro-
portionately broad and lingering influence. Among other effects, it
furnished the rationale for a wave of political terrorism which marked
much of the next decade; it generated a mystique of mock-brutal
theatrics ("terrorist chic") which has continued to spin off malicious
variations into the eighties; it nurtured the morbid growth of an
assortment of authoritarian cults—worshipping God, Satan, or the
founder himself—which culminated in the holocaust at Jonestown;
and, not least of all, it fostered in the name of personal liberation
(specifically that of sexuality and more broadly of morals) an aggressive self-indulgence so comprehensive in its scope and so contemptuous in its execution as to signal the advent of a new age—not this time
of Aquarians but of barbarians.

Much has been written about the more notorious of these offshoots
of the debased counterculture over recent years, and about the *fin de
siècle* atmosphere of decadence and narcissism which has encouraged
their growth. Comparatively little attention has been given, however,
to what may be the most pervasive and destructive expression of the
barbarian spirit in contemporary life: the *pop culture of nihilism,* as
reflected in the brutalization of genre movies, the degradation of
rock, and the decivilizing of sport. Accordingly it is to these graphic
symptoms of cultural decay that the following chapters of our study
are addressed.

6

THE VIOLENT ARTS: POP GOES THE CULTURE

AT LAST THE WORLD'S FIRST COMEDY HORROR
MOVIE. 13½ MURDERS + 1423 LAUGHS = "STUDENT BODIES"
—*Newspaper Advertisement*

T HE ABOVE AD for a 1982 Hollywood film was not, of course, quite
accurate historically. The comic treatment of horror is a venerable convention of the movies (and still more ancient in other theatrical traditions such as the carnival, with its often grisly displays and its enduring "funhouse" of spooks and cobwebs). During the silent era there were numbers of famous clowns, like Harold Lloyd and Chester Conklin, as well as such popular teams as Wheeler & Woolsey and Dane & Arthur, who made something of a specialty of converting fear into fun. The arrival of the talkies reinforced the convention, in parallel with a new invigoration of the serious horror genre; during the forties, in particular, it seemed that Abbott and Costello were forever "meeting" Frankenstein, or Dracula, or the Wolf Man, or all

of them together, in the matinee at the Bijou. And in the fifties, as the "imagination of disaster"[1] grew to encompass both outer space and lower depths, the comic confrontations with evil shifted to Bikini Beach, where Annette and Fabian humorously fended off a variety of scaly creatures with their beachballs and surfboards. During the sixties the comedy of horror was epitomized by the elegant villainy of Vincent Price, who played Poe for laughs (e.g., *The Raven*) and created an archetype of the mock-fiend in *The Abominable Dr. Phibes.* The seventies witnessed a voguish succession of farcical Frankensteins and dapper Draculas, culminating (if that is the word) in the black-comical "Inquisition" number of Mel Brooks' *History of the World Part One.* Nor should one forget the relatively recent development of the Comedy Horror *Musical,* as exemplified most ghoulishly by Brian DePalma's *Phantom of the Paradise* (1974) and the low-camp classic *The Rocky Horror Picture Show* (1976).

But if the 1982 *Student Bodies* was hardly the world's first comedy horror movie, it was among the first feature films to embody a disturbing new trend—one in which violent assault, rape, and murder (often repeatedly and multiply performed) are presented as not only amusing but acceptable, approvable, and applaudable. This contemporary vogue—which has been variously labeled "terrorist chic," "cruelty cult," and just plain "punk"—is not limited to the movies but runs like a crimson thread throughout the realm of popular culture all the way from rock music through the wide world of sports to the cellophane-sealed contents of the new pornography.

The New Show of Violence

It is not the mere presence of cruelty and terror in popular culture—the show of violence has always been there in some form—but the insistent and almost voluptuous manner of its presentation that characterizes the new trend. While specific themes and motives vary widely from medium to medium (e.g. in punk-rock the purpose is to outrage the audience, or at least the audience's parents, while in killflicks the objective is to provide cheap thrills), the effect is essentially the same: to provide a validation of violence, if not an exaltation of evil, through a set of attitudes and an angle of vision which at once dignify the violent act, trivialize its human consequences, and desensitize the audience. Even these callous perspectives toward violence are not, to be sure, entirely without precedent; in greatly attenuated form they were always a staple of the patriotic war movie, the classic western, and the cops-and-robbers melodrama. But there are significant differences. The good soldier, for example, was defending his country, and although he might kill one or many of the enemy (who were savages or barbarians after all) he was rarely portrayed as enjoying his violent performance; the occasional soldier who took too eagerly to his job—like Franchot Tone in *They Gave Him a Gun* (1937) or George C. Scott in *Patton* (1970)—was seen to be morally tainted if not thoroughly evil. The approved violence was a matter of duty, a demonstration of courage and prowess (Hemingway's "grace under pressure"), and in short an act of heroism. The westerner in the old movies, as critic Robert Warshow described him in a definitive essay on the genre, was no less than "the last gentleman": one who lived and died by a code of honor and a distinct sense of chivalry.[2] But whether it was the code of the West, or of the police academy, or of the officer who was also a gentleman—and however remote it surely was from the actual world of the frontier, the battlefield, or the mean streets—it drew a clear unwavering line, which the youngest movie fan could follow, between the opposite poles of virtue and villainy, of right conduct and the Right Stuff versus foul play and dirty tricks. John Wayne never shot anyone in the back.

But the Duke is gone—and his place has been taken by Dirty Harry. There is more than a change of role models in this devolution of the violent hero; there is a profound shift in sensibility which amounts to an altered state of moral consciousness. It is not only the hero that has been dehumanized; it is also the dramatic vision, the moral esthetic, which underlies the new fables of aggression, vengeance, and terror—and which evidently motivates their fabulators. Thus film historian Robert F. Moss has called attention to the emergence in the seventies of a "new breed of brutalist directors," for whom

> the city is a pit of vice, grimly polluted and inhabited by the worst kinds of predators and human refuse: rapists, murderers, muggers, junkies, weirdos. Violence has become reflexive, an inherent part of the urban rhythm. Human relationships

have hardened along battle lines, drained of almost every feeling but rage, lust, and horror.[3]

And social critic Michael Selzer, drawing upon a wider cesspool of pop-cultural phenomena in the same decade, has clustered them all under the heading of "Terrorist Chic": "Through a wide range of artifacts and posturings, Terrorist Chic expresses fascinated approval of violence, brutality, sadomasochism, evil, and degeneracy in general; it apotheosizes meaninglessness and indecency."[4]

The dehuman syndrome, which we have previously examined in its real-life career, has found its corresponding mirror image in the magic theater of the popular arts: an image enlarged by technology, enriched by imagination and distorted by exploitation, but still recognizably inhuman and fundamentally faithful to the worst that is in us. The theme of violent dehumanization, in one or another ugly variation, has so permeated the media of mass entertainment as to become a major motif and conventional stock in trade. It is most blatant, of course, in the orchestrated fascism of punk-rock and much of the musical "new wave"; in the blood-dimmed tide of horror movies flooding the drive-in market; in the relentless brutalization of professional sports led by boxing, hockey and football; and in the proliferating subcultures of pornographic "liberation," where nothing is sacred and nothing is profane—an Orwellian underworld in which pain is pleasure and vulgarity is style, where the elites of sadism and masochism meet to beat.

But the impulse of defilement has not been contained within these authorized red-light zones; like a cancer of the spirit it has metastasized swiftly and spread its poisons into the mainstream of popular culture. In Hollywood films it has transcended the cut-rate cinema of horror and made its way into major productions of award-winning caliber, as well as into traditional "family fare" such as westerns and space operas. On television it has penetrated the defensive perimeter of network censors and become visible on prime time, thanks largely to the competitive inroads of unexpurgated cable TV. Even the child-oriented world of video games, always marred by an abstract violence of cartoon-like slaughters and obliterations, has been invaded alike by X-rated sexual fantasies (in the form of "adult" games) and by sadistic scenarios of grotesque ingenuity, like the notorious "Custer's Revenge," in which players score points by sexu-

ally assaulting an Indian maiden. (Item, from a *Newsweek* report on
electronic toys: "Mego's Fireman Fireman [$40], for instance, seems
to be cashing in on the public's taste for the macabre: its object is to
position a safety net on the screen to catch babies falling from a
burning building. The more babies a player saves, the higher the
score. With every miss, a tiny baby splats on the 'ground' and a little
angel appears in a corner. Three angels, and you're out.")[5]

For all the diversity of its images and expressions, the dehuman
syndrome in the popular arts exhibits a number of central themes and
common symptoms. One of the most significant of these, in the
American context, is the theme of *vengeance*—which carries with it a
distinctive historical legacy, an ethical rationale, and a psychological
purpose.

Retaliatory Violence: The Return of the Vigilante

The vigilante tradition, a peculiarly American phenomenon
without parallel elsewhere in the world, has remained alive and active in one or another part of the country for more than two
centuries—ever since it emerged from the swamps of South Carolina
about 1760 to compensate for the absence of law and order.[6] Once
established, however, vigilantism survived the arrival of sheriffs and
judges by developing its own romantic mystique within the broader
American mythology of self-reliance and rugged individualism (a
mystique which has since received practical and powerful reinforcement through the efforts of the National Rifle Association). The continuous legitimation of vigilante violence through popular fiction, and
later through the movies, has its origin in the widespread acceptance
of the custom by respectable elements of society throughout the
nineteenth century; indeed, as historian Richard Maxwell Brown has
demonstrated, it was often the leading citizens who organized
"committees of vigilance."[7] Moreover, vigilante movements generally arose in response to actual or perceived increases of crime and
violence, thereby reinforcing their aura of respectability as legitimate
instruments in the defense of persons and property. Hence the vigilantes were not usually regarded as outlaws, though they were
plainly outside the law, nor as vengeance-seeking killers and terrorists, but rather as good citizens taking up arms in the "American
way" to serve the cause of justice and civilization. Their illegal

violence—invariably bloody, frequently murderous, replete with lynchings, tarrings and featherings, and assorted tortures—was made to appear not only legitimate but positively high-minded and moral. As sociologist Graeme Newman has observed: "Apart from its violence, the central feature of vigilantism would appear to be its highly moralistic stance, and it is the latter . . . that is more prototypically American than is the violence per se."[8]

Nor was it only the vigilante bands that were thus apotheosized in the public imagination; there soon appeared the heroic figure of the solitary self-appointed vigilante, the archetype of the Lone Ranger, an early favorite of pulp westerns who would later find his urban counterpart in the four-color fantasies of Superman. This character of the Avenger, the Nemesis in relentless pursuit of his evil prey under the stalking moon, has been a favorite of pulp fiction from the dime novels of Ned Buntline to the dollar novels of Mickey Spillane. (According to Frank Gruber, an authority on westerns, the "revenge story" is one of the seven basic plot-lines to be found in that specialized subliterary and cinematic genre.)[9] The moral point underlying the formula is, of course, that revenge is a sufficient reason for violence: the end justifies the means. Given the crime to be avenged (typically the gruesome murder of the avenger's father, wife, and/or child), the ordinary rules of civil behavior and the tiresome procedures of the law are tacitly, not to say gleefully, set aside. With this absolution of conscience and suspension of the superego, almost any violent action, any display of retaliatory brutality, becomes acceptable and approvable; the reader or moviegoer is enabled, without guilt or shame, to participate vicariously in the cathartic act of retribution.

That element in the revenge story, then, is nothing new. What has altered, over time, is the focus of attention, the point of interest, and the quality of vengefulness itself. In traditional westerns and crime stories, it was enough for the vigilante hero, having caught up with his prey, to shoot him cleanly or otherwise vanquish him in some form of fair combat. But with the advent of realism in fiction, beginning in the 1920s, such decorous behavior became swiftly obsolete. The change occurred almost simultaneously in the separate spheres of serious literature (exemplified by the early stories of Ernest Hemingway) and pulp fiction (epitomized by the *Black Mask* stories of Dashiell Hammett), in both of which it became permissible for the physical details of killings, beatings and maimings to be meticulously and minutely described. By the forties the hardboiled style of un-flinching naturalism in the literary portrayal of violence had devel-oped to the point where so blasé a critic as George Orwell found himself nauseated by the trend. (His reaction to a fairly typical thriller in the Hammett tradition, James Hadley Chase's *No Orchids for Miss Blandish,* was summed up in the remark: "Now for a header into the cesspool.")[10] In the more sophisticated school of realism pioneered by Hemingway, the extent to which squeamishness had been overcome in the narrative of revenge by the late thirties was illustrated by Irwin Shaw's short story, "Sailor Off the Bremen," in which a group of Americans corner a Nazi who had blinded a buddy of theirs in one eye:

> Charley [the wounded man's brother] worked very method-ically, getting his two hundred pounds behind short, accu-rate, smashing blows. . . . When he got through with the nose, Charley went after the mouth, hooking along the side of the jaw with both hands, until teeth fell out and the jaw hung open, smashed, loose with the queer looseness of flesh that is no longer moored to solid bone. . . .
>
> When he started on Lueger's eye, Charley talked. "You bastard. Oh, you lousy goddamn bastard," came out with the sobs and the tears as he hit at the eye with his right hand, cutting it, smashing it, tearing it again and again, his hand coming away splattered with blood each time. . . . And he kept hitting with fury and deliberation at the shattered eye.[11]

The revenge story in popular fiction reached an apogee of blood-lust, brutality, and plain mayhem during the fifties in the sensation-ally successful works of crime novelist Mickey Spillane, featuring a rogue cop turned private detective (well-named Mike Hammer) who has dedicated his life to hunting down and executing any and all crooks, Communists, or kooks of his own choosing who have man-aged to elude the hesitant arm of the law. But unlike previous incar-nations of the vigilante-enforcer, Hammer is without compunction or compassion. As historian Russell Nye has described him,

He is not out to enforce the law or to serve justice. He is his own law (as *I, the Jury* makes clear), his own judge, prosecutor, and executioner. . . . His motives are morally simple. He never kills anyone who isn't "someone who needed knocking off bad." The way to handle a crook when the law can't is to "plunk one right in his gut and when he's dying on the floor kick his teeth in."[12]

Although sexual acts are nearly as rampant in the Spillane novels as killings and beatings (according to one account his first five books contained 48 killings, 21 beatings, and 21 sex acts)[13]—and although the sexual encounters are rendered in crudely pornographic images invariably degrading and contemptuous toward the female partners—the truly erotic component of these stories is not in the lovemaking but in the death-dealing: i.e., in their undisguised and celebrant sadism. "Violence as orgasm," in John Cawelti's apt phrase, is the central theme and obsessive concern of the Spillane fables; the delivery of pain, the spectacle of broken bodies and agonized faces, the sound effects of the victims' moans and gurgles, all are sensually depicted and elaborately drawn out in much the same way as a different connoisseur might describe the savory details of an orgy. Hammer clearly loves his work, and Spillane loves to picture it for us, leaving nothing out. Here is a representative sample:

> The goddamn bastards played right into my hands. They thought they had me nice and cold and just as they set to carve me into a raw mess of skin, I dragged out the .45 and let them look down the hole so they could see where sudden death came from.
> It was the only kind of talk they knew. The little guy stared too long. He should have been watching my face. I snapped the side of the rod across his jaw and laid the flesh open to the bone. He dropped the sap and staggered into the big boy with a scream starting to come up out of his throat only to get it cut off in the middle as I pounded his teeth back into his mouth with the end of the barrel. . . . The punk was vomiting on the floor, trying to claw his way back under the sink. For

laughs I gave him a taste of his own sap on the back of his hand and felt the bones go into splinters. He wasn't going to be using any tools for a long time.[14]

There was nothing in the Hollywood films of the fifties to match the ferocity and pure viciousness of Spillane's avenger-hero (not even in the movie versions of the same novels, which muted the violence and censored the sex). Within the genre of crime films Hammer's like was not to be seen until 1971, when the urban vigilante returned with a vengeance in the persons of two renegade police detectives, Harry Callahan (of *Dirty Harry*) and Popeye Doyle (of *The French Connection*), whose smoldering tempers and penchant for brutality placed them in a direct line of descent from the Hammer prototype. But by the time these fascist cops appeared on the screen they were already vaguely familiar figures; for the parallel genre of movie westerns had accomplished the same degradation of heroic style several years earlier. The trend surfaced first, curiously enough, not in Hollywood films but in the "spaghetti westerns" produced in the sixties by Italian director Sergio Leone, mainly starring the American actor who was later to rematerialize as Dirty Harry (Client Eastwood). The Roman vision of the American West broke radically and almost scornfully with every tradition of nostalgic chivalry which had graced the classic western from the pioneering morality plays of William S. Hart to the long high noon of Gary Cooper and John Wayne. As film historian Philip French has summarized its contribution, the Italian western was characterized by "a taste for ultra-violence, a strong line in calculated sadism, a penchant for over-emphatic images and over-loaded sound tracks, a characteristically continental *nostalgie de la boue* that can pass for unflinching realism, and a slick line in simplified Marxism."[15] At the hands of the Italian master, the colorful landscape of the Old West turned suddenly dark and repellent, its towns barren and scabrous, their sullen inhabitants brutalized by corrupt and lecherous figures on both sides of the law; and through those villages of the damned rode the squinting Eastwood character, the Man With No Name, a high plains drifter ready to hang 'em high for a fistful of dollars—and a few dollars more. In this Italian inversion or perversion of the traditional western hero-image, moreover, the protagonist was not only mercenary but merciless; to give him sufficient motivation for the bloodbath to come he was equipped with a mission of dark vengeance. As Cawelti has described him, "If the hero has any motive beyond money, it is usually to perform some terrible revenge for a long past deed, a revenge that commonly seems more like a dehumanizing obsession than a justifiable moral purpose."[16] The Italian western replaced the familiar cinematic Old West, epitomized by the big sky and purple sage of John Ford's beloved Monument Valley, with an unrelieved vision of hell straight from Dante's *Inferno*.

But this strange interlude of the Spaghetti Western, which flourished for less than a decade before it flickered out, might have warranted only a footnote in the history of western films except for one all-important fact: it worked. The dark and cynical scenario of Leone and his imitators—their transformation of the Winning of the West into *Grand Guignol*—struck a responsive chord with American audiences and produced a boxoffice bonanza. It made an international star of Clint Eastwood (and to a lesser degree of Lee Van Cleef); and it provided the model for a "brutality chic" in filmmaking which was to leave its permanent mark not only upon Hollywood's westerns but also upon its urban cowboys, eastern outlaws, and ghetto vigilantes.

The curious popularity of this alien and thoroughly unsympathetic revision of one of the most honored of American myths requires some explanation. The formula would almost certainly have failed in an earlier decade; but the timing of the Italian invasion was auspicious. It took place in the late sixties, at a time when America was experiencing an extraordinary degree of violence and confrontation—in the streets, on the campuses, in the country roads of the South and the nightmare alleys of the North. And in the living rooms of nearly every family, where an interminable and inexplicable war involving their sons and neighbors was continuously on display. The reality of violence—and the violence of reality—was beyond the capability of ordinary citizens to resolve or deal with, let alone to comprehend. But these explosive new movies, with their orgies of retaliation and their fantasies of revenge—with their slow-motion epiphanies of mutual slaughter in which the good, the bad, and the ugly were alike blown up in stereoscopic displays of retribution and apocalypse—these movies provided a kind of therapeutic resolution. Vengeance is thine, saith the filmmaker.

The Cute Cutups

The Americanization of the Italian horse opera may be said to have been completed with the appearance of *The Wild Bunch* (1969), in which director Sam Peckinpah outperformed Leone himself in both the extent and intensity of exquisitely choreographed slaughter. (In fact, Peckinpah, along with writer-director John Milius, seems to have made a conscious and persistent effort to copy the successful formula of the Cinécitte hemophiliacs.) But much the same effect was accomplished two years earlier in the trend-setting *Bonnie and Clyde*, the cinematically brilliant romantic tragedy directed by Arthur Penn which contrived somehow to blend the seemingly incompatible modalities of the western and gangster genres. It did so, however, in a manner that broke resoundingly with the restraints of both traditions. According to Robert Moss, *Bonnie and Clyde* stands as "the landmark film that established a director's right to blow his characters away in whatever fashion he chooses and in whatever state of dismemberment."[17] While the film abounded in closeup revelations of maiming by gunshot, what was most shocking to moviegoers of the time was the grand climacteric of the final episode; as recalled by film historian David A. Cook, ". . . nothing could prepare audiences in 1967 for the apocalyptic violence of the ending, in which Bonnie and Clyde are ambushed after a romantic interlude and their bodies ripped apart by machine-gun slugs in a protracted ballet of agony and death. . . . Bonnie and Clyde are not simply killed; they are destroyed."[18]

Bonnie and Clyde was a premonitory event in more than one way. Not only did it "glorify" violence cinematically, by making it more bloodily picturesque than ever before; it also glorified violence morally, by luring audiences into a sympathetic identification with the gangster protagonists, who were portrayed as romantic young lovers out on a lark. ("They're young! They're in love! And they kill people!" declared the ads.) They did indeed kill people, in the process of robbing banks all over the midwest; but audiences were induced to forgive them their sins, not only because they seemed such nice kids but because their violent actions were glazed over with a countercultured mystique of pseudo-populist revolt against the System. Bonnie Parker and Clyde Barrow, who in real life had been among the most vicious of modern-day American criminals, were thus elevated to the hip pantheon of folk heroes, their crimes metamorphosed through the magic of the silver screen into the right-on rebellion of easy flivver riders in search of freedom and the good life. The people they shot and brutalized during the course of their career of pillage were observed to be total squares, either contemptible or loathsome; while handsome Clyde and pretty Bonnie, with their poetic natures and touching vulnerability, remained lovable to the bitter end.

This pair of killers were only the first of their breed to be redeemed and canonized by the cinematic counterculture; they were soon joined by the frolicsome outlaws of the once-infamous Hole-in-the-Wall gang from the turn of the century, as reimagined by director George Roy Hill in *Butch Cassidy and the Sundance Kid* (1969), a film even more dazzlingly seductive to moviegoers which not only copied its predecessor in bringing sweetness and humor to raw violence but recapitulated the same terminal slow-motion apocalypse of overkill. Following the enormous success of these cute-couple outlaw films, Hollywood capitalized upon the trend by churning out a succession of comedy capers, heists, break-ins and blowups, usually involving the clean getaway and happy enrichment of the crooked but colorful pair—with the residual litter of corpses, injured persons and demolished property receding gently into the background of forgettable misdemeanors. (Peckinpah's *The Getaway* [1972], for example, featuring Steve McQueen and Ali McGraw as the attractive crooks, was simply *Bonnie and Clyde* without tears.)

Another landmark in the escalation of movie violence, and in the desensitization of audiences, was *The Wild Bunch*, in which the moral viewpoint of director Peckinpah moved beyond the relatively light-handed cynicism of his earlier work toward a dark vision of unrelieved nihilism which had not before been witnessed on American screens and which has not since, or not yet, been surpassed. The degradation of the western hero which had begun with Leone and Eastwood here reached its ultimate denouement; the saga of the Old West was emptied out of whatever had been left of the chivalric code or of any moral differentiation between good and evil. *The Wild Bunch* both began and ended with spectacular massacres on an unprecedented scale—the first involving the slaughter of the entire population of a Texas town, the second portraying the demolition of a Mexican village along with rival gangs of outlaws. In between were scenes of individual killings, tortures, and assorted cruelties—

performed indiscriminately by the outlaw "heroes," by the official villains, and even by children (demonstrating the innate wickedness of the human animal). Critic David Shaw has well emphasized the main visual theme of the movie:

> In *The Wild Bunch,* blood spurted all over the screen. In one especially gruesome (and gratuitous) scene, a man's throat was slit—the knife slashing across the wide screen in agonizing verisimilitude, the blood cascading forth as from an exploding ketchup bottle. Those viewers who didn't jerk their heads away and close their eyes sat drinking it all in, proud of the machismo that enabled them to watch the gore, unblinking.[19]

But that was only the appetizer. What made a landmark of Peckinpah's antiwestern was the vast improvement of its ending, technically and kinesthetically, over the terminal blood-bathos of *Bonnie and Clyde*; for here it was not just two individuals who were destroyed, in slow-motion closeup, but unnumbered people, combatants and noncombatants alike, both the innocent and the damned, women and children and elders conspicuously included—their wounds and agonies observed from every artistic angle, with the entire widescreen spectacle orchestrated and choreographed (by cinematographer Lucien Ballard) with the precision of a classical ballet. "The final massacre," writes David Cook, "has about it a sort of mad, orgasmic ecstasy, as the slaughter grows more and more intense until it reaches Eisensteinian (or Bunuelian) proportions; we see more people die than could possibly fill the small village; we see the same people die over and over again."[20] By comparison with this grand mal climacteric, the erotic violence of Mickey Spillane resembles affectionate foreplay.

Peckinpah had yet another ace of spades up his sleeve. It was *Straw Dogs* (1971), which derived its powerful and peculiar shock effect from what might be called the domestication of violence: the killings and maimings were brought indoors, into the setting of a contemporary household with which audiences could fearfully identify themselves. But their identification went deeper than that; their sympathies were drawn to the lead character (played by Dustin Hoffman), a mild-mannered Clark Kent-like intellectual who was instantly transformed by the gang-rape of his wife into an implacable avenging angel consumed by a rage so total that its expression evinced a kind of sexual pleasure. Although filmed on a more intimate scale than *The Wild Bunch, Straw Dogs* managed to seem (in the words of one critic) even "more violent, more graphic, more bloody."[21] Its violence was also more personal, more "real," to viewers by virtue not only of its familiar setting but of its combination of two themes that were coming into renewed vogue in the seventies: the Vigilante Story, with which we have dealt, and the "Violation Movie" (to use John Fraser's descriptive label).[22] The latter theme typically has involved the invasion of the home or other private space of ordinary "decent" people by one or more violent intruders carrying with them the threat of pillage, rape and murder. The theme of violation had, in fact, been an early favorite of American readers, especially during the pioneer period when "captivity stories" based on Indian raids were as often real as imaginary and furnished the basis for the "first authentically popular American novels."[23] The theme later surfaced repeatedly in the public arts—a notable example being the flood of "white slavery" films and fiction early in the present century following a series of metropolitan crackdowns on prostitution. In every cycle the theme of violation has conveyed the symbolic conflict of good against evil, civilization against barbarism, innocence against depravity; and its resonance is always greatest in periods when that conflict is felt to be not imaginary but actual, immediate, and uncertain in outcome. Such was the case in the seventies, when many Americans came to believe that all their streets had turned mean and their neighbors had gone bad, when muggings had become a part of the daily routine and rape only waited until dark. "The United States is the most violent country in the world," rationalized B-movie producer Roger Corman: "We have the most murders and assaults. We have been called the rape capital of the world. I think the function of the artist is to reflect the times."[24] (Corman was eminently true to his word, if not to his art; among his more noteworthy productions in the sixties and early seventies were *Bloody Mama, The St. Valentine's Day Massacre, Bucket of Blood,* and the irresistible *Attack of the Crab Monsters*.)[25]

In its ardent rendering of the theme of violation, *Straw Dogs* was neither the first nor the worst of the feature films to emerge in the new crimson wave. *In Cold Blood* and *Wait Until Dark* had both preceded it by four years; Stanley Kubrick's *The Clockwork Orange* (1971) was at once the most artistic and the most sadistic of them all in its lurid depiction of a gang rape-murder; and Alfred Hitchcock, the old master of terror who might arguably be credited with having started the whole trend in *Psycho* (1960), brought it to a kind of voyeuristic climax with his elaborately drawn-out, up-close rape-murder in *Frenzy* (1972). But *Straw Dogs* did set a precedent of sorts in its juxtaposition of the twin themes of violation and vigilantism. Its most important successor in this vein was *Death Wish* (1974), in which another mild-mannered professional (played by Charles Bronson) was transformed into a deadly avenger by the savage muggings of his wife and daughter, which left the former dead and the latter comatose. Here, significantly, the film undertook a departure from convention; instead of seeking out the actual culprits the protagonist appoints himself Lord High Executioner Without Portfolio and goes gunning for all the crooks and delinquents he can find in the subways and on the streets, shooting them down one after another, almost casually, with a pair of old-fashioned pearl-handled revolvers. As his terrorist exploits are publicized by the press, the anonymous lone ranger becomes a heroic figure to the Manhattan populace—so much so that when the police finally establish his identity they can do no more than banish him to a distant city, where in the final sequence we observe him raising a cocked finger smilingly in the direction of a departing mugger. This latter-day Zorro, we are given to understand, will assuredly rise again to perform his civic duty (see *Death Wish II*, 1982); he has been not only absolved but apotheosized. And he has provided an admirable role-model for would-be snipers, future klansmen, potential terrorists, and closet assassins.

That was not, in the original conception at least, how the story was supposed to go. As a subsequent magazine article reported:

> One writer who is concerned about the impact of violence is Brian Garfield, who wrote the novel *Death Wish*. He intended the novel as a cautionary tale about the dangers of the vigilante mentality; the hero began by killing muggers and ended by killing children. Garfield explains, "I wanted to show that when you begin to act as a vigilante, it quickly goes out of control. The movie changed the novel to show vigilantism as a heroic act. And I was alarmed by the effect the movie

had. I saw it on Times Square, and the audience reaction was terrifying. People stood up and cheered, 'Kill that mother!'" Garfield points to cases where real-life killers imitated the hero of "Death Wish," and he says, "I feel a degree of responsibility for the victims of the violence." Recently, Garfield tried to stop CBS from showing *Death Wish* in prime time; he failed.[26]

In the case of *Death Wish,* the movie deliberately reversed the moral point of the novel. But, in the light of other and later films on the same theme, it might be questioned whether audiences would have reacted any differently if the movie had been altogether faithful to the author's intent. For the figure of the vigilante, as we have seen, works a powerful magic; he embodies our own furtive fantasies of retaliation and revenge against all those out there who would disturb our peace and menace our well-being—all the muggers and crazies, the violators and vandals, real or imagined, who lurk in the shadows of our lives, whispering obscenely on the phone, peering through the window, walking invisibly behind us in the night. The vigilante is the enemy of our enemy; and so he becomes our ally, our avenger, even our guardian angel. Whatever his flaws of character, his past sins or present eccentricities, it is hard not to cheer him on.

Which brings us to *Taxi Driver* (1976), the ultimate vigilante picture—an intentionally ironic fable (written by Paul Schrader and directed by Martin Scorsese) about a simple-minded New York cabbie named Travis Bickle (played by Robert De Niro) who commits himself to a one-man war against crime and corruption, identified in his view with the fringe population of his inner-city world: "whores, queens, fairies, dopers, junkies." As in his earlier *Mean Streets* (1972), which also starred De Niro, Scorsese fairly revels in the dank atmosphere of urban rot and human viciousness which surrounds the taxi driver and incites him to his mad crusade. Travis's disgust, if not his loathing, becomes ours also as we ride with him in his cab through the city of dreadful night where, as one critic has observed, "Red lights and steam rising through sidewalk gratings are a Dantean reminder of human decay."[27] Moreover, Travis's madness, when he finally embarks upon his orgy of vengeance, is not without moral method; for his purpose is to rescue a child prostitute from the clutches of the pimps and parasites who live off her earnings. His mission is accomplished in a climactic shootout, a phantasmagoria of blasted bodies and bursting arteries, which afficionados of movie violence have ranked among the bloodiest ever filmed. It was not simply bloody, however; the soundtrack resounded not only with gunfire but with the agonized screams, cries and mumblings of the maimed and butchered: an appalling stereophonic spectacle of slaughter which left many in the audience shaken and nauseated, utterly repelled by the cruel insanity of the carnage.

That was presumably the effect intended by the director and writer. But there were others in the audience, no small number, who cheered Travis on in his vengeful rampage and laughed at the suffering of the victims. Scorsese is reported to have reflected afterward: "The movie provoked different reactions from what I anticipated. When I was filming it, I never thought there would be such strong responses to the violence."[28] That may have been somewhat disingenuous, under the circumstances; for whatever the intended irony of the scenario, and however paranoid the protagonist, his quest was undeniably in the tradition of chivalry—to rescue a damsel in distress—and those whom he dispatched were clearly worse and meaner rascals than himself. Indeed, in a last curious attempt at irony, the filmmakers have their demented killer declared a public hero, and the movie ends with the sound track recording the humble thanks of the prostitute's parents, sentimentally reunited with their wayward child. It may be that in this mockery of pop heroism, as a critic has remarked, "Scorsese and Schrader seem to be laughing up their sleeve at society."[29] But they should not have been surprised to find that their sardonic joke was over the heads of many in the audience who felt themselves irrationally stirred by the bravado of the tenement vigilante, impressed by his existential loneliness and dedication, and thus both relieved at his survival of the immolation he himself had unleashed and heartened by his public vindication. For these viewers, the supposedly ironic ending only served to confirm their favorable judgment of the man and his act; Travis Bickle deserved to be enshrined in the pantheon of latterday folk heroes, taking his rightful place alongside Butch Cassidy, Clyde Barrow, Dirty Harry Callahan, Don Corleone, and William Calley.

As the world now knows, at least one moviegoer literally adopted Travis as a role model and sought to duplicate his heroic feats. The character of the teenage prostitute who was rescued by Travis from durance vile had been played by a young actress named Jodie Foster; and it was in order to win the love of Miss Foster that John W. Hinckley, Jr., set out on his own misguided quest for recognition. Like Travis, he accumulated an arsenal of small arms; and, also like Travis in an early segment of the movie, he plotted the assassination of a prominent public figure. Indeed he outdid Travis in his selection of a target: none other than the President of the United States. And he also bettered Travis in the assassination attempt; Hinckley actually got off one shot and wounded his victim. But from that point on his personal movie, publicly enacted and instantly replayed across the land, went off track; he failed both to get his man and to get his girl. Life may imitate art, but it is not always as happy in its ending.

Hinckley was not the first movie fan to seek to re-enact on a wider stage the violent exploits of Hollywood heroes and antiheroes. In 1952 a Canadian youth, after seeing a film called *The Sniper,* picked up a rifle and shot eleven women. (The filmmakers were subsequently sued on behalf of one of the victims, but were absolved of responsibility by the Canadian Supreme Court.)[30] In 1960, after viewing *Psycho,* a young lab technician killed three women in Los Angeles.[31] Later in the decade, *Bonnie and Clyde* apparently inspired a number of youthful outlaws; 21-year-old Yancey Morris, for example, who liked to call himself "Clyde" and his girl friend "Bonnie," pulled off some thirty-four robberies before being apprehended.[32] And another youth, immediately after seeing the same film, went out on his own and murdered the owner of a drive-in grocery store.[33] In 1972 a former busboy and janitor named Arthur Bremer shot and permanently crippled Alabama Governor George Wallace after viewing Stanley Kubrick's *A Clockwork Orange* (although it appears probable that the film only furnished added incitement to a mind already twisted by hatred for public personages, by admiration for earlier assassins like Harvey Oswald and Sirhan Sirhan, and by a diet of fantasies drawn from *Gun Digest, Playboy,* and pornographic comics).[34]

Movies made for American television—where sex and language are delicately monitored but violence is generally given free rein—have almost as frequently triggered "copy-cat" crimes, including rape and murder. *Born Innocent,* a 1974 TV movie, contained a scene in which a girl is raped with a broomstick by her reformatory classmates. The day after its showing in California, four children raped two little girls (eight and nine years old) in the same way.[35] A 1973 TV movie entitled *The Fuzz* included a scene in which an individual was doused with gasoline and set afire. A few days after its airing, six Boston youths forced a young woman to douse herself with gasoline, then lit a match to her body; the charred victim lived just long enough to report the incident.[36] Shortly afterward a separate group of teenage boys poured gasoline over a homeless drifter and laughingly watched him burn. It was only a prank, they told police—a small improvement on their previous hobby of setting cats afire.[37]

Fear and Loathing in Hollywood

The point here is not that movie violence inevitably, or even usually, begets its replica in live violence. It is highly probable that these spectacular displays of carnage and cruelty "turn off" many more viewers than they "turn on"—and that filmmakers like Lawrence Gordon are correct in supposing that "most people who see these violent films will be so horrified that they wouldn't think of going near a knife or a gun. The people who see *Taxi Driver* are going to be revolted by violence."[38] Yet they did go to see the film, in sufficient numbers to make Scorsese's urban nightmare (to his apparent surprise) one of the biggest hits of the year. But it was small potatoes compared to the phenomenal successes achieved by *The Godfather* (1972), *The Exorcist* (1973), and *Jaws* (1975), each of which in turn set all-time records at the boxoffice. These three vastly dissimilar films had only two qualities in common: violence and terror. Moviegoers may have been repelled by their pyrotechnics of blood and thunder, but it is obvious that they were attracted even more. As a result of the vast fortunes these blockbusters won for their makers and their studios, the twin themes of violence and horror— already recognized as eminently bankable—became a consuming passion of the Hollywood moguls and poverty-row producers (rivaled only, toward the end of the seventies, by the recycled genre of the space opera). As film after film tumbled noisily forth in imitation of the precedent-setters, several variations on the master theme became recognizable. There was, for example, the *natural disaster* film (a specialty of producer Irwin Allen), such as *The Poseidon Adven-*

ture (1972), *Earthquake* (1974), and *The Towering Inferno* (1975). There was also the film of *unnatural disaster,* typically of occult origin—e.g., *Carrie* (1970), *The Omen* (1976), *The Fury* (1978), *The Amityville Horror* (1979), and *The Shining* (1980). What was different about these films, in the long tradition of the ghost story, was not their supernaturalism but their super-realism; *The Exorcist,* with its child self-abuse by bloody crucifix, seemed only to whet the imaginative appetites of the Cormans and De Palmas. The scriptwriter of *The Omen,* David Selzer, testified frankly concerning his own artistic aspiration: "I was very conscious of including the most repulsive scenes I could imagine. I wanted to write a commercial movie."[39]

There were other new-minted varieties of cinematic sadism as well. The *violation movie,* as suggested earlier, came into particular vogue during the seventies and early eighties—growing ever more aggressive and obsessive in its favorite exercises of stabbings, throat-cuttings, and general dismemberment. Among the more lurid of these assaultive films were *The Texas Chainsaw Massacre* (1976), *Lipstick* (1977), *Looking for Mr. Goodbar* (1977), *Halloween I, II,* and *III* (1978, 1980, 1982), *Friday the Thirteenth* (1980), and *Dressed to Kill* (1981). This subgenre specializing in the torture and killing of young women took a novel and significant direction in the seventies, to which we shall return.

But we are not yet done with the proliferating versions of the new cinema of violence. That familiar staple, the *war movie,* once the comfortable haven of patriots, lost its innocence in the wake of the Vietnam disaster; and a new generation of filmmakers raised and schooled in the counterculture articulated their disenchantment and dismay through a succession of unrelieved portrayals of combat carnage—as in, most powerfully of all, Michael Cimino's *The Deer Hunter* (1978) and Francis Ford Coppola's *Apocalypse Now* (1979), both of which delivered emotional shock after shock to their audiences on a scale unimaginable in any earlier period (even in the strongly antiwar period of the thirties, which had produced *All Quiet on the Western Front* [1930]). Nor was this repudiation of traditional heroics and romantics limited to the antiwar film; it was no less conspicuous in the emergence of the *macho-game* film, with its dark interpretation of "bloodsports" as a form of interpersonal warfare symbolizing the descent of civilization into savagery: notably *Rollerball* (1976), *Death Race 2000* (1975), and in a slightly different vein

The Warriors (1979) and *The Road Warrior* (1982). Although the old romanticism still flourished in such films as *Rocky* (1976), the flip side of that athletic American dream was brutally demonstrated in *Raging Bull* (1980), as well as in the earlier and less pretentious *Hard Times* (1975).

In all of these variations on violence, a new kind of "hero" was emerging on the American screen. He was something more and different from the so-called "anti-hero" of the fifties and sixties, who had been typically a populist rebel with or without a cause on the order of James Dean, or else a scruffy street urchin on the order of Dustin Hoffman; in either case he was merely a contemporary recycling of the tough character with the heart of gold familiar to movie audiences from the days of Wallace Beery and Monte Blue to those of John Garfield and Humphrey Bogart. The new "hero" of the seventies, on the other hand, had no redeeming qualities of heart or soul, no saving grace of charity or conscience; he was typically a killer, invariably a man of ruthless violence, who would only yesterday have been perceived by moviegoers as the unmistakable villain of the piece. But now, by a strange alchemy of emotional reponse, he had become sympathetic; he had won our hearts. This inverted hero-figure had been pioneered by Clint Eastwood's "Man With No Name," and later by the same actor's "Dirty Harry." He was visible in the person of the vigilante-killer, as we have seen; but he was also visible in a new and more disturbing guise, that of the hit man or contract killer—once regarded as the most repellent and despicable of criminal types. Again, Eastwood's spaghetti-western character foreshadowed the trend; but it became firmly established in a contemporary setting by such films as *Hard Contract* (1969) and *The Mechanic* (1972), in both of which the protagonist drew the sympathy of audiences while remaining coldly and unremorsefully a mercenary assassin. In *The Killer Elite* (1975), director Peckinpah updated the basic theme of *The Wild Bunch* by setting killer against killer within the context of a kind of Murder, Incorporated. And in *The Godfather*, Parts One and Two, director Coppola faithfully rendered the perverse morality of Mario Puzo's pulp novel about a devoted Mafia "family." In these films there were no morally redemptive resolutions, no terminal regrets or deathbed conversions—no apologies whatever for the cold-blooded killings routinely carried out—yet audiences were subtly drawn into a powerful bond of empathic involvement with the leading characters. These became the heroes of the movie, not because of any moral virtue on their part, but simply because of their possession of a greater supply of what are still miscalled the "manly virtues": prowess, efficiency, skill, and above all strength. As Pauline Kael remarked of the decadent western genre, the hero has become identifiable only as the one who is still standing after all the others have been slain.

Witnesses for the Persecution

For the so-called "general audience," the sordid matter might be said to rest there: that is, with the profound moral slippage involved in the passing of the chivalric hero and his replacement by the Man With No Name—and No Code. But for specialized audiences, comprising at least two distinct and substantial groups of movie fans, there has been a further development which carries the theme of dehumanization into another dimension. Simply put, this is the trend toward approval and endorsement of (and psychological identification with) the *villains* of the terror films in their ghoulish depredations. These audiences have long since obliterated the thin red line separating heroism from villainy: they have opted eagerly for the bad, the ugly, the unadulterated evil. They need no rationalizations or equivocations; they are not interested in heroics, let alone in ethics. They want only the kill, preferably the multiple kill in full Sensearound, the more the merrier, the louder the better. They are the cultists of cruelty, the gourmets of gore.

The larger of these select audiences may be designated simply as the youth, or teenage, market—the drive-in, as distinguished from the carriage, trade. It is this very broad segment of the total audience for whom the makers of violence-exploitation films calculatedly package and promote their product; and it is from this audience, or more precisely from the market research done on it, that the basic themes and formulas of the new pop violence are derived. Prominent among the psychological devices involved is that of playing upon the vulnerable emotions of youth such as envy, jealousy, and anxiety; thus, for example, the intended victims in the movie may be depicted as arrogant, snobbish, or otherwise unlikable. This manipulative effect is often prefigured in advertising campaigns, so that potential viewers may anticipate the emotional catharsis in store for them. *Happy Birthday to Me* (1982) was accompanied on its release by posters and newspaper ads luridly describing both the manner of its successive killings and their motivation. One ad showed a terrified youth about to be murdered with a foodladen shish-kebab skewer, and proclaimed in bold headlines: "John will Never Eat Shish Kebab Again. Steven will never ride a motorcycle again. Greg will never lift weights again. *Who's killing Crawford High's snobbish top ten?*"[40] The rationale for this media blitz was provided by the studio's head of marketing and research:

"People like to root against somebody. People don't like to see people get killed at random, no way. To have people killed, they have to be people you're rooting to have killed. So that became part of our campaign—'The 10 Snobs at Crawford High.' Nobody likes snobs."[41]

Another studio executive was even more direct in his assessment of audience interest in this charming drama: "You're going to the movie to see somebody get it with a shish kebab," he said.

Thus the preconditioned audiences for these exploitation formula films are maneuvered not only into sympathy for the devil but into antipathy toward the victim. A recent variation on the unlikable-snob-victim, which various critics have remarked upon, is the character of the "uppity woman"—the female cast member who is a bit aloof, or independent, or merely intelligent enough to be vaguely threatening to some male viewers—and whose inevitable doom at the hands of the mad slasher or monster of the midway comes to seem a matter of just deserts. Moreover, the inclination on the part of macho moviegoers to relish such assaults has been reinforced in recent exploitation films (such as the two sequels of *Halloween*) by the device of utilizing the camera as the "eyes" of the killer as he stalks his vulnerable (and snobbish) female prey; hence the film literally adopts the *point of view* of the villain and subtly induces the viewer to take his role and join him on his escapades.

In addition to the teenage market, there is a more sophisticated audience which not merely enjoys the trash films of horror and violence but celebrates them as a distinctive form of artistic expression.

This is the self-styled *avant-garde* of movie buffs—connoisseurs of sadism and decadence whose general style was aptly designated by Michael Selzer as "Terrorist Chic." One relatively innocuous version of this attitude—that which has made a cult film of *The Rocky Horror Picutre Show*—was delineated by Susan Sontag in the sixties as the "Camp Sensibility."[42] In the main, however, the horror movie buffs take themselves and their esthetics very seriously; it was they, for example, whose critical praise led to a special showing at the Museum of Modern Art of the *Texas Chainsaw Massacre*. Although small in numbers, the circle of film buffs around the country is large in influence; according to novelist and critic Stephen Koch they "form a quite coherent and by no means powerless subculture of the general intelligentsia, and they have played a very real role in the formation of modern taste."[43] This esthetic (or counter-esthetic) subculture has developed its own peculiar "version of radical will," to use Sontag's phrase; it has chosen to make a vogue of senseless brutality and mindless violence in much the same way as its predecessors of pop art, like Andy Warhol, thought it fun to celebrate all that was most vulgar and tasteless in the commerce of mass culture. And like the decadent radicals of the sixties counterculture—the Yippies and the Weathermen—the film buffs of the seventies and eighties not only pride themselves on their ability to watch the worst of ruddy-gore without flinching, but declare it to contain dramatic beauty and a kind of existential truth. At the least, as Stephen Farber has maintained, "Buffs evaluate movies purely in sensory terms, and they exalt the brutal movies made by the American action directors."[44] In so doing they provide a rationale, if not a coherent philosophy, for the *public* enjoyment of forbidden fantasies and perverse pleasures which have doubtless always existed but were formerly relegated to the secret chambers and back alleys of the imagination. Thus Selzer writes of this development in its wider context:

> Yet in one respect Terrorist Chic is quite novel, for it has succeeded in transforming into a *publicly* acceptable posture what hitherto had existed only in furtive and antisocial privacy. Degenerate fantasies of sex and violence are not new; making them into a fashionable pose *is* something of a departure in the history of culture. It is only in the context of

Terrorist Chic that it becomes permissible, even appealing, for
Penthouse to offer the *bon mot* "Fucking and killing are the
same" to its three and a half million readers.[45]

And when the devotees of movie violence graduate from mere
buffdom to writing and directing their own films, as has happened in
some celebrated cases—when they leave their seats in the audience
and take an active place onstage—their influence is vastly extended.
They are now in a position to convert their private vices into what
will be widely seen as public virtues. And whether they are regarded
as stern realists (a la Scorsese and Schrader) or magical fantasists (a la
Romero and De Palma), they will be taken seriously by the world of
buffs and treated respectfully as *auteurs* of the American New Wave.
No matter if their imaginations remain arrested at the level of the
children's matinee, or if their perceptions of the human condition are
as warped as the pulp comix that were once their primers; like the
hero of Jerzy Kosinski's novel and film *Being There,* their retarded
state is likely to pass as enlightenment. "[M]any of these new
filmmakers," writes Farber, "regard the humanism and the social
concern of the last generation of filmmakers as hopelessly old-
fashioned. They want to reproduce the violent genre pictures that
they loved as children. To them violence is part of the magic of
movies, and they are unconcerned about the effect these movies may
have on audiences."[46]

At their worst, as in the kidflicks churned out by writer-director
Mark Lester (*Class of 1984, Roller Boogie, Truck Stop Women,* etc.),
the ultraviolent rays are rationalized unconvincingly in promotional
blurbs as radiating "subtle commentary on contemporary American
life." The real commentary of these films, of course, is not on life but
on death, or more exactly on the obsession with violent death shared
by the filmmakers and their specialized audiences. *Class of 1984*
(1982), for example, contains the following graphic highlights, as
described by critic Jack Kroll in *Newsweek*:

Timothy Van Patten's gang starts things off by stomping a
rival drug pusher all over the john. Freaked out on coke, one
of Van Patten's teen-age customers leaps from the school
flagpole to his death, wrapped in the Stars and Stripes. The
victim's friend is knifed in the kidney in the school cafeteria.

. . . [Outraged music teacher Perry King] smashes up Van Patten's snazzy sports car. Swearing vengeance, Van Patten's gang destroys the lab of King's friend, biology teacher Roddy McDowall, slaughtering and hanging his precious animals. McDowall tries to run them down in his car but is killed when it crashes and explodes.

While King is preparing to conduct the student orchestra in Tchaikowsky's immortal "1812 Overture," the gang breaks into his home, attacks and gang-rapes his pregnant wife. The crazed King goes after the gang, which beats him to a pulp. Depulping himself, King pursues the creeps. Cornering the first creep in the carpentry shop, King slices off his arm and then kills him with a buzz saw. Moving on to the automotive class, King incinerates another with a blowtorch and crushes two more under a car. After this tour of Lincoln High's vocational courses, King finds Van Patten, who is sent crashing through a skylight, hanging himself on a rope just above the student orchestra banging away at Tchaikowsky.[47]

Apocalypse Here: The Culture of Nihilism

By the early 1980s the graphic presentation of violence in Hollywood films, cheapies and extravaganzas alike, had grown to the point where it was no longer merely a convention but was becoming, for more and more producers, an imperative. Nor was it enough by then to display a simple shooting or two. As the example of *The Class of 1984* nicely illustrates, the slaughter preferably should be multiple and recurrent while the manner of its execution should be ingenious and inventive: here a chainsaw, there a shish kebab (everywhere a chop-chop). In the search for bigger and bolder climaxes, the brutalist filmmakers appear to have employed all the horsemen of the apocalypse as technical advisers. Disaster buffs, for example, have demonstrated a penchant for earthquakes, floods, holocausts, and explosions which can annihilate entire populations; others have gone in for shipwrecks, airplane crashes, and highway collisions which with any luck may dispatch a cast of hundreds. In recent years there has been a vogue of what might be called the zoological-disaster film, possibly inspired by Hitchcock's classic *The Birds* (1963); prominent among the animal assassins have been bees, ants, spiders, cock-roaches, crabs, sharks, piranhas, alligators, snakes, wolves, dogs—and, in a memorable instance, killer tomatoes.[48] Filmmakers with a mechanical bent have made imaginative use of numerous engines of destruction: notably cars (an endlessly recurrent *diabolus ex machina*), trucks, tractors, bulldozers, motorcycles, helicopters, robots, computers, nuclear reactors, elevators, chainsaws, dentist's drills . . . and almost anything both electrical and sharp.

Through all of these scenarios of pain and terror, of death and demolition, there runs a common theme to which Pauline Kael has given the label of *nihilism*. Writing in the mid-seventies, she declared:

> I often come out of a movie now feeling wiped out, desolate—and often it's a movie that the audience around me has reacted to noisily, as if it were having a high, great time—and I think I feel that way because of the nihilism in the atmosphere. It isn't intentional or philosophical nihilism; it's the kind one sometimes feels at a porn show—the way every-thing is turned to dung, oneself included. . . . Hits like *The Exorcist* give most of the audience just what it wants and expects, the way hard-core porn does. The hits have some-thing in common: blatancy. They are films that *deliver*. They're debauches—their subject might almost be mindless-ness and futurelessness.[49]

Kael went on to point to a particularly powerful example of the nihilist attitude, in the form of a widely praised 1974 film which combined cinematic artistry with moral cynicism:

> The success of *Chinatown* . . . represents something dialec-tically new: nostalgia (for the thirties) openly turned to rot, and the *celebration* of rot. . . . [Director] Roman Polanski seals the picture with his gargoyle grin; now evil runs ram-pant. The picture is compelling, but coldly, suffocatingly compelling . . . you don't care who is hurt, since everything is blighted. Life is a blood-red maze. Polanski may leave the story muddy and opaque, but he shoves the rot at you, and large numbers of people seem to find it juicy. . . . The nihilis-

tic, coarse-grained movies are telling us that nothing matters to us, that we're all a bad joke.[50]

Where *Chinatown* turned nostalgia for the past into "rot, and the celebration of rot," another set of nihilist movies has done the same for the appreciation of the present—and still another set has turned the anticipation of the *future* into rot and its celebration. Filmmakers like De Palma, Scorsese, Schrader, and Walter Hill have generally shared a morbid fascination with contemporary city life which by its very depravity, as Robert Moss maintains, "seems to intoxicate the brutalist [directors] and they excitedly pass the bottle around to the rest of us, inebriating moviegoers with the sight of slaughter and degradation . . . these filmmakers plunge into it with gusto."[51] Meanwhile others have given us a vision of the future which is, if anything, still more dehumanized and desolate—one that might be called the post-apocalyptic view. Thus Stanley Kubrick, whose epochal *2001* (1968) had portrayed the future as essentially a banal parody of the present, extended that viewpoint into nihilism with *A Clockwork Orange* (1971). It may well have been the titillating shock waves from the latter film that stimulated the tidal flow of malevolent futurist fantasies which followed it in the seventies. And it is worthy of note at this point that Kubrick's gruesome projection of man's coming inhumanity to man was no mere passing fancy of the director—nor for that matter of his star, Malcolm McDowell. They both believed profoundly in what they were doing in *A Clockwork Orange*—not only in its dramatic qualities but in its existential truth. Their avowed intent in celebrating the human rot of sadism, rape, murder, and raw violence was to acknowledge and exhibit "the eternal savagery of man." In an interview, Kubrick declared: "I'm interested in the brutal and violent nature of man because it's a true picture of him." And on another occasion he added: "Man isn't a noble savage; he's an ignoble savage. He is irrational, brutal, weak, silly, unable to be objective about anything where his own interests are involved . . . Any attempt to create social institutions on a false view of the nature of man is doomed to failure." McDowell, in a letter to the *New York Times,* went even further than his director: "People are basically bad, corrupt. . . . Liberals, they hate *Clockwork* because they're dreamers, and it shows them the realities, shows 'em not tomorrow but *now. Cringe,* don't they, when faced with the bloody truth."[52]

Other filmmakers with a bloodshot eye to the future have since elaborated ingeniously on this dire view of the human condition and the catastrophic shape of things to come. In such films as *The Omega Man* (1971), *THX 1138* (1971), *Soylent Green* (1973), *Rollerball* (1975), *Alien* (1979), *Quintet* (1979), *Escape from New York* (1981), *Outland* (1981), *The Road Warrior* (1982), *Blade Runner* (1982), and numerous others, the future is displayed as a terminal wasteland of the spirit populated by a dehumanized race of predators engaged in deadly games of survival—a neo-social-Darwinian jungle in which, as sociologist Neil P. Hurley has written concerning some of these films, "man can only prevail precariously in a paranoid state as an alert vigilante, always on the defensive and with force at his beck and call."[53] The recurring nightmare of these scenarios is essentially the same; nor is it anything new but rather the oldest and darkest of human premonitions—the dread anticipation of universal "closing time" which portends the triumph of evil, the final wages of original sin, the dusty death of a wicked race. Each of these nihilist movies constitutes a dramatic variation on the ancient theme enunciated most powerfully by Thomas Hobbes three centuries ago—that of the human "state of nature" as a war of each against all, a struggle of power after power that ceaseth only in death: "No arts, no letters, no society, and, which is worst of all, continual fear and danger of violent death, and the life of man solitary, poor, nasty, brutish, and short."[54]

What is most significant about these dark sagas from what someone has labeled "Outer Hollywood" is not their predictive or prophetic quality but their naked exposure of a desperate contemporary state of mind. As movie star McDowell put it, such a film shows audiences "the realities, shows 'em not tomorrow but *now.*" And let the pointy-headed liberals cringe at the bloody truth. It is apparent that the gore-drenched, death-obsessed projections of the nihilist filmmakers are not really about the future at all but about *us* here and now, our brutalized state, our incorrigible savagery, and the strategies of survival in the jungle of the present. These pictures are not then to be placed in the humane tradition of sci-fi classics like *Things to Come* (1935), *The Day the Earth Stood Still* (1951), *The Time Machine* (1960), and latterly of *Star Wars* (1977), *Close Encounters of the Third Kind* (1977), and *E.T.* (1982). Rather they are of a piece with *Mean Streets, Taxi Driver,* and *The Exterminator*—and for that matter with the drive-in dreck of *Friday the Thirteenth, Kill and Kill Again,* and *The Class of 1984*—and their underlying coded message is exactly the same as these: get off, get yours, and above all get them before they get you—any which way you can.

Overkill: The Death of the Senses

We have reviewed, in preceding pages, the progressive elaboration and intensification of the show of violence in American films over two decades. It remains to estimate their psychic consequences. One school of thought, dear to the hearts of the violence devotees, holds that if these movies have any effect at all it is surely beneficial. This is the "catharsis" theory (dignified by its association with Aristotelian dramaturgy), which maintains in effect that if monkey see, monkey will not do; in other words, watching a film or other show of violence is a kind of emotional purgative, rather like an orgasm, affording a harmless discharge of aggressive or hostile feelings and terminating in an amiable state of *post-coitum triste.* Anything is possible, of course, in life as in the movies; but some things are less probable than others, and this convenient hypothesis of the soothing effects of mass-mediated violence carries roughly the same factor of probability as the belief that poverty is good for the soul or (closer to the bone) that war is the health of the state. The cathartic theory has its counterpart in the notion that sadomasochistic pornography, with its voluptuous fantasies of assault and battery, is "good" for the enthusiast because it induces masturbation rather than imitation. (The truth would seem to be, as the ads for S-M clubs and dating bureaus in porn publications attest, that it induces both—and that the two are mutually reinforcing.)[55] The difficulty with the cathartic theory is not that simulated violence (or simulated sex) is never orgasmic in its effect but that it very often is—and that the experience of viewing it, far from relieving aggressive or vicious impulses, stimulates and strengthens them. As experimental psychologist H. J. Eysenck observes in *Sex, Violence and the Media,* it is likely that "exposure to pornography may further increase the strength of the unacceptable urges, and there seems no reason why sooner or later the person will not want to act out his fantasies . . . [especially in the case of] the more 'active' and involved sex crimes such as rape and sadism."[56]

But if the repeated viewing (not to say the obsessive observation) of simulated physical and sexual violence is unlikely to result in the purging of aggressive tension, it may well lead to a hardening of the heart and a deadening of the senses. The evidence for this effect of desensitization, drawn both from laboratory experiments and practical training exercises, is compelling—and alarming. The essence of the desensitizing process is in the axiom that familiarity breeds contempt (read indifference); or, put another way, that the more one sees of violence and suffering the less one is moved by it. It is an old insight, to be sure—one which the modern conditions of mass communication and entertainment have only confirmed on a new scale. "Begin with a torn robe or a broken cup," wrote the Stoic Epictetus, "and say, 'I don't care.' Go on to the death of a pet dog or horse and say, 'I don't care.' In the end you will come to the stage where you can stand beside the bed of your loved one and see that loved one die, and say, 'I don't care.' "[57]

It should be acknowledged that the process of desensitization, in its natural form, functions as an adaptive mechanism of defense against stresses and shocks which might otherwise immobilize the individual through "sensory overload"—that is, through more anguish than he can handle, more suffering than he can bear to see, more evil than he can face and stay sane. But this natural defense mechanism can be manipulated into grotesque forms of dehumanized behavior—can be rendered maladaptive—through the turning off and tuning out of the equally natural responses of compassion, empathy, and concern. This process may still be considered adaptive, of course, in extreme situations such as a battlefield or a gang war. It is the kind of discipline which the young Gordon Liddy, so he tells us, practiced on himself in order to be transformed into a "killing machine." It is also the sort of conditioning carried out under the label of "stress reduction training" by various military and quasi-military units seeking, as journalist Peter Watson has put it, to "take the feeling out of killing." A program conducted by a U.S. naval psychologist, Thomas Narut, resembles a black-humor parody of the theater of violence and its effects upon viewers. As described by Watson, Dr. Narut

> . . . employs "Clockwork Orange" techniques, in which
> men have their head clamped in a vise, their eyelids propped

open, and they are then shown horrific films. With such techniques the aim is to completely desensitize the men to pain or suffering, to remove any emotion associated with it that might interfere with killing. According to Commander Narut, men have been trained in the U S forces in this way—for use as special combat units for rapid assassinations.[58]

The way this program works is that the trainee-victims, held firm in their head clamps and eyelid props, are forced to watch a succession of films involving torture and maiming, each more gruesome than the one before; the key elements in the formula are repetition and intensification. Eysenck and Nias report similar projects under American military auspices in which the physiological reactions of subjects have been carefully monitored so as to register with scientific precision the progressive deterioration of feeling and the slow death of the senses. At first, they observe laconically, "these reactions are quite marked, and indicate severe emotional upheaval. Gradually these reactions become less severe, until finally there is almost no reaction of an emotional kind to the sight of such scenes."[59] At that point the military trainees can, in the language of the James Bond trade, be officially licensed to kill—to terminate the careers of others "with extreme prejudice," to inflict pain and witness suffering without a qualm or quiver. And their basic training for this dehumanized condition, be it noted, has been nothing more than the repetitive watching of increasingly violent motion pictures.

Punk Chic: The Death Rattle of Rock

It is not only the movie show of violence that in recent years has come to celebrate rot (in Pauline Kael's phrase) and to desensitize audiences to the display of cruel and unusual punishments. The dominant musical form among contemporary youth—that which was once known as rock-'n-roll and now is more simply labeled rock—was infiltrated during the seventies by a wave of adolescent nihilism which has not merely favored muck and putrefaction but has exalted them into a creed to live by. This is, of course, the school of "punk," and, in a later recycling, "new wave" music—an English import in the arts field which is not likely to be confused with Masterpiece Theater. Nor should it, apart from its roots in the rock tradition, be confused with any previous variety of popular music; it is, if not *sui generis,* at least unique in its motivation, its message, and its morality. But if it is not much like its predecessors it can be usefully compared with them in its verbal and visual images—both of which present instructive variations on certain familiar themes. Typical of these is the dilemma of the frustrated youth unable to compete successfully in the dating game—a common enough problem which forty years ago led the Ink Spots to popularize a lyric that concluded: "I'd rather have a paper doll to call my own, than have a fickle-minded real-life girl." The same predicament is resolved somewhat differently by the contemporary punk group T.S.O.L. in a song entitled "Code Blue" in which the youths proclaim their desire to "fuck the dead," because of their inability to get along with girls in their school.

Before proceeding further into the necrophilous depths of the punk philosophy, it should be noted that this musical posture for all its unique pathology is only the extreme expression of a state of consciousness that pervades much of the contemporary adolescent subculture anchored in pop-rock. To be sure the punks, and various of their new-wave spinoffs, have gleefully descended from mere narcissism into total nihilism (and frequently, as we shall see, into the rhetorics of fascism). The nihilism and fascism are their peculiar contribution; but the underlying narcissism is broadly shared with their less audacious peers—as well as with a great many of their elders, as Christopher Lasch and others have pointed out.[60] That self-obsessed "Me generation" (Tom Wolfe) of the "new narcissists" (Peter Marin) which arose from the ashes of the older activist counterculture has found perhaps its most typical and illuminating expression in the mainstream popular music of today's youth. Lyric after lyric keens a mournful message of emotional deprivation and emptiness, of a yearning to feel something, preferably something sexual, voiced almost invariably in terms of receiving rather than of giving.

The portrayal of oneself in the mechanistic terminology of John B. Watson ("an organic machine, ready to run") is a recurrent image in the lyrical repertoire of contemporary rock groups whose concert performances are at least as notable for their high-tech engineering as for their musical content, and whose lifestyle seems often to be a mixture of zen and the art of motorcycle maintenance. But the imagery of the machine has a deeper resonance than that: it is a metaphor for self-dehumanization, a clue to the absence of genuine feeling in the very act of simulated and trumpeted passion. Thus a perceptive observer of the youth subculture, Mark Crispin Miller, has declared that the present-day "obsession with feeling betrays nothing more than a panicked inability to feel. . . . To liken oneself to a whole or broken mechanism is to renounce, however, subtly, the desire for autonomy." The real desire is not for an autonomous but an automaton existence, providing escape from freedom and protection against feeling: "If we could only become like a robot, we too might exist forever, given periodic tuneups by some great technician."[61] And where the robopathic fantasy takes the form of a sexual machine, the goal becomes that of efficient and tireless performance, getting it up, coming on, and getting off, unencumbered by emotion.

The self-centered sentiments of vulgar narcissism and emotional drouth appear innocent and almost affectionate by contrast to the confessions of indifference and acompassion in the songs of various punk bands. The insistent refrain of "I Don't Care" (the title of a single by The Ramones) suggests that the affective state of these "talking heads" is less like that of the robot than that of the zombie, the living dead.

More often the indifference to others turns into contempt, as in The Ramones' "I'm Against It," in which the vocalist lists all the things (human, vegetable and mineral) that he is against and concludes: "I don't like anyone . . . All I care about is me." Yet for all their scorn and defiance, this group of musicians is candidly and almost poignantly aware of their dehumanized condition. In an alarming number entitled "Teenage Lobotomy," the singer laments that he is "a real sickie" with "no mind to lose"; and in another number the reiterated refrain (and the title) proclaim: "I wanna be well!"

Such songs as these, of course, represent only the bottom line of punk rock and punk theater; they are poetic statements of confession, of self-diagnosis. On this foundation have been built the gaudier and more dramatic settings of low life and high anxiety. "We're not into pretty or smooth, man," explains a punk musician. "We're into life. Life is ugly. Life is mean."[62] The favored subjects have been enumerated by a close observer of the scene as follows: "They sing about anarchy, alienation, violence, drugs, sex, teen rebellion—in short, any and every lesion on the dark, ripe underbelly of American life."[63] Some lesions, however, are more popular than others, as may be

surmised from the anatomical and recreational orientations proclaimed by such punk group names as the Sex Pistols, Sic Fux,
Sniveling Shits, Buzzcocks, Blowjobs, Slits, Tubes, Cramps, Germs,
Lewd, Vibrators, and Human Sexual Response. Something more
sinister is suggested by other group labels: The Dead Kennedys, Dead
Boys, Dead Commies, Clash, Criminals, Grenades, Stilettos, Hot
Knives, Vultures, Jerks, Dogs, and Kinks. And the preferred politics
of punk—if any doubt remains—is not oversubtly indicated by such
song titles as "Storm Troopin'," "Master Race Rock," "Blitzkrieg
Bop," and a hit single of the late seventies with the catchy title,
"Deutschland Über Alles." These ditties were typically performed by
groups like The Dictators, Shrapnel, and Black Flag. Finally, mention
should perhaps be made of a few of the more colorful stars of punk-
dom: Johnny Rotten (a recent dropout), the late Sid Vicious (who
ended a suicide), Rat Scabies, Ron the Ripper, Richard Hell, and Alan
Suicide.

How the punk phenomenon came about, and why, is a matter of
speculation and some dispute among subculture historians. On its
merely rebellious and iconoclastic side, its roots may be traced to the
first wave of rock 'n roll in the fifties; in terms of rhetorical and
gestural violence, according to one account, "the movement broke
ground in the longhair 1960s with the Rolling Stones and with the
excesses of the Who and Jimi Hendrix, smashing guitars and setting
them afire."[64] The Stones' Mick Jagger, in particular, sang of violence, degradation, and reverse morality in such famous numbers as
"Sympathy for the Devil" and "Let It Bleed." And, of course, there
were the many radicalized groups, like the Jefferson Airplane and the
Grateful Dead (mentioned in the preceding chapter), who flaunted
their outlaw image and advocated ripping off the establishment.
Flamboyant haberdashery and joyously vulgar behavior were intrinsic to the sixties youth movement; but it was not from the left-
wing counterculture but from the increasingly fascistic counter-
counterculture, the spawning ground of the Yippies and the Manson
family, that the school of punkmanship appears to have drawn its
major inspiration. And although there were premonitory rumbles of
the punk sound to be heard in the early seventies in the dissonances of
such groups as the New York Dolls and the Velvet Underground, the
most direct antecedents were probably such British rockers as the

indefatigable Who, The Kinks, David Bowie and the Diamond Dogs, and most blatantly Alice Cooper—all of whom were flourishing by mid-decade. It was the colorful transvestite Cooper who acquired the greatest notoriety and the most enthusiastic audiences through a series of concerts and albums featuring songs like "Love It to Death," "Killer," and especially "Dead Babies." As one observer recalls the memorable scene:

> As most American teenagers knew, when Alice Cooper gave a live performance of "Dead Babies," he hacked a doll to pieces on stage with an axe, drawing a shower of simulated blood. Then, for the *piece de resistance,* he hurled limbs to a howling audience.[65]

The significance of this sacrificial rite—the ritual murder of infants—is a matter for social psychiatrists and urban anthropologists to ascertain; but it is noteworthy that Cooper's act of symbolic infanticide has since been widely imitated by rock groups of the punk persuasion.

The songs "I Hate Children," by a group called Adolescence, and "I Kill Children" by the Dead Kennedys sufficiently demonstrate the hostility which pervades the lyricism of the punk genre. But, as their live audiences know, the aggression is not merely rhetorical; it is very often physical as well. An astute historian of rock and roll, Jim Miller, has defined punk itself as "beginning with a confrontation: its medium hostility, its aim to shock."[66] The confrontation is commonly between the musicians and their audiences; following the lead of Alice Cooper, the punks have devised ingenious ways of taunting and abusing their fans. Patti Smith spits on them, Johnny Rotten vomited on them, most groups throw things at them, and Richard Hell wears a T-shirt inviting them to "Please Kill Me." In the early eighties the theme of audience participation was carried to new depths with a phenomenon called "slam dancing," a Los Angeles innovation in which fans slam into one another and musicians hurl themselves bodily from the stage into the audience. Something of the ambiance of this exotic tribal rite is conveyed by a newspaper account of the scene during a 1981 "concert" by the Dead Kennedys in San Francisco:

> In a combat zone in front of the stage, aptly named "the pit," a mob of young people in leather jackets and torn T-shirts surged in a sweaty sea, pushing each other, flailing with arms and elbows like a herd of human livestock eagerly anticipating a trip to the slaughterhouse.
>
> The distorted, over-amplified rock set one young punk whirling and bounding up and down, slamming his body into another punk who ricocheted into a barechested kid who lashed out at someone else. . . .
>
> "We are gathered here tonight to pay tribute to our lord," [lead singer Jello] Biafra screamed into the microphone before hurling himself onto the shoulders of the crowd, smacking a kid in the back with a boot, bashing an open hand into the face of a teenage boy in a leather jacket and shaking himself as if he had an epileptic seizure while the audience held him aloft.[67]

In its origins punk-rock was distinctively British—owing something to the fifties tradition of the angry young playwrights and the mod youth gangs, and something else to the sixties conventions of the bad-boy Rolling Stones, but arising more immediately from the frustrations of working-class youth in the depressed decade of the seventies. Thus an early observer of the movement characterized British punk as the "music of working-class rage—at the empty promises of the welfare state, at the eternal dole and the double-digit inflation and the double-digit unemployment, all of which leaves young working-class Brits holding the empty bag."[68] There was no mistaking this socioeconomic determinism in the case of the original punk group, the Sex Pistols, who played their first concert at an English art school in November, 1975—and had the plug pulled on them after five minutes by an appalled social secretary.[69]

If the punk sound and the punk message were of English origin, however, they were quickly Americanized—without appreciable loss of tempo or temper. Working-class rage was merely supplanted by middle-class *Angst*. Like the earlier British invasions of the U.S. rock-music scene—the Beatles, the Stones, the Who, the Bee Gees, and the rest—the angry young Brits of Brixton inspired a new wave of musical and behavioral fashion which by the eighties had spread across the land as far as Hawaii and whose underlying theme was graphically expressed by one John Holstrom, editor of *Punk* magazine and author of the "Punk Manifesto": "The rock 'n roll guitar is like a gun. Rock 'n roll is a form of war, a rock concert is like an assault, you know. What the kids want is World War III, and we're giving it to them."[70] In visual and auditory terms the assault was upon the senses of audiences; in physical terms the assault was alternately upon the bodies of fans (as in slam dancing), upon the bodies of the musicians themselves (assorted self-carvings and mutilations), upon instruments and furniture and selected icons of the hated adult culture such as TV sets and automobiles (notably by the axe-wielding Wendy O'Williams and The Plasmatics). It was all theater, of course, a theater of nihilism with more than a touch of the absurd, an overamplified explosion of petulance and meanness, an orchestrated exercise in malicious mischief: mere child's play, perhaps, but child's play with a vengeance. Sid Vicious and Johnny Rotten had the appearance of mean little kids, to be sure, the bastard brothers of Peck's Bad Boy; but their pranks were neither merry nor harmless, and the rot they celebrated still continues to spread. Their song may have ended (as the old pun has it), but the malady lingers on.

Malice in Wonderland: The Punk as Trickster

In a perceptive study entitled *The New Gods: Psyche and Symbol in Popular Art,* Harold Schechter has called attention to the curious reincarnation of the ancient mythic figure of the Trickster in various forms of contemporary popular culture—notably in movies (e.g., *Animal House*), television shows ("Sergeant Bilko"), and animated cartoons (Bugs Bunny and his numerous kin).[71] Wherever the trickster has appeared, from the simplest aborigine tribe to the most complex civilization, he is at best a creature of insolence and mischief and generally a symbol of demonic forces intent on social disruption and personal harm. According to Carl Jung, the great psychoanalytic interpreter of myth and symbol, the primordial trickster gods were "brutal, savage beings" notorious for their "pointless orgies of destruction."[72] In Jungian terminology, the trickster is the embodiment of the "shadow archetype"—the dark side of both the individual and the collective unconscious harboring those "wild, untamed" impulses which are too outrageous and threatening to be acknowledged and must, therefore, be repressed. Denied conscious recognition, these destructive inclinations find an outlet in dreams and in myths. They also find an outlet in tribal rituals and communal revels, such as the nearly universal occasion of "acting-out" known as Carnival. In the time of carnival, normal restraints are swept aside and forbidden impulses unleashed; the festival represents, according to folklorists, "a boisterous communal celebration" featuring, among other things, "masquerades, . . . dances, fireworks, noisemaking, and tomfoolery which often reaches a point of nuisance and licentiousness."[73] Carnival is thought to have descended from the Roman Bacchanalia, Lupercalia, and Saturnalia—all orgies in the grand manner, sanctioned excuses for debauchery, the breaking of idols and the profaning of sacred cows. The addition of obscene songs (*cante carnascialesche*), incidentally, is said to have been refined into an art by Lorenzo de Medici. Successive cultures have developed their own versions of carnival, but the essential elements of iconoclasm, obscenity, and collective catharsis have remained constant. More than a few observers of the contemporary rock-music scene have interpreted the massive public concerts of major performers as communal celebrations by the "tribes" of attuned youth (as in the "Woodstock Nation"). When to the orgy of carnival is added the mischievous presence of the trickster, the resultant equation takes on a darker dimension. Thus Schechter describes the early Rolling Stones as the "bad boys" of rock, countering the niceness of their compatriots the Beatles at every turn of the turntable with a satanic or obscene musical gesture of their own. There were badder boys even then, of course, more defiant and more destructive—groups like the Fugs, the Jefferson Airplane, and that British band called the Deviants, mentioned earlier, whose biggest hit was "Let's Loot the Supermarket." But if the Stones were not the baddest, they were the best of a bad lot; they created the model of the trickster with guitar and went on rolling and rocking across the land through nearly two decades of communal concerts, drawing hundreds of thousands of the faithful at nearly every one-night stand. Until the mid-seventies they virtually owned the carnival; but then came Kiss, Alice Cooper, Davie Bowie, and the utlimate apotheosis of the Dirty Trickster in the form of the Punk.

It is remarkable how closely the personae of punk performers (the Richard Hells, Alan Suicides, Johnny Rottens, etc.), their onstage antics and their musical fantasies, correspond to the plots and escapades of the archetypal trickster-figure. Not only is the malice there in abundance, the desire to hurt people and wreck property; so is the erotic lust, the combined role of attacker and victim, and the dark undertone of obsession with death and the dead. Thus we are told by folklorists that

> Characteristically the trickster is greedy, erotic, imitative, stupid, pretentious, deceitful; he attempts trickery himself in many forms, but is more often tricked than otherwise. In a sense, trickster is nearly always on the side of evil; if people die, he votes that they stay dead . . .[74]

Similarly, punk groups give themselves names like the Dead Boys and the Dead Kennedys and sing happily of dead babies, of killing children, and of fornicating with corpses. In their imaginations (and ritual enactments) they are sometimes murderers, as in the Talking Heads' "Psycho Killer" and the Dead Boys' "Son of Sam" ("I am Son of Sam, I got death breathing from my hand"). More often their wish is to start a riot, create panic, and generally disturb the peace; thus a Hawaii-based group called The Squids sang delightedly of a "Tourist Riot" climaxed by the burning of Honolulu; The Clash uttered a plea for a "White Riot" ("I wanna riot, white riot, riot of me own"), and the Sex Pistols proclaimed a state of general anarchy ("I wanna destroy passersby"). And through it all runs the deadly litany of tricksterism, as when the Dead Kennedys recite their favored strategies of doing children in: feeding them poison candy on Halloween, sneaking a lethal drug into the kids' ward, shooting the tires of the schoolbus, and offering them "a helping hand of open telephone wires." Even Thyl Eulenspiegel himself would not have applauded these merry pranks.

7

ENDGAME:
THE DECIVILIZING
OF SPORT

SportsWorld is a sweaty Oz you'll never find in a geography book, but since the end of the Civil War it has been promoted and sold to us like Rancho real estate, an ultimate sanctuary, a university for the body, a community for the spirit, a place to hide that glows with that time of innocence when we believed that rules and boundaries were honored, that good triumphed over evil, and that the loose ends of experience could be caught and bound and delivered in an explanation as final and as comforting as a goodnight kiss.—*Robert Lipsyte*

Every heavyweight fight is a simulated death struggle. Those fans who rise up in primeval blood lust and beg their favorite to "Killim! Killim!" may be more in earnest than they know. Death in the ring is not an everyday occurrence, not every month or even every year. But it always adds a titillating sense of danger and drama to all the matches that follow. For the sadism and cruelty of the Roman circus audience still peers out through eyes of the modern fight crowd. There is not only the conscious wish to see one man smash another into insensibility, but the subconscious, retrogressive urge to witness violent tragedy, even while the rational mind of the spectator turns away from excessive brutality.—*Budd Schulberg,* The Harder They Fall

T HE TWO QUOTATIONS ABOVE represent polar aspects, the sunny side and the dark side, of the schizoid obsession with sports which characterizes the contemporary public consciousness in America, and, to a lesser or greater degree, in all the nations of the modern world. On the one hand, there is the springtime illusion summoned up by Robert Lipsyte, composed of childhood memories of pure play and breathless excitement—"of the wide free field," as an early fabulist of sport put it, "the smell of early grass, the ripple of soft breeze on flushed faces, the damp give of springy turf . . ."[1] These are such things as dreams are made on, and dreams turned into books—bearing titles like *The Joy of Sports, The Sweet Science, The Boys of Summer*. And this is the shimmering image, larger than life, that inspires and sustains our faith in the good works and moral purposes of the competitive sporting life: how it builds character and instills discipline, teaches teamwork and produces loyalty, and generally is synonymous with ancestral values such as integrity, fair play, decency, friendship, honor, patience, fortitude, humility . . . and, well, virtue.

But there is also that other side of the coin, when the toss comes up tails. Then the shimmering image darkens, the wide free field turns into a gladiatorial arena, the players into combatants, the audience into a mob; the contesting faces are no longer flushed but bloody; the sound is not of laughter but of cries and curses. We know this alternative scenario at least as well, if not as fondly: it is the *film noir* where nice guys finish last, where winning is the only thing, "tying is like kissing your sister and losing is nothing."[2] It is not a recollection in tranquillity of that Championship Season; it is a harrowing tale of the Nightmare Season. It has spawned its own literature, which does not speak of joy and sweetness but of mayhem and meanness: books like *Blood and Guts, War Without Weapons, Violence Every Sunday, Blood on the Ice, Slashing!, Football Hooliganism, Knuckle Sandwich, Good Clean Violence, Rip Off the Big Game*—and, of course, *Nice Guys Finish Last, Winning is the Only Thing* (on Vince Lombardi), and *The Nightmare Season*.[3] This is the tarnished image which gives the lie to our first fine rapturous vision of the wide world of sport and turns it inside out, exposing its naked spleen and releasing the accumulated contents of its bowels and bladder.

Each of these contradictory impressions carries its own degree of truth, of course. The celebrant image, like a Norman Rockwell poster, conveys a nostalgic panorama of a realm of playful sport which, for Americans at least, is as deeply imbedded in the national psyche as the comparable myth of the Old West with its purple sage and chivalric code. "Sportsworld" is a domain of the imagination which, as Lipsyte points out, "has been promoted and sold to us like Rancho real estate"—and which, once bought and occupied and fenced, is defended as loyally and fiercely as if it were God's little acre. The reference to the divinity is not altogether frivolous; more than a few philosophical observers have maintained that sport has become the modern religion (complete with "immortals," shrines, weekend rituals, and annual observances of the super-sacred ceremony). However that may be, sport has indisputably become a major, if not dominant, form of entertainment in the media age, a version of drama more popular and more compelling than the theater, an essential part of the evening news and the morning chatter, a spiritual need and an emotional fix—in short, virtually a way of life. "Intellectually and philosophically, emotionally and psychologically, sexually and physically," writes Neil D. Isaacs in *Jock Culture U.S.A.*, "sport governs our lives. It is not quite enough to recognize . . . the great influence of sports on our system. We must go further and recognize that our system as a whole has become, that the U.S.A. is, a jockocracy."[4]

Few true believers, of any faith, of course, are likely to suppose that it is the devil they worship. The cultists of sport have their own preachers and evangelists—in the form of broadcasters and commentators—who make it a point to see no evil, hear no evil, and speak no evil. (A few of these, to be sure, like Howard Cosell in 1982, have given up their pulpits rather than avert their eyes and voices; in Cosell's case, it was professional boxing he could no longer pretend to celebrate.) In any case it is easy for the fans to regard the souring of a sweet science with benign neglect and selective inattention; they are not close enough to the action or conversant enough with its inside moves to perceive the difference. And there is one thing more to cloud the issue: for many of the spectators, perhaps a majority (and possibly the vast majority), the sourer it gets the sweeter it is. The taste for violence is enhanced and sharpened by the spectacle of violence: "There is not only the conscious wish to see one man smash another into insensibility," as Budd Schulberg put it, "but the subconscious, retrogressive urge to witness violent tragedy . . ."

There is indeed a tradition of civility—a legacy of pure play and an ideal of fair play—to be found in the annals of sport, and even in its contemporary practice. This residue provides the kernel of truth, and the semblance of credibility, which still give precarious support to the conventional rhetoric of sportsmanship and the lingering image of the gallant champion: that ultimate athlete who, when the "One Great Scorer" comes to write against his name, marks "not that he won or lost—but how he played the game." But there is also another tradition at work in the arena of modern sport—openly avowed, assiduously cultivated, and zealously carried out—which was succinctly defined in the statement of Coach Woody Hayes that "I'd rather die a winner than live a loser," and was nicely demonstrated in the testimony of an ex-professional lineman (Alex Karras) that "I hated everyone on the football field, and my personality would change drastically when I got out there. . . . I had a license to kill for sixty minutes a week. My opponents were all fair game, and when I got off the field I had no regrets. It was like going totally insane."[5]

Fair game is a long way from fair play.

Play, Sport, and War

It is a common practice nowadays among those concerned with organized athletics—both the ardent advocates and the hostile critics—to draw analogies between competitive sports (especially football) and modern warfare. Of course, the intentions are different on either side; the "jocks" wish to emphasize the strategic and tactical (and earnest) dimensions of sport, while the anti-jocks wish only to point up its ferocity. Both sides, however, share the sense of this comparison as an *analogy,* the very power of which derives from the recognition that sports and war are two very different spheres of human activity—curiously parallel in certain peripheral and linguistic ways but fundamentally distinct. For sports, as everybody knows, are *games*—forms of play—while war is serious business, not at all playful. Hence the apologists for big-time sports hasten to qualify their paramilitary metaphors and similes by stressing the pacific and cooperative qualities of "sportsmanship"; while the critics maintain that the degree to which athletic contests become "war-like" is a measure of their degradation from the norm of pure sport: an "Olympian" ideal, above the battle, disinterested in victory or reward, mere child's play writ large.

This distinction between the play-world of sports and the real world of practical affairs (the realm of business, politics, and war) is an old one, to be sure; but it was given perhaps its most impressive and influential expression in Johan Huizinga's classic study of the "play-element in culture," *Homo Ludens* (Man the Player), published in 1938. For Huizinga all the forms of play—including games, sports, and contests—take place in a realm of "free activity standing quite consciously outside 'ordinary' life as being 'not serious,' but at the same time absorbing the player intensely and utterly."[6] The element of freedom refers to the voluntary character of all play: "Play to order is no longer play; it could at best be but a forcible imitation of it."[7] The forms of play are also free in another sense, according to Huizinga; they are free from any material consideration of profit, from the taint of commerce, which would remove them from the independent sphere of play to the "seriousness" of business. On the other hand, play—at least in its higher and social forms—is not pure spontaneity or random activity either: "It proceeds within its own proper boundaries of time and space according to fixed rules and in an orderly manner."[8] Of all the characteristics of the play forms the most fundamental and distinctive is that "play is not 'ordinary' or 'real' life. It is rather a stepping out of 'real' life into a temporary sphere of activity with a disposition all of its own."[9]

Huizinga's definition of the play element, specifically embracing what used to be called the sporting life, has come to be generally adopted (with certain technical qualifications and emendations) by later students who have focused their attention mainly on sport.[10] In its emphasis on the non-reality and nonseriousness of play, the definition has also entered popular consciousness where, as we have seen, it lends sharpness to "analogies" drawn between the free play of sport and the grim business of war. But the relationship between these two disparate realms of human action was, for Huizinga, much more complex and intimate than the simple popular distinction comprehends. In fact he perceived the element of play as an intrinsic part of war, at least in its advanced or "civilized" form; and in a chapter on "Play and War" he suggested that the athletic contest and the martial encounter are so closely related as to be virtual "blood brothers"—sharing a common origin, a common purpose, and a common psychology. But it is not this sibling relationship to war that characterizes the *degradation* of modern sport, in Huizinga's analysis; rather, that decline parallels the degradation of modern war itself: for both have resulted from the progressive "de-civilizing" of the activity, as contesting nations and contesting teams alike have come to toss out the civilized rulebook page by page, and therewith to descend into barbarism and savagery.

The historical analysis is cogent and persuasive. In Huizinga's view, the history of warfare is one of the gradual elaboration of rules and conditions, culminating in international law, which has increasingly distinguished acts of war from mere brawls and assaults, and has converted them into contests of strength and skill subject to a variety of limitations. With the elaboration of rules comes the civilized concept of "fair play" and the concomitant values— variously defined in advanced cultures but invariably present—of honor, virtue, and justice. These ethical considerations are, literally and figuratively, *refinements* of the simple acts of fighting and killing; they represent what Huizinga calls the "agonistic" (contest or ritual) character of warfare. They were not always there, of course:

> In the very earliest phases of culture fighting lacked what we would call fair play—that is, it was largely non-agonistic. The violence of savage peoples expresses itself in predatory expeditions, assassinations, man-hunts, head-hunting, etc., whether it be from hunger, fear, religion or mere cruelty. Such killings can hardly be dignified by the name of warfare. The idea of warfare only enters when a special condition of general hostility solemnly proclaimed is recognized as distinct from individual quarrels and family feuds.[11]

The conception of war, of military engagement, as a *contest* is most clearly illustrated in the numerous cases of single or limited combat by selected antagonists, opposing "champions," as in the biblical encounter of David and Goliath. (The Philistines might well have objected that the underhanded methods of the Israelite contender "weren't cricket.") The elements of sport and of battle, however distinctive in various ways, have been thoroughly mixed up through history in such passages-at-arms as trials by combat, gladiatorial contests, knightly challenges and jousting tourneys, duelling in general and the "royal duel" in particular, and innumerable conflicts between picked adversaries evenly divided on both sides (as in the fourteenth-century "Combat des Trente" fought in Brittany and the "Disfida di Barletta" of 1503, pitting 13 Italian knights against 13 French counterparts).[12] To be sure, this courtly approach to war was limited, even in the age of chivalry, to circumstances of perceived equality between the foes; it was never operative in the "extermination" of those defined as subhuman or otherwise beyond the pale:

> We can only speak of war as a cultural function so long as it is waged within a sphere whose members regard each other as equals or antagonists with equal rights; in other words its cultural function depends on its play-quality. This condition changes as soon as war is waged outside the sphere of equals, against groups not recognized as human beings and thus deprived of human rights—barbarians, devils, heathens, heretics and "lesser breeds without the law."[13]

Even within the family of nations or kingdoms espousing the principles of fairness and common restraint, of course, the code of honor was always more an ideal than a reality. Much of the legendary chronicle of noble battles beautifully fought, as Huizinga points out, has been the stuff of folklore. But the ideal was not without its own force: "Even if it were no more than a fiction, these fancies of war as a noble game of honour and virtue have still played an important part in developing civilization, for it is from them that the idea of chivalry sprang and hence, ultimately, of international law."[14] It should not be forgotten that this system of jurisprudence contained not only a law of nations but a law of war, replete with rules and constraints representing a specialized tradition of civility (e.g., captive officers must not be put to labor), which ultimately gave rise to the sophisticated concept of "war crimes"—a phrase that would seem redundant to a savage of any historical period. As long as the principles of international law held sway among nations, in this view, war retained its ludic function—its civilized character as a contest, however deadly, "played" according to rules respected on both sides. The law of nations provided a system of restraints both rational and ethical in nature, "recognizing as it did the ideal of a community of mankind with rights and claims for all, and expressly separating the state of war—by declaring it—from peace on the one hand and criminal violence on the other."[15]

But that precarious structure, and the faith which supported it, were seen by Huizinga to have been betrayed and undermined in the present century by doctrines hostile to its essential spirit. Writing in the 1930s, with a vivid recollection of the first world war and a clear premonition of the second, Huizinga (along with other observers such as Walter Lippmann) traced the breakdown of the civilizing process to the spirit of "totalism" which found expression in the theory of total war, the institution of the total state, and the goal of unconditional surrender (with its counterpart of total victory).

> Things have now come to such a pass that the system of international law is no longer acknowledged, or observed, as the very basis of culture and civilized living. As soon as one member or more of a community of States virtually denies the binding character of international law and, either in practice or in theory, proclaims the interests and power of its own group—be it nation, party, class, church or whatsoever else—as the sole norm of its political behavior, not only does the last vestige of the immemorial playspirit vanish but with it any claim to civilization at all. Society then sinks down to the level of the barbaric, and original violence retakes its ancient rights.[16]

Curiously enough, despite his recognition of the kinship of sport and war, Huizinga did not fully perceive the same process of de-civilization operating in the realm of sport as in that of war. But he was writing in a time now regarded as the "golden age of sport," an era of relative innocence (despite recurrent scandals) in the evolution of modern athletics. Even then he was able to discern a marked decline of the "play-spirit" in sports—and inferentially of the spirit of fair play—through the infiltration of professionalism and its concomitant features of management, calculation, and "over-serious" business: "In the case of sport we have an activity nominally known as play but raised to such a pitch of technical organization and scientific thoroughness that the real play-spirit is threatened with extinction."[17] What Huizinga was not yet able to anticipate was that the extinction of the play-spirit would carry with it the extinction of the spirit of fair play, the circumvention of rules, the abandonment of civility, the retreat of honor, and the increasingly pervasive brutalization of sports. He could not, in other words, foresee the occurrence in the realm of sport of that subversive doctrine of *totalism*—of total victory, winning at any cost—which had overtaken modern war and reduced it to barbarism, to the state where "original violence retakes its ancient rights."

Although Huizinga did not envision the ultimate decivilizing of sport, he was ahead of his time in perceiving its retreat from the spirit of play into the mood of serious business and deadly earnest. Even as he wrote, in the late thirties, an early sociology of sport was taking form on the basis of a diametrically opposed assumption: namely, that modern sport was still evolving progressively onward and upward toward more civilized forms and practices. A pioneer expositor of this encouraging thesis was the Swiss sociologist Norbert Elias, who came to consider sport as one of the central "civilizing processes" of the modern world.[18] Both theories were agreed on one point: that there had been a definite historical progress from uncontrolled brawling to controlled competition, from collision to contest. But where Huizinga (whose major work was on the waning of the Middle Ages) located the fateful turning point in the premodern period, Elias and his school placed it in the late modern period— specifically, in the nineteenth and twentieth centuries. This difference in dating was more than an academic quibble over temporal details; it conveyed a profound disagreement concerning the impact of *modernity* on sports (as well as on life generally). To Huizinga the modern temper, with its accent on organization, technique and professionalism, instigated the corruption of the spirit of play—of "amateurism," spontaneity, nonseriousness, and ungoverned freedom. To Elias the same modern temper, through its installation of rules and protocols, was the essential civilizing process in the development of sport; the more regulated and rationalized it was, the more civilized it became. Given this assumption it followed that, as Elias's student and collaborator Eric Dunning has put it, "the principal sociological problem posed by the genesis of modern sports is that of explaining their civilized character relative to the 'sports' of earlier ages."[19]

Those earlier "sports," all the way from classical Greece to medieval England, were easily shown to have been lacking in the civilized graces; they were not so much sporting contests as "semi-institutionalized fights," rituals of violence staged for the purpose of releasing tensions and resolving inter-group conflicts. Graphic illustrations of their casual cruelty and barbaric temper were invoked by the civilized-process school to dramatize the gulf between these early practices and their politer modern counterparts. Thus, in a particularly lurid example drawn from the classical period, Elias pointed out that "Boxers did not only fight with their fists. As in almost all older forms of boxing, the legs played a part in the struggle. Kicking the shins of an opponent was a normal part of the boxing tradition in antiquity."[20] Again, concerning the Greeks:

> This agonistic type of boxing, as one can see, accentuated the climax, the moment of decision, of victory or defeat, as the most important and significant part of the contest, more important than the game-contest itself. It was as much a test of physical endurance and of sheer muscular strength as of skill. Serious injuries to the eyes, ears and even to the skull were frequent; so were swollen ears, broken teeth and squashed noses.[21]

And Elias quoted the observation of an historian of the ancient Olympics: "Like their colleagues in the wrestling and the pancreation, the boxers were determined to win at all costs."[22]

The attentive reader will have noticed an oddly familiar ring to these descriptions of the uncivilized character of early sports. They could, of course, equally well describe the state of the martial and manly arts today, with only technical qualifications here and there. The use of the legs for kicking (long permitted in the French form of boxing known as *savate,* as well as in Chinese and Thai boxing and Okinawan karate) has not found its way back into the western boxing ring, to be sure, but it is the distinctive feature of one of the most popular new sporting pastimes in America and Britain: the exquisitely named "martial arts," and in particular the lethal variation known as "full contact karate" (which is commonly advertised by promoters as a no-holds-barred "fight to the kill").[23] Meanwhile, in the squared circle of the other fight game, injuries of the dreadful kind attributed to the ancients are today so routine as to seem the least of the potential misfortunes awaiting the professional boxer.

"Win or Die"

Still more familiar to modern sports fans, and more heavily ironic, is the refrain of the historians which emphasizes the crass motivation of the contestants of long ago to "win at all costs"—their unchivalrous accentuation of "the moment of decision, of victory or defeat," as "more important than the game-contest itself." We have heard those phrases before, over and over—not from the annals of oldtime bloodsports but from the mouths of our own anointed heroes and official spokesmen of the contemporary jock culture. The phrases have come to form a litany, a new book of common prayer, repeated so often in high places and low that their mindlessness has been transmuted into revelation. The famous version of this gospel (the Apollo Creed?) uttered by the immortal Vince Lombardi—"Winning isn't everything, it's the only thing"—had been pronounced at least as far back as 1940 by a lesser luminary (Vanderbilt coach Red Sanders); but what doubtless added the ultimate symbolic grace note to the cretinous remark was that it was spoken on the silver screen, louder than life, by the Duke himself. The golden moment occurred in a 1953 movie, *Trouble Along the Way*, in which John Wayne was cast in the role of a football coach at a small Catholic college (a reincarnation of the immortals' immortal, Knute Rockne) to whom the leading lady, true to type, fed the innocent cue: "Is winning everything to you?" The Duke, as we knew he would, paused only long enough to get a bead on her: "No, ma'am," he drawled—and fired the verbal shot heard 'round the world.[24]

This knee-jerk chauvinism is not, of course, the peculiar characteristic merely of obsessive-compulsive coaches like Lombardi, Woody Hayes, George Allen, Darrell Royal, and the rest of their fanatic breed. It is rather a specialized version of the aggressive temperament actively fostered and continuously reinforced by those cultures old and new which have oversold the virtues of competition, overvalued the ends of power, and overprized the feats of the champion: the warrior, the gladiator, the king of the hill. (Nor is the competitive syndrome unique to capitalist countries; it is as rampant in East Germany and Cuba, let alone the USSR, as it is in America, Australia, or Taiwan.) But there is a peculiarly virulent American strain, long since isolated and identified by researchers. "Americans have always loved a winner," as General George S. Patton told his troops, "and have always hated a loser." The same sermon has been preached by evangelists ("Jesus is Number One") and intoned by statesmen (even those as politically distinct as Lyndon Johnson and Richard Nixon, thereby making the winner's creed a bipartisan domestic policy). Gerald Ford, the famous Michigan lineman, made the point with his usual perspicacity:

> We have been asked to swallow a lot of home-cooked psychology in recent years that winning isn't all that important any more, whether on the athletic field or in any other field, national and international. I don't buy that for a minute. It is not enough to just compete. Winning is very important. Maybe more important than ever.[25]

The psychology of total winning carries implications that are not at all abstract but as plain as the broken nose on an opponent's face. ("I broke a kid's nose in Juniors with a punch," said hockey enforcer "Wild" Willie Trognitz: "That was the biggest thrill I had as a kid.") Winning at any cost means there will in fact be costs, human costs, measured in broken bodies, crushed spirits, and ruined lives. It has been estimated that some 32 college and high school football players are converted into paraplegics every year, that 28 are killed outright, and that no less than 86 of every 100 high school gridders are sidelined for a week or more by injuries. "Any boy who plays the game throughout both high school and college," according to Don Atyeo, "stands a 95 percent chance of a serious injury."[26] The ranks of the professionals are, of course, especially decimated by the violence of the game. A few years ago it was estimated that a player in the National Football League suffered 2.5 injuries every season and that four out of every 22 in action were playing with serious injuries. One veteran of the pro wars has maintained that in the latter part of every season, "from around the tenth game on, 80 percent are playing with some kind of injury, either minor pulls or bruises or a serious injury."[27]

Statistics like these are usually shrugged off by celebrants of the joy of sports with the truism—which is unfortunately true—that it is all part of the game. "Football isn't a contact sport," as one coach put it, "it's a collision sport. Dancing is a contact sport." But as the pathology of total winning has overtaken the game, the collisions have not only accelerated but turned dirty; the tactics and motives of the mugger and hoodlum have emerged from the back alleys and found a welcoming reception on the wide free field. In more or less conscious emulation of the degraded sport of ice hockey, pro football has entered the Age of the Cheap Shot. (A "cheap shot," in the parlance of the game, is an illegal or unnecessary hit upon an unsuspecting adversary, usually after the play has ended or entirely apart from the action.) The crippling of Darryl Stingley is only the most conspicuous of recent episodes of aggravated assault by players who, more frequently and openly than ever, take pride in their Mafia-type roles as "enforcers" and "hit men" for the Family-team. Stingley was a brilliant wide receiver for the New England Patriots before he made the error of intruding, albeit in the line of duty, upon the personal turf of defensive back Jack Tatum of the Oakland Raiders; today Stingley is a paraplegic. Another member of the Raiders' swat team, George Atkinson, defined the territorial imperative under which these human predators operate: "I treat pass receivers the way you would treat a burglar in your home," he said, just after he had given Lynn Swann a cerebral concussion from one of his patented cheap shots.[28]

And the beating goes on. Wrists are slapped by league officials, fines are assessed against those offenders clumsy enough to get caught *in flagrante delicto*, and hands are wrung throughout the stadium. But other hands are also clapping; the reputation of enforcer and intimidator is sought after by numerous athletes, and the sobriquets of "assassin," "killer," and especially of *"mean"* (as in "Mean Joe" and "Mean Gene") are coveted like medals of valor. Soon after his maiming of Stingley, the Raiders' Tatum was persuaded to write a book about his exploits, entitled *Call Me Assassin*; his infamies had made him famous. Tatum's success has evidently served as an inspiration to various of his peers and colleagues, who seem intent on matching him shot for cheap shot. Following an especially vicious incident during the 1982 season, involving Stan Blinka, a linebacker for the New York Jets, reporter Bob Rubin filed the following commentary:

> Blinka should have to take the place of the nurse who feeds Stingley, the paralyzed former New England Patriots' receiver, and lifts his withered limbs to simulate normal motion. Perhaps then Blinka would fully realize the terrible con-

sequences that might have resulted from his shocking cheap shot to the head of Green Bay Packers' wide receiver John Jefferson.

Once severed, the human spine stays severed. Forever.

Jefferson never saw Blinka coming. Blinka had several yards of open field to build up momentum and time enough to choose a course of action. He almost decapitated Jefferson with a vicious forearm shot. . . .

Only Blinka knows his intent for sure, and one hesitates to accuse a man of deliberately trying to maim another. But circumstantial evidence against him mounted greatly in the next game when he hit Detroit Lions' superstar Billy Sims twice in the head during the second quarter.[29]

The doctrine of "total sports," like that of total war, is at once a symptom and a causative factor in what is coming to be seen as a precipitous decline of civilized values and codes of conduct in the western world. By elevating victory—at any price, by any means—into the overriding *raison d'etre* of sports, the new gospel has subverted not only the spirit of play but the ethics of fair play: all the time-honored considerations of decency, tolerance, honesty, friendliness, and restraint. In pursuit of the holy grail of victory no quarter must be given, no sympathy displayed, no limits imposed, no questions asked. The end sanctifies the means; might makes right; win, only win, for Winsocki or Woody or the shade of the Old Gipper, and all thy trespasses and cheap shots will be not only forgiven but hailed as virtues of the conquering hero. The familiar epic poem of Grantland Rice is in process of undergoing a mutation; now, when the One Great Scorer comes to write against your name, he appears to mark not whether you won and they lost, but how big you won and how viciously you played the game. "It bothers me," said Jack Lambert of the Pittsburgh Steelers, "to have kids asking how they can be as mean as me. They write and say, 'I love the way you kill people.'"[30]

The Children's Crusade

Football has long since become established as America's favorite spectator sport, if not its favorite form of entertainment; and professional football is the prestige model at the top of the line. (In 1983, the pro game became virtually a year-round entertainment, not including reruns, through the creation of the springtime United States Football League.) But the unscrupulous pursuit of victory, and the complementary inability to accept defeat, which pervades the professional game today is scarcely less conspicuous in intercollegiate football and has rapidly spread its contagion downward through the high schools all the way to what James Michener has termed the "jungle world of juvenile sports competition"—specifically, Pop Warner Junior League Football. Indeed the corruption of the macho syndrome has so thoroughly penetrated the lower ranks (in baseball and other sports as well as football) that the poison now spreads upward as well as down: it begins with overzealous parents, coaches, and parasitic publics who demand a winning season and indoctrinate their wards with the do-or-die spirit. That is the source of the hysteria which surrounds the competitive playground, converts recreation into production, and graphically fulfills Huizinga's prophecy of the imminent death of the play-spirit. Before long the external pressures on the performing moppets are joined by the internal pressures of the peer group; it is now the rare school, at any level above the elementary (and in some places the kindergarten), in which the popularity of male students is not measured significantly in terms of athletic prowess. There is simply no other role-model in contemporary society which compares with that of the athlete in terms of intrinsic appeal, of social approval, or of continuous media reinforcement. As psychiatrist Arnold Beisser has pointed out:

> American youth is explicitly prepared for the athlete's role in exquisitely accurate miniaturizations of the professional team. Little League baseball and Pop Warner football are almost exact duplications of major professional sports. The uniform, the publicity, the arduous practice, the complex plays, and, most of all, the pressure of adult expectation, make the role of professional athlete not only a future possibility, but a present reality.[31]

It would be difficult to say which is the more victimized child, the physically gifted or the physically inept, by this authoritarian social system of athletically based rewards and punishments. The boy without natural ability or interest in the competitive world of juvenile sports suffers by enforced exposure to it—at best by feelings of inadequacy and inferiority, at worst by acquiring the permanent self-image of a "loser" through internalization of the felt disapproval of significant others. (Nor is it, of course, only boys who are subject to this shaming label: as Janis Ian's poignant lyric to "Seventeen" demonstrated, the high-school girl who is maladroit at basketball may suffer her own form of obloquy.) Rather less apparent, because more gradual and subtle, is the victimization of the athletically inclined youngster—the winner—who is thrust at an early age into the apprenticeship system of the jockocracy. The most obvious price to be paid is the probability (now approaching 100 percent) of serious injury somewhere along the way; but there are more subtle forms of damage, no less serious, inflicted by the athletic assembly line—such as the burn-out suffered by overtrained and overpressured youths while still in their teens, a common affliction even in noncontact sports such as tennis, swimming, baseball (pitchers), track, and gymnastics. Even without terminal burn-out, the monomaniacal devotion to the sports regimen and its narrow values which the system imposes upon its juvenile recruits tends to produce a stunting of mental and emotional growth in direct inverse correlation to their accelerated physical development. Whatever the special advantages of this distinctive modern caste—in terms of prizes, privileges, and pampering—it involves a largely segregated and sheltered life conducted within a tight circle of demands and limitations, giving a poignant reality to the "loneliness of the (juvenile) long-distance runner."

In their comprehensive account of the spreading corruption of juvenile sports, *Winning Is Everything and Other American Myths,* Thomas Tutko and William Bruns provide copious evidence of the dehumanizing effects of this paranoid strain in American athletics. The enclosed and watery world of the competitive swimmer (typically in the early teens or younger) furnishes a graphic illustration—with its year-round training, two-a-day workouts, authoritarian coaches, spartan privations, and recurrent if not continuous pain. "It's like a mileage race to nowhere," remarked a swimmer's mother; and Tutko has been led to wonder at the possible justification of what looks less like healthy exercise than a sophisticated form of child abuse:

> Objectively speaking, one has seriously to question the claims that swimming is a healthily adjusted sport. I feel that

it requires a neurotic approach to competition and to living one's life. The sport is a complete preoccupation in which nearly every other aspect of normal living is eliminated. . . . Once a youngster makes a commitment to the sport, she (or he) is forced to narrow her experiences and her behavior. She loses social interaction away from the pool and the ability to develop social graces; dating is something you do after you retire. Of the thousands of things she could be doing, all she knows about is swimming. Not only that: the longer she stays in swimming, and the better she becomes, the more her obsession must grow to meet the ever-increasing competitive pressures.[32]

It almost goes without saying that this ruthless regimentation in the name of sports has severed the last tenuous connection with the free spirit of play. It is no wonder that young athletes are led, in increasing numbers, to detest their so-called sport and to abandon it altogether before they have reached maturity. "Every semester," reports Tutko, "I have students come up after a class to tell me, 'You know, I just don't like to swim anymore. I started swimming when I was six and when I was twelve I was burned out!'" The play element has been driven off by the work ethic; spontaneity, frolic, joy have been blown away by the cold breath of the achieving society. Huizinga would surely have wept to find his worst anticipations so thoroughly and so soon confirmed. That technological imperative which we have seen to intrude its criteria of efficiency and calculation into other dimensions of life and leisure has now taken command of play itself—reaching into the kindergarten if not yet into the nursery to pluck its conscripts and line them up for basic training. In his prophetic critique of technical civilization, written in the fifties, Jacques Ellul accurately identified the manner of the takeover: "A familiar process is repeated: real play and enjoyment, contact with air and water, improvisation and spontaneity all disappear. These values are lost to the pursuit of efficiency, records, and strict rules."[33]

When the spirit of play has been banished, the spirit of fair play is certain to follow it off the field. Whatever is left of civility or decency in the serious business of sports, as in other areas of modern life, becomes increasingly exploited and victimized by the exponents of strategic gamesmanship: i.e., the dirty tricksters. George Orwell, writing forty years ago, went directly to the heart of what was the matter: "Serious sport has nothing to do with fair play. It is bound up with hatred, jealousy, boastfulness, disregard for all rules, and sadistic pleasure in witnessing violence: in other words, it is war minus the shooting."[34] Another Englishman of the period, the humorist Stephen Potter, wryly outlined the emerging forms of unsportsmanlike conduct in a series of writings on gamesmanship and "one-upmanship"—the gist of which was that the manners and conventions of fair play could be subtly manipulated to enable an inferior player to defeat a superior without really trying.[35] Potter's intention was, of course, to expose and satirize the hidden weapons of all the artful dodgers of the sports world (as was apparent in the title of a derivative film, *School for Scoundrels*); but in doing so he was unwittingly giving aid and comfort to the enemy, for his gentle and ironic essays became huge bestsellers on both sides of the Atlantic—giving rise to a spate of superficially similar books conceived in deadly earnest (e.g., *Winning Through Intimidation*) and purporting to reveal the strategic secrets of how to succeed at practically anything with no other talent than that of the swindler.

The decay of sportsmanship has proceeded so far in various fields of athletic competition that the old-fashioned standard of behavior has virtually ceased to exist in the minds of sports enthusiasts (jockaholics)—coaches, athletes, and fans alike. "Show me a sportsman," said baseball manager Leo Durocher, "and I'll show you a player I'm looking to trade." The corollary of the adage that nice guys finish last is the conventional wisdom that mean guys get the bonuses. Illustrations of this existential truth abound on every sports page; here is one selected almost at random from the morning paper. "MR. MEAN," blares the headline: "Micheaux Would Like to Tattoo Louisville." The accompanying story on a college basketball star, entirely enthusiastic in tone, reads in part:

> . . . Micheaux has a reputation to live up to. His nickname is Mr. Mean and he even has shaved his head at times to foster that intimidating image.
>
> Micheaux has been the terror of Houston practices all season, especially since coach Guy Lewis does not like to blow the whistle once the scrimmaging starts. No blood, no foul. His teammates have even asked him to lighten up.
>
> Micheaux just laughs. "I guess I was pretty awesome in

practice," he said. "I don't take no mess. I just picked up the name Mr. Mean from our assistant coach . . .

"I want to intimidate everybody we play," he said.[36]

Head Hunting and Other Games

Intimidation is an elementary form of one-upmanship; if you can make the adversary tremble, the contest is half won. And fear is the name of the game for those accomplished terrorists, in any sport, who make a personal style of the sucker punch and the sneak attack, the backhanded blow, the gouge in the eye, the twist of the knee, the elbow to the head, and other refinements of what is fast becoming a high art of the killing ground (formerly the playing field). Most enforcers and intimidators are specialists, each with his favorite cheap shot or limited repertoire; a few of the more talented, like the fearsome All-Pro guard Conrad Dobler, go on to become jocks of all trades. The ultimate goal, of course, is to put the opponent out of commission, to blow him away for good: "If you can get Lawrence McCutcheon or James Harris out of there when you play the Rams," said one defensive specialist, "then you've got a hell of a chance to win, and that's what it's all about." So that's what it's all about: winning through attrition—with three brownie points perhaps for a fallen quarterback, two for a running back, and one each for wide receivers. Short of actually maiming the opponent, the tactical objective (serious students please note) is to secure a competitive advantage. "You get in a good lick around the head area, it rattles the man," said another pro gridder: "You can beat a dazed man easier than an alert one. It's that simple." But there is also the pure joy of sport, the sweet smell of success, the deep-down satisfaction of a job well done: "The harder I hit people the better I like it," said still another professional. "When you hit a guy and he hits the ground hard and his eyeballs roll and you see it and he looks up at you and knows you see it, then you've conquered him. It's a great feeling."[37] (To be sure, a few players have had misgivings about this pleasurable sadism. Dave Meggysey, a former pro linebacker, wrote that "the conditions that made me feel a confused joy at breaking up another man's body gradually became just one of the many reasons why I decided to quit the game.")[38]

One of the standard tactics in the modern pastime of "endgame" is that of head hunting. "Concussion," according to Don Atyeo, "is the common cold of football." Many professionals, especially the quarterbacks, accept these "dings" almost routinely, and there are even some who take pride in their accumulation (as many as ten or more over a career), much like the old-fashioned duelist with his saber scars. (They might be less proud if they were fully aware of the high risk of brain damage from successive blows to the head; more than three such concussions are considered by experts in sports medicine to represent the point of no return.) That is not the worst of it; if concussion has become the common cold of football, head and neck injuries (many resulting in death or permanent paralysis) are becoming its black plague. Numerous studies have documented both the frequency and severity of these combat wounds; one four-year survey of high school football found approximately 13 percent of all injuries to be those affecting the head and neck, while another lengthy study turned up 65 deaths from a total of 139 craniocerebral injuries and another 16 fatalities out of 78 spinal cord injuries.[39] The head is not only the target in this lethal recreation but the weapon as well—particularly since the advent in the sixties of the hard plastic helmet (lately outlawed by high schools), which has inspired the popular new method of attack known as "spearing," where the helmet (rather than shoulders or arms) carries the brunt of the assault and players "are taught to aim for the side, throat, knee or any other vulnerable area . . ."[40] The only problem with this tactic is that the hunter who uses his head is as vulnerable to injury as the hunted; his "best weapon" (as Jerry Kramer regarded it) is also his worst enemy.

What has descended upon bigtime football with the acceptance of these vicious tactics is not just the night of the hunter, but the day of the jackal. The low blows and sneak attacks of the new breed of gridiron gangsters—the self-acclaimed assassins, intimidators, enforcers, and hit men—are not, of course, acts of courage but of cowardice, not feats of skill or prowess but the cynical and sinister methods of what would elsewhere be recognized instantly as criminal assault. And the men who deliberately and systematically perform these atrocities, on the gridiron or the hockey rink or the basketball court, are not *players*, in any meaningful sense of the term, but muggers. They are not "playing" at what they do, and there is nothing "playful" about their purpose and their execution of it; they are in deadly earnest. In plain fact they have no choice; survival in their weekend jungle depends on resourceful aggression, instant retribution, and cunning maneuvers. He who hesitates is not just lost but clobbered. If this is most blatantly the case in hockey—where rookies or foreign players new to the American pro game are literally broken in or broken up by veterans intent on exploiting any weakness[41]—it is barely less conspicuous in pro football, and is becoming increasingly apparent in the semi-professional game played by the football colleges (like the southwestern institution praised by its president as one the football team could be proud of). But perhaps most telling of all is the rapid descent of the once gentle sport of basketball into a form of martial arts—complete with its enforcers and muscle men, intimidators and head hunters, and its own expanding bag of lethal inside moves. For this was the graceful recreation purposely created and crafted by its nineteenth-century inventor, the Rev. Dr. James Naismith, as a *non-contact* sport—a safe refuge from the rough games of tackling, blocking, and colliding. Almost any interference with an opponent, the slightest encroachment upon his person, was designated (with a nice gentility) a "foul." No wonder that basketball was appreciated, almost from its inception, as a proper recreation for young ladies as well as young gentlemen. That may still be the way it is understood and played in seminaries; but it bears little relation to the modern game either at the professional or intercollegiate level. The descriptive language now speaks of survival, the defense of territory, of "contact" in the form of shots to the rib, elbows in the small of the back, fingers to the eye, assorted blows, kicks, trips, and other cheap shots.[42] Injuries are almost as rife on the court as on the football field, and almost as often deliberately caused or contrived.

The degeneration of basketball into a collision sport, just another American variation on the martial arts, is only the latest symptom of the deeper degenerative disease afflicting major competitive sports. In some cases the malaise has already proved terminal: the earliest recorded casualty was that of professional wrestling, scarcely even mourned any longer by a generation with no living memory of Frank Gotch (let alone of "Farmer" Burns), of the German strong boy Gus Hackenschmidt, of the ageless Stanislaus Zybisko and the original "Strangler" Lewis. An ancient art and complex craft, with its own amazing grace—possibly a sweeter science in its season than the prizefight ever was—became a victim of the big money and the carni-

val spirit, of the audience's thirst for spectacle and melodrama, leading to the swift degradation of an honorable sporting tradition. Pro
"rassling" today competes only with the Roller Derby on the lowest
rung of debased athletic performance—and on nearly the lowest rung
of debased theatrical performance, barely above the residual
sideshow of Freaks and the fading remnants of Old-Fashioned Burlesque. Perhaps that is not quite the destiny in store for the dominant
sports of today; but the lesson which the sad clowns of grappling
provide is that the twin motives to win big and to put on a good show
of violence contain the seeds of a corruption that is not likely to be
checked or contained before it has destroyed both the credibility of
bigtime sport and the credulity of its innocently believing fans.

OUT OF THE NIGHT: TOWARD <u>HOMO</u> <u>HUMANUS</u>

The hour is very late, and the choice of good and evil knocks at our door.—*Norbert Wiener*

Therefore let us consider miracles.—*Lewis Mumford*

THIS BOOK might be represented metaphorically as a guided tour through the badlands of modern culture: not the whole of that vast living desert, to be sure, nor all of its lowest dives or most grotesque exhibits. There is too much there to take in on one trip. But we have gone down some indisputably mean streets, crowded with the walking dead—and we have peered into various dark alleys of the imagination, harboring nightmares of a crafty and sullen art. We have also paused to inspect some garish display windows advertising the fashions of decadence. It has been hard traveling, but we never promised you a rose garden. There are foul deeds aplenty in these chapters—both mindless acts of viciousness and coolly rational administrations of fear. And there are foul mouths aplenty, chorus after chorus of them, crying havoc and exalting degradation; they are the voices of nihilism, foreshadowing the acts of barbarism.

What these widely diverse episodes and events have in common is that all are manifestations of what we have termed the dehuman syndrome. The culture of nihilism has been shown to operate at numerous levels of social reality and social fiction—some of them blatantly outrageous, others subtly disguised, and still others masquerading publicly as virtue. Modern evil, we have seen, wears no horns—or, alternatively, wears them so flagrantly and flauntingly that we are equally deceived. The devil at four o'clock is just an ordinary citizen, or only a brash kid.

Our study has been a limited exercise in the identification and elucidation of certain aspects of a major social problem: the spreading contagion of dehumanization. It is a book of criticism—not a book of revelation. We have sought to cast light on the dark corners of modern culture, some that are foully festering and others that smell like a rose. If intelligence is, as Santayana described it, "one centrifugal ray, darting from the slime to the stars," we hope to have furthered its work. Our goal has been that of stimulating a modest increase of awareness—and of vigilance. That may not be enough, of course, to cope with the self-destructive genius that animates our age. It may be that the modern world will not survive its Promethean discoveries in the realm of technics—its theft of thunder and the ultimate lightning from the gods. The fate of the earth, as Jonathan Schell has made us know, hangs by a thread of moral recognition.[1] And if we do somehow avert Armageddon, the race of man and woman may not survive its Frankensteinian discoveries in the realm of the self (body and mind): its new power to transfigure itself utterly, or merely to clone its own monsters. (See, for illustration, *The Boys from Brazil*.)

In any case, it is later than we like to think. Indeed the hour is very late, as Norbert Wiener understood a generation ago, at the dawn of the apocalyptic era. In his warning that the choice of good and evil knocks at our door, he was thinking of the terrible gap that lies open like a knife wound between our high-tech brains and our confused sensibilities. Like Siegried Giedion in the same period of history, he saw civilization standing by, a spectator at the excavation site, while mechanization took command. Like Lewis Mumford before him (and like Lewis Mumford after him), Wiener knew that we must therefore consider miracles. But the voices of these prophets, as we now know, were crying in the wilderness. In 1952 William H. Whyte, Jr., published a little book entitled *Is Anybody Listening?* No one seems to have read it. The world was too busy then with lovely wars (hot and cold) and diverting conspiracies to be distracted by the consideration of miracles. The great fear was there, of course, even then (those who looked up from their backyard fallout shelters on a clear day could almost see the sword of Damocles hanging in the sky); but, as the great fear was too much to bear in the absence of faith, and too much to comprehend in the absence of leadership, it took the form of the great blandness: that happy consciousness of the cheerful robot, the Man from Glad, whom we have met in the course of our investigation. Instead of considering miracles, people decorated their cars with bumper stickers reading "Expect a Miracle." Whatever the inexplicable problem was, if there was a problem, it was out of their hands. Let George (that is, God played by George Burns) do it.

There have been, however, some hopeful portents of a change of mind, if not yet a change of heart, in the last two decades. In both America and western Europe, the first indications of an altering state of consciousness—in the form of the mixed bag of aspirations known as the counterculture—were not, of course, faint whispers but loud and clamorous protests. If those youthful voices were finally seduced by their own innocence and rage into the cesspool of what we have termed the counter-counterculture, if the rock music they stepped to and the different drummer they heard led them out of Woodstock and into Altamont, into sympathy for the devil, that should not abolish the memory of their brief moment of truth and courage: their Great Refusal (in Marcuse's term) of the juggernaut with the smiling face. In any case the moment passed; the juggernaut assumed the posture of the astronaut (radiating the "banality of virtue," as Mumford put it); the interminable senseless war wound finally down; two successive presidents who had made a calling of meanness were pressured out of the presidency; and we had seen the moment of our greatness flicker. What followed in America was called a "time of healing"; in reality, of course, it was a time of forgetting, or burying the live along with the dead, of pellmell return to the era of "normalcy" dear to Harding and Gerald Ford. Robinson Jeffers had anticipated the mood of the seventies a generation before:

While this America settles in the mold of its vulgarity, heavily
    thickening to empire,
And protest, only a bubble in the molten mass, pops and sighs out,
    and the mass hardens . . .[2]

It was a time, we remember, for singing "Where Have All the Flowers Gone?" and odes to all the sad young men. The times were once again a-changing, in the silent seventies, and what was now blowing in the wind was not worth writing lyrics about except in punk circles. The culture of narcissism was in full swing, from the decadent discos of Manhattan to the exotic hot springs of Big Sur; and the vaunted exploration of self and actualization of the human potential which marked the therapeutics of joy were mostly frivolous where they were not plainly fraudulent. But not the whole of it. It was not all vanity of vanities; there was a small living core, at the bottom of this applied humanistic psychology, of earnest searching for a healthier self and a saner way of living. Fun could be made, of course, then as now, of the trendy life-stylists of all the middle-class Marins who went from transcendental meditation to primal scream without a quiver and apparently without a clue in their faddish pursuit of instant satori, or at least of total orgasm. They have been firmly put in their suburban place by a succession of formidable critics; there is little need to Lasch them further.[3] But hold on a minute. There is a baby, in that bathwater from the hot tub, which should not be casually thrown out. It is the underlying psychology of humanism that gave original authority, not to say inspiration, to the so-called Awareness Movement of the seventies; if it came to be soon debased on the heady atmosphere of spiritual power trips and media hype, it should at least be distinguished from its numerous illegitimate offspring. It has nothing to do, for example, with the therapeutic fascism of "est" and related exploitations of mind control; it was never at ease in the hot springs, with Bob & Carol & Ted & Alice— who almost certainly had never heard of this psychology and couldn't care less if they had. (Who's afraid of Virginia Satir?) And, whatever else it may have been, it was surely not an "Aquarian Conspiracy." Nothing so romantic or titillating. The real humanistic psychology, which had begun to find its voice in the fifties, was not so much insurgent as it was resurgent in its message; it presented rare old philosophical wine in new laboratory bottles.[4] It called us back to ourselves, away from the toolbox and the calculator. This new psychological humanism dared to speak openly of the self—that old spook so long ago exorcised from the house of intellect; and worse yet, it spoke *well* of the self. Nearly all the entrenched and mired orthodoxies of behavioral science were now challenged and jostled, if not quite overturned. Among them was the ancient doctrine dear to instinctivists of the doom carried in our genes, the scientific version of original sin; although this image of *la bete humaine* continues to hold a peculiar fascination for morbid or despairing minds, it has been effectively repudiated in theory and refuted by research.[5] The humanist alternative holds that man's fate, his course of conduct for good or ill, is not preprogrammed but self-determined: Man at some time is master of his fate; the fault, dear humans, is not in our stars or in our genes but in ourselves that we are . . . whatever we become.

More than that. The new psychology, and its equivalent formulations throughout the arts and sciences of man, maintains not only that the responsibility for life is ours—to make or break, to exalt or debase, to murder and create. It holds that the capability is ours as well: that there is nothing within us or without to prevent an act of self-transformation, an evolutionary leap, if that is what is called for. It is the arrogant belief of this theory of humane science that man is the creator no less than the creature of his culture; that he is an actor upon his world and not just a play-actor in it; that in simple fact, as V. Gordon Childe put it, "man makes himself."

The time has come for remaking. *Homo Sapiens* has had his day on earth—and has failed. The great lesson now beginning to be learned by the overmechanized and overmobilized world, a world of power inhabited by a powerless race, is that sapience is not enough to save us. Mind divorced from feeling, rationality without mercy, is not a divine gift but a devil's bargain. The enveloping culture of nihilism, and the new dark age of dehumanization, reflect a fatal disorder of the modern world, generated systematically out of the mainsprings of advanced industrial society and nurtured by a purely technical intelligence cut off from those balancing attributes of human nature invidiously categorized as sentimentality. The coming of the Fifth Horseman of the Apocalypse coincides with the triumph of the computer and the disinheritance of the senses. No, mind alone cannot save us in this extremity; what is needed now is *minding*—the marriage of thought and feeling. Out of that marriage may come more than a new balance, a new sanity; it holds the prospect of a new and higher consciousness. As Alan McGlashan has written in his prophetic work, *Savage and Beautiful Country*, "Out of the royal union of thinking and feeling will be born the inner force that alone can pull man back to safety from the high and narrow window ledge on which he now stands, screaming silently."[6]

The possible attainment of full humanness—the transformation of the species from *Homo sapiens* to *Homo humanus*—rests upon our recovery of the lost world of fellow feeling, the source of all human connection. Before thinking of new horizons, before planning any bold new enterprises, we must come back to our senses—or perish senselessly.

NOTES

Preface

1. Erich Kahler, *The Tower and the Abyss* (New York: Viking Compass Books, 1967), p. xiii.
2. Melvin Maddocks, *Honolulu Advertiser,* August 16, 1980.
3. Rollo May, *Power and Innocence* (New York: Norton, 1972), p. 21.
4. Erich Fromm, *The Revolution of Hope: Toward a Humanized Technology* (New York: Bantam, 1968), p. 41.
5. Christopher Lasch, *The Culture of Narcissism* (New York: Norton, 1978), p. xiii.

Introduction

1. Eric and Mary Josephson, editors, *Man Alone: Alienation in Modern Society* (New York: Dell, 1962), pp. 16–17.
2. Lewis Mumford, *The Transformations of Man* (New York: Harper Torchbooks, 1972), p. 39.
3. *Man Alone,* p. 17.
4. Peter Laslett, *The World We Have Lost* (New York: Scribner's, 1965), p. 21.
5. Quoted in Alexandre Koyré, *From the Closed World to the Infinite Universe* (New York: Harper Torchbooks, 1958), p. 29.
6. Ibid., p. 4.
7. E. A. Burtt, *The Metaphysical Foundations of Modern Science* (Garden City: Doubleday Anchor Books, 1955), pp. 238–239.
8. Lewis Mumford, *Technics and Civilization* (New York: Harcourt, Brace and World, 1934).
9. Paul Halmos, *Solitude and Privacy* (London: Routledge & Kegan Paul, 1952), p. 27.
10. Ibid., p. 29.
11. Quoted in Halmos, p. 31.

12. Ralph Waldo Emerson, "Works and Days," *Society and Solitude* (New York: William H. Wise & Co., 1929), p. 159.
13. Henry Adams, *The Education of Henry Adams* (Boston: Houghton Mifflin, 1973 [1918]), p. 380.
14. "Works and Days," p. 163.
15. Ibid., p. 164.
16. Ernest Samuels, "Introduction," *The Education of Henry Adams*, p. vii.
17. *The Education of Henry Adams*, pp. 388–389.
18. Quoted in Lewis Mumford, *The Pentagon of Power* (New York: Harcourt Brace Jovanovich, 1970), p. 232.
19. W. B. Yeats, "The Second Coming," *A Little Treasury of Modern Poetry*, edited by Oscar Williams (New York: Scribner's, 1946), p. 459.
20. Jacques Ellul, *The Technological Society* (New York: Knopf, 1964), p. 6.
21. Viola W. Bernard, Perry Ottenberg, and Fritz Redl, "Dehumanization: A Composite Psychological Defense in Relation to Modern War," *Behavioral Science and Human Survival*, edited by Milton Schwebel (Palo Alto: Science and Behavior Books, 1965), p. 66.
22. *Newsweek*, November 8, 1982, p. 82.
23. Susan Sontag, *On Photography* (New York: Farrar, Straus & Giroux, 1977); Daniel J. Boorstin, *The Image: A Guide to Pseudo-Events in America* (New York: Harper Colophon, 1964).
24. Erving Goffman, *The Presentation of Self in Everyday Life* (New York: Doubleday, 1959), pp. 252–253.
25. Stanford M. Lyman and Marvin B. Scott, *The Drama of Social Reality* (New York: Oxford University Press, 1975); Stanford M. Lyman and Marvin B. Scott, *A Sociology of the Absurd* (Pacific Palisades, Calif.: Goodyear, 1970).
26. John Lofland, "Interactionist Imagery and Analytic Interruptus," in Tamotsu Shibutani, *Human Nature and Collective Behavior* (Englewood Cliffs, N.J.: Prentice-Hall, 1970).
27. Alvin W. Gouldner, *The Coming Crisis of Western Sociology* (New York: Basic Books, 1970), pp. 380, 381.
28. Ludwig Gumplowicz, *The Outlines of Sociology* (Philadelphia: American Academy of Political and Social Science, 1899), p. 156.
29. Wayne Hield, "The Study of Change in Social Science," *British Journal of Sociology* (March 1954); Gouldner, p. 206.

Chapter 1

1. Robert Bierstadt, *The Social Order* (New York: McGraw-Hill, 1957), p. 20. For closely similar asseverations see Arnold Green, *Sociology* (New York: McGraw-Hill, 1956), pp. 8, 10; E.B. Reuter, *Handbook of Sociology* (New York: Dryden, 1941), p. 12.
2. Ernest Becker, *The Structure of Evil: An Essay on the Unification of the Science of Man* (New York: Braziller, 1968); Ernest Becker, *Escape from Evil* (New York: Free Press, 1975); William Ernest Thompson, *Evil and World Order*

(New York: Harper & Row, 1976). See also Karl Menninger, *Whatever Became of Sin?* (New York: Hawthorn, 1973).

3. Stanford M. Lyman, *The Seven Deadly Sins: Society and Evil* (New York: St. Martin's Press, 1978), p. viii.

4. Hannah Arendt, *Eichmann in Jerusalem: A Report on the Banality of Evil* (New York: Viking Press, 1963), p. 451.

5. Lewis Yablonsky, *The Violent Gang* (New York: Macmillan, 1962), p. 7.

6. *The Seven Deadly Sins,* p. 273.

7. Erich Fromm, *The Anatomy of Human Destructiveness* (New York: Holt, Rinehart and Winston, 1973), p. 339.

8. Charles E. Silberman, *Criminal Violence, Criminal Justice* (New York: Random House, 1978), pp. 64–65.

9. G. Gordon Liddy, *Will* (New York: St. Martin's Press, 1980), p. 60.

10. Albert Camus, *The Stranger* (New York: Vintage, 1946), p. 169.

11. *The Seven Deadly Sins,* p. 5.

12. Ibid., p. 18.

13. Michael Selzer, *Terrorist Chic: An Exploration of Violence in the Seventies* (New York: Hawthorn, 1979), p. 193.

14. Ibid., pp. 132–133.

15. Ibid., p. 192.

16. Lewis Yablonsky, *Robopaths* (Indianapolis: Bobbs-Merrill, 1972), p. 6, *passim*; Lyman, *The Seven Deadly Sins,* p. 40; Fromm, *The Anatomy of Human Destructiveness,* p. 332.

17. *The Seven Deadly Sins,* p. 40.

18. See, for example, Fritz Pappenheim, *The Alienation of Modern Man: An Interpretation Based on Marx and Tönnies* (New York: Modern Reader Paperbacks, 1959).

19. See Heinz Kohut, *The Analysis of the Self: A Systematic Approach to the Psychoanalytic Treatment of Narcissistic Personality Disorders* (New York: International Universities Press, 1971); Sigmund Freud, *Civilization and Its Discontents* (London: Hogarth Press, 1930).

20. This European sociological tradition and its viewpoint are well discussed and exemplified in C. Wright Mills, editor, *Images of Man* (New York: Braziller, 1963).

21. *Robopaths,* p. 7.

22. Ibid., p. 6.

23. Ibid., pp. 14–15.

24. Ibid., p. 15.

25. Quoted in Yablonsky, ibid., p. 35.

26. Vincent Bugliosi with Curt Gentry, *Helter Skelter: The True Story of the Manson Murders* (New York: Norton, 1974), p. 126.

27. *Will,* p. 210.

28. *The Anatomy of Human Destructiveness,* p. 352.

29. *Will,* p. 4.

30. Ibid., p. 11.

31. Ibid., p. 12.

32. Ibid., p. 17.
33. Ibid., p. 24.
34. Ibid., p. 26.
35. Ibid., p. 190.
36. Herman Wouk, *The Caine Mutiny* (Garden City: Doubleday, 1951).
37. *Will*, p. 55.
38. Ibid., p. 97.
39. Ibid.
40. Ibid., p. 148.
41. Ibid., p. 208.
42. Ibid.
43. Ibid., p. 348.
44. Stanley Milgram, *Obedience to Authority: An Experimental View* (New York: Harper & Row, 1974), p. 8.
45. Ibid., p. 11.
46. Ibid., p. 188.
47. Ibid., p. 50.
48. Ibid., p. 6.
49. Ibid., p. 188.

Chapter 2

1. C. Wright Mills, *The Sociological Imagination* (New York: Oxford University Press, 1959), p. 170.
2. Ibid., p. 174.
3. Herbert Marcuse, *One-Dimensional Man* (Boston: Beacon Press, 1964), p. 76.
4. Ibid., p. 79.
5. William H. Whyte, Jr., *The Organization Man* (Garden City, N.Y.: Doubleday Anchor, 1957), p. 384f., *passim*.
6. Alan Harrington, *Life in the Crystal Palace* (New York: Knopf, 1959), p. 7.
7. Harvey Swados, "The Myth of the Happy Worker," in Harvey Swados, *A Radical's America* (Boston: Little, Brown, 1957).
8. Tom Wolfe, *The Pump House Gang* (New York: Bantam Books, 1969), pp. 8–9.
9. Ibid., p. 53.
10. Ibid., p. 55.
11. Ibid., p. 58.
12. Ibid., p. 61.
13. Mildred Edie Brady, "The Strange Case of Wilhelm Reich," *New Republic*, May 26, 1947, pp. 20–23.
14. Stephen Kern, *Anatomy and Destiny: A Cultural History of the Human Body* (Indianapolis: Bobbs-Merrill, 1975), p. 125.
15. Lionel Trilling, *The Liberal Imagination: Essays on Literature and Society* (New York: Viking, 1950), p. 231.

16. See Ashley Montagu, *Sex, Man, and Society* (New York: Putnam's Sons, 1969), esp. chap. 6, "Where Kinsey Went Wrong."
17. Rollo May, *Love and Will* (New York: W. W. Norton, 1969), p. 43.
18. Quoted in May, ibid., p. 44.
19. Ibid., p. 43.
20. *Anatomy and Destiny*, p. 138.
21. Ruth Brecher and Edward M. Brecher, editors, *An Analysis of Human Sexual Response* (London: Andre Deutsch, 1967), p. 119.
22. Ibid. Quoted in George Frankl, *The Failure of the Sexual Revolution* (London: Kahn & Averill, 1974), p. 132.
23. Patrick M. McGrady, Jr., *The Love Doctors* (New York: Macmillan, 1972), p. 281.
24. *The Failure of the Sexual Revolution*, p. 134.
25. Ibid., p. 131.
26. Wardell B. Pomeroy, quoted in David Holbrook, *Sex and Dehumanization* (London: Pitman Publishing, 1972), p. 142.
27. Ibid.
28. Leslie H. Farber, *Lying, Despair, Jealousy, Envy, Sex. Suicide, Drugs, and the Good Life* (New York: Basic Books, 1976), p. 137.
29. *Sex and Dehumanization*, p. 139.
30. See McGrady, *The Love Doctors*, p. 283f.
31. "M," *The Sensuous Woman* (1970); "J," *The Sensuous Man* (1971) . . . (tbs)
32. Farber, pp. 138–139.
33. Ibid., p. 140.
34. Erich Fromm, *The Anatomy of Human Destructiveness* (New York: Holt, Rinehart and Winston, 1973), p. 350.
35. George Steiner, "Night Words: High Pornography and Human Privacy," in *Perspectives on Pornography*, ed. by Douglas A. Hughes (New York: St. Martin's Press, 1970), pp. 96–108.
36. Ortega y Gasset, *The Dehumanization of Art* (Garden City, N.Y.: Doubleday Anchor, n.d.). The title essay was first published in 1949.
37. Kenneth Clark, *The Nude: A Study in Ideal Form* (Princeton: Princeton University Press, 1972), p. 8.
38. See Siegried Giedion, *The Eternal Presence: The Beginnings of Art* (New York: Bollingen Foundation, 1962), p. 4.
39. Joseph Campbell, *The Hero with a Thousand Faces* (Princeton: Princeton University Press, 1949), pp. 302–303.
40. Norma Nichols, *The Mirrors of Eve: Changing Images of Women in American Art, 1670–1980*. Unpublished dissertation, University of Hawaii Department of American Studies, 1982, p. 234.
41. See Robert Hughes, *The Shock of the New* (New York: Knopf, 1981); Barbara Rose, "Filthy Pictures: Some Chapters in the History of Taste," *Artforum*, May 1965, pp. 20–25.
42. William H. Gerdts, *The Great American Nude: A History in Art* (New York: Praeger, 1974), pp. 196–197.
43. Ibid., p. 207.

44. Ibid., p. 201.
45. *Mirrors of Eve,* p. 131.
46. Ibid., p. 132.
47. *The Shock of the New,* p. 55.
48. Erich Kahler, *The Disintegration of Form in the Arts* (New York: Braziller, 1968).
49. See William H. Gerdts, *The Great American Nude* (New York: Praeger, 1974), pp. 192–196.
50. *The Dehumanization of Art,* p. 21.
51. Ibid., p. 37.
52. John P. Sedgwick, *Discovering Modern Art* (New York: Random House, 1966), p. 14.
53. Ibid., p. 17.
54. Ibid., p. 18.
55. Ibid., p. 21.
56. Ibid., p. 22.

Chapter 3

1. Quoted in Vance Packard, *The People Shapers* (Boston: Little, Brown, 1977), p. 25.
2. Such an approach has been taken especially by Werner Jaeger, *Paideia: The Ideals of Greek Culture* (New York: Oxford University Press, 1944), Vol. II.
3. Aldous Huxley, "Foreword," *Brave New World* (New York: Bantam Books, 1953), p. xi.
4. Ibid., p. xii.
5. Ibid., p. xv.
6. Ibid., p. xvii.
7. Aldous Huxley, *Brave New World Revisited* (New York: Perennial Library, 1958), p. 4.
8. Bruce Barton, *The Man Nobody Knows* (Indianapolis: Bobbs-Merrill, 1924).
9. *Brave New World,* p. 20.
10. On Pavlov, see Gardner Murphy, *Historical Introduction to Modern Psychology* (New York: Harcourt, Brace, 1951), p. 255f.
11. John B. Watson, "Kinaesthetic and Organic Sensations: Their Role in the Reactions of the White Rat to the Maze," published in *Psychological Review* (1907), Vol. VIII, Monograph Supplement No. 2, pp. 1–100.
12. John B. Watson, *Behaviorism* (Chicago: University of Chicago Press, 1930), p. 159.
13. Ibid., p. 160.
14. Ibid., p. 161.
15. Ibid., p. 162.
16. Ibid., p. 167.
17. John B. Watson, *The Ways of Behaviorism* (New York: Harper, 1926), p. 9.

18. John B. Watson, *Psychology from the Standpoint of a Behaviorist* (Philadelphia: Lippincott, 3rd edit., 1929), p. 7.
19. *Behaviorism*, p. 11.
20. Ibid., p. 303.
21. Ibid.
22. John B. Watson, *Psychological Care of Infant and Child* (New York: Norton, 1928).
23. Luther Emmett Holt, *The Care and Feeding of Children: A Catechism for the Use of Mothers and Children's Nurses* (New York: Appleton-Century, 15th ed., 1935). See also the updated version, edited by L. E. Holt, Jr., *Holt's Care and Feeding of the Child* (New York: Appleton-Century, 1948).
24. Watson, *Psychological Care of Infant and Child,* pp. 81–82.
25. Ashley Montagu, "Breastfeeding and its Relation to Morphological, Behavioral, and Psychocultural Development," in Dana Raphael, ed., *Breastfeeding and Food Policy in a Hungry World* (New York: Academic Press, 1979), pp. 189–197; Gerald E. Gaull, "What is Biochemically Special About Human Milk?" ibid., pp. 217–227; Jane Pitt, "Immunological Aspects of Human Milk," ibid., pp. 229–232. More generally, see Ashley Montagu, *Touching: The Human Significance of the Skin* (New York: Harper & Row, 2d ed., 1978); Ashley Montagu and Floyd Matson, *The Human Connection* (New York: McGraw-Hill, 1979), chap. 4.
26. Quoted in Lewis M. Andrews and Marvin Karlins, *Requiem for Democracy? An Inquiry into the Limits of Behavioral Control* (New York: Holt, Rinehart and Winston, 1971), p. 3.
27. *Behaviorism*, p. 44. (Emphasis added.)
28. Ibid.
29. Jacques Ellul, *The Technological Society* (New York: Knopf, 1964), pp. 350–351.
30. Elton Mayo, *The Social Problems of an Industrial Civilization* (Boston: Harvard University Press, 1945), chap. 1.
31. Ibid., p. 5.
32. William H. Whyte, Jr., *The Organization Man* (Garden City: Doubleday Anchor Books, 1957), pp. 40–41.
33. *The Technological Society,* p. 353.
34. The key work in the revival of human relations is Douglas McGregor, *The Human Side of Enterprise* (New York: McGraw-Hill, 1960). For critical discussion, see Christopher Lasch, *The Culture of Narcissism* (New York: Norton, 1978), pp. 182–186.
35. Korzybski was one of the earliest proponents of human engineering, in his *Manhood of Humanity: The Science and Art of Human Engineering* (New York, 1921). His ambitious program of "verbal engineering" was announced in *Science and Sanity: An Introduction to Non-Aristotelian Systems and General Semantics* (New York, 1933). Cf. Stuart Chase, *The Tyranny of Words* (New York, 1938); S. I. Hayakawa, *Language in Action* (New York, 1941). For an early critique of what has been called the "semantic-depressive" syndrome, see Barrows Dunham, *Man Against Myth* (New York, 1949).
36. Peter Schrag, *Mind Control* (New York: Pantheon Books, 1978), p. 14.

37. Adolf A. Berle, Jr. and Gardner C. Means, *The Modern Corporation and Private Property* (New York: Macmillan, 1934); James Burnham, *The Managerial Revolution* (New York: John Day, 1941). The updated version of this thesis, for the 60s and after, is found in John Kenneth Galbraith, *The New Industrial State* (Boston: Houghton Mifflin, 1967).
38. Max Lerner, *America as a Civilization* (New York: Simon & Schuster, 1957), p. 236.
39. For details see Floyd Matson, *The Broken Image: Man, Science and Society* (New York: George Braziller, 1964), esp. chapters 1, 3.
40. Talcott Parsons, *The Social System* (Glencoe, Ill.: Free Press, 1951); David Easton, *The Political System* (Chicago: University of Chicago Press, 1954). Cf. Marion J. Levy, *The Structure of Society* (Princeton: Princeton University Press, 1952). For criticism of these models, see C. Wright Mills, *The Sociological Imagination* (New York: Oxford University Press, 1959), chap. 2; and citations following.
41. Wayne Hield, "The Study of Change in Social Science," *The British Journal of Sociology* (March, 1964), reprinted in N. J. Demerath III and Richard A. Peterson, editors, *System, Change, and Conflict* (New York: Free Press, 1967), pp. 258–259.
42. Alvin W. Gouldner, *The Coming Crisis of Western Sociology* (New York: Basic Books, 1970), p. 206.
43. B. F. Skinner, *Beyond Freedom and Dignity* (New York: Knopf, 1971), p. 215.
44. B. F. Skinner, "Behaviorism at Fifty," in T. W. Wann, editor, *Behaviorism and Phenomenology* (Chicago: University of Chicago Press, 1964), p. 84.
45. *Behaviorism*, pp. 5–6.
46. Quoted in Robert S. Woodworth, *Contemporary Schools of Psychology* (New York: Ronald Press, 1948), p. 215.
47. Clark L. Hull, *Principles of Behavior* (New York: Appleton-Century, 1943), p. 27.
48. Julien Offray de la Mettrie, *L'Homme machine* (1748); quoted in Joseph Needham, editor, *Science, Religion, and Reality* (New York: George Braziller, 1955), p. 236.
49. Holbach, as rendered by Ernst Cassirer, *The Philosophy of the Enlightenment* (Boston: Beacon Press, 1955), p. 69.
50. B. F. Skinner, *Science and Human Behavior* (New York: Macmillan, 1953), pp. 447–448.
51. Ibid., p. 6.
52. B. F. Skinner, *Walden Two* (New York: Macmillan, 1948), p. 214.
53. Ibid., p. 289.
54. *The Center Magazine* (published by the Center for the Study of Democratic Institutions), 5 (March-April 1972), pp. 63–65.
55. Robert L. Geiser, *Behavior Mod and the Managed Society* (Boston: Beacon Press, 1976), p. 107.
56. Erving Goffman, *Asylums* (Garden City, N.Y.: Doubleday, 1961), p. 51.
57. D. T. Fullerton, H. Fahs, and T. Sayles, "Motivating Chronic Patients Through

a Token Economy," *Hospital and Community Psychiatry*, September 1971, p. 289.

58. See Geiser, *Behavior Mod and the Managed Society*, p. 34.
59. Ibid.
60. Ibid., p. 36.
61. Ibid., p. 35.
62. Ibid., p. 34.
63. Skinner, *Science and Human Behavior*, pp. 447–48.
64. Skinner, *Beyond Freedom and Dignity*, pp. 200–201.
65. Quoted in Schrag, *Mind Control*, p. 205.
66. U.S. Congress, Senate, Subcommittee on Constitutional Rights of the Committee on the Judiciary, *Individual Rights and the Federal Role in Behavior Modification*, 93rd Cong., 2nd sess., November 1974 (Washington, D.C.: U.S. Government Printing Office, 1974).
67. See Anatol Rapoport, *Strategy and Conscience* (New York: Schocken Books, 1969), chap. 6, "Prisoner's Dilemma."
68. *Mind Control*, p. 152.
69. Samuel Chavkin, *The Mind Stealers: Psychosurgery and Mind Control* (Boston: Houghton Mifflin, 1978), p. 23.
70. *Mind Control*, p. 163.
71. Chavkin, *The Mind Stealers*, p. 23.
72. Ibid., p. 24.
73. Quoted in ibid., p. 25.
74. *The Mind Stealers*, p. 25.
75. Peter R. Breggin, "The Return of Lobotomy and Psychosurgery," *Congressional Record* 118 (February 24, 1972), 5567–5577.
76. Ivan Illich, *Medical Nemesis: The Expropriation of Health* (New York: Pantheon Books, 1976), p. 40.
77. Chavkin, *The Mind Stealers*, p. 26.
78. A. E. Bennett, quoted in Schrag, *Mind Control*, p. 176.
79. The Oxford Universal Dictionary, with its careful dating of various significations of the noun "disorder," indicates that the public references ("disturbance, commotion, tumult") preceded by several centuries the use of the term to describe an internal "disturbance of mind." The latter meaning is traced to 1838, the heyday of restraint and force in the treatment of mental conditions.
80. Watson, *Behaviorism*, p. 36.
81. Ibid., pp. 184–185.
82. *Mind Control*, p. 151.
83. Ken Kesey, *One Flew Over the Cuckoo's Nest* (New York: Viking, 1964).
84. *Mind Control*, p. 154.
85. Ibid., p. 155.
86. Ibid., p. 154.
87. Quoted in Chavkin, *The Mind Stealers*, pp. 76–77.
88. Quoted in Schrag, *Mind Control*, pp. 150–151.
89. *Behaviorism*, p. 185.
90. Ibid., pp. 185–186.

91. See Jan Wojcik, *Muted Consent: A Casebook in Modern Medical Ethics* (West Lafayette, Indiana: Purdue Research Foundation, 1978), chap. 4, "Behavior Control—Psychotropic Drugs, Behavior Modification, and Psychosurgery."

91A. Ibid.,

92. Michael Crichton, *The Terminal Man* (New York: Bantam Books, 1973), p. 246.

93. Vernon H. Mark and Frank R. Ervin, *Violence and the Brain* (New York: Harper & Row, 1970), p. 160.

94. Vernon H. Mark et al., "The Destruction of Both Anterior Thalamic Nuclei in a Patient with Intractable Depression," *Journal of Nervous and Mental Disease* 150 (1970), pp. 266–272. For discussion see Breggin, "The Return of Lobotomy and Psychosurgery"; Schrag, *Mind Control*, p. 166.

95. *Violence and the Brain*, p. 93.

96. Vernon H. Mark and Frank R. Ervin, "Is There a Need to Evaluate the Individuals Producing Human Violence?" *Psychiatric Opinion* (August, 1968), p. 34.

97. *Violence and the Brain*, pp. 96–97. For extended discussion of this case, see Stephan L. Chorover, "Psychosurgery: A Neuropsychological Perspective," in *Psychosurgery: A Multidisciplinary Symposium,* ed. Samuel Fried (Lexington, Mass.: Lexington Books, 1974), pp. 24–28.

98. Peter R. Breggin, "Professional Bulletin, a Complement to the FAS Public Interest Reports," published by Federation of American Scientists, vol. 2, no. 2 (February 1974); quoted in Chavkin, *The Mind Stealers*, p. 18.

99. J. A. Meyer, "Crime Deterrent Transponder System," *EEE Transactions,* vol. AES-7, no. 1 (January 1971); quoted in Chavkin, *The Mind Stealers,* p. 143.

100. Ralph K. Schwitzgebel, "Issues in the Use of an Electronic Rehabilitation System with Chronic Recidivists," *The Law and Society Review,* vol. 3, pp. 597–611. See discussion in Chavkin, pp. 140–142.

101. Geiser, *Behavior Mod and the Managed Society,* p. 59.

102. See Chorover, "Psychosurgery: A Neuropsychological Perspective"; Valenstein, *Brain Control,* pp. 266–277, *passim*; Chavkin, *The Mind Stealers,* chap. 6.

103. See, for example, Robert Neville, "Pots and Black Kettles: A Philosopher's Perspective on Psychosurgery," in *Psychosurgery: A Multidisciplinary Symposium,* pp. 127–140. For a concise summation of the major criticisms, see Schrag, *Mind Control,* chap. 6, "Ultimate Weapons," and chap. 8, "The Lessons of Intervention."

104. Eliot S. Valenstein, "The Practice of Psychosurgery: A Survey of the Literature (1971–1976)," in *Psychosurgery: Report and Recommendations.* The National Commission for the Protection of Human Subjects of Biomedical and Behavioral Research. DHEW Publication No. (OS) 77-0001 (Washington, D.C.: U.S. Government Printing Office, 1977), p. I–17.

105. "The Practice of Psychosurgery," pp. I–12, I–13.

106. Quoted in Jerome J. Shestack, "Psychiatry and the Dilemmas of Dual Loyalties," in *Medical, Moral and Legal Issues in Mental Health Care,* edited by F. J.

Ayd, Jr. (Baltimore: Williams & Wilkins, 1974), p. 12. See also, in the same volume, Nicholas N. Kittrie, "The Flowering and Decline of the Therapeutic State?" pp. 81–96.

Chapter 4

1. George Lichtheim, in *Current,* May 1968, p. 16.
2. John Kenneth Galbraith, *The New Industrial State* (Boston: Houghton Mifflin, 1967), p. 3.
3. Christopher Lasch, *The Culture of Narcissism* (New York: Norton, 1978), p. 53. See also Michael Maccoby, *The Gamesman: The New Corporate Leaders* (New York: Simon and Schuster, 1976).
4. *The New Industrial State,* p. 200.
5. Ibid., p. 202.
6. Joe McGinnis, *The Selling of the President* (New York: Trident, 1969), p. 178–179.
7. Jacques Ellul, *Propaganda: The Formation of Men's Attitudes* (New York: Knopf, 1965), p. 15.
8. Herbert Marcuse, *One-Dimensional Man* (Boston: Beacon, 1964), p. xvi.
9. Michael Novak, "Television Shapes the Soul," in Gary Gumpert and Robert Cathcart, eds., *Inter/Media: Interpersonal Communication in a Media World* (New York: Oxford University, 1979), p. 328.
10. Harry J. Skornia, "TV Debases Everything It Touches," in Robert J. Glessing and William P. White, eds., *Mass Media: The Invisible Environment Revisited* (Chicago: Science Research Associates, 1976), p. 29.
11. Rose K. Goldsen, *The Show and Tell Machine: How Television Works and Works You Over* (New York: Dial, 1977), p. 14.
12. C. Wright Mills, *The Power Elite* (New York: Oxford University, 1956), p. 305.
13. Richard Sennett, *The Fall of Public Man* (New York: Vintage, 1978), p. 261.
14. Daniel J. Boorstin, *The Image: A Guide to Pseudo-Events in America* (New York: Harper Colophon, 1964), p. 13.
15. Susan Sontag, *On Photography* (New York: Farrar, Straus and Giroux, 1977), p. 157.
16. Daniel Schorr, *Clearing the Air* (Boston: Houghton Mifflin, 1977).
17. Jules Henry, *Culture Against Man* (New York: Knopf, 1963), p. 47.
18. Ibid., p. 48.
19. Paul F. Lazarsfeld and Robert K. Merton, "Mass Communication, Popular Taste and Organized Social Action," in Wilbur Schramm, ed., *Mass Communication* (Urbana: University of Illinois, 1960), pp. 492–512.
20. Quoted in Dennis K. Davis and Stanley J. Baran, *Mass Communication and Everyday Life* (Belmont: Wadsworth, 1981), p. 53.
21. Jim Hougan, *Decadence: Radical Nostalgia, Narcissism, and Decline in the Seventies* (New York: Morrow, 1975), p. 180.
22. Quoted in Davis and Baran, p. v.

Chapter 5

1. Charles A. Reich, *The Greening of America* (New York: Random House, 1970). See also William Braden, *The Age of Aquarius: Technology and the Cultural Revolution* (Chicago: Quadrangle, 1970); Theodore Roszak, *The Making of a Counter Culture* (New York: Doubleday Anchor, 1969); Philip Slater, *The Pursuit of Loneliness: American Culture at the Breaking Point* (Boston: Beach, 1970); George B. Leonard, *The Transformation* (New York: Harper and Row, 1971).
2. Reich, p. 13.
3. *Communication Company,* Bulletin, August, 1967. Quoted in Jesse Kornbluth, ed., *Notes from the New Underground* (New York: Viking, 1968), p. 247.
4. Richard Neville, *Play Power: Exploring the International Underground* (New York: Random House, 1970), p. 34.
5. Kornbluth, pp. 247–249.
6. *Village Voice,* October 19, 1967.
7. Ibid., November 30, 1967.
8. *East Village Other,* September, 1969; quoted in Neville, p. 119.
9. *San Francisco Oracle,* February, 1967; reprinted in Kornbluth, p. 166.
10. *San Francisco Good Times,* September 18, 1970; reprinted in Harold Jacobs, ed., *Weatherman* (San Francisco: Ramparts Press, 1970), pp. 517–518.
11. Tom Wolfe, *The Electric Kool-Aid Acid Test* (New York: Bantam, 1969), p. 93.
12. Ibid., pp. 334–335.
13. Ibid., p. 77.
14. William Burroughs, "Academy 23: A Deconditioning," *Village Voice,* July 6, 1967; reprinted in Kornbluth, pp. 110–114.
15. Quoted in David Felton, ed., *Mindfuckers* (San Francisco, Straight Arrow Books, 1972), p. 11.
16. Quoted in Sherri Cavan, *Hippies of the Haight* (St. Louis, Mo.: New Critics Press, 1972), p. 117.
17. Kenneth Leach, *Youthquake: The Growth of a Counter-Culture Through Two Decades* (London: Sheldon Press, 1973), p. 49.
18. Quoted in Leach, p. 61.
19. Felton, p. 10.
20. Quoted in Felton, p. 11.
21. Michael Selzer, *Terrorist Chic: An Exploration of Violence in the Seventies* (New York: Hawthorn Books, 1979), p. 196.
22. William L. O'Neill, *Coming Apart* (New York: Quadrangle/New York Times, 1971).
23. David E. Cooper, ed., *The Manson Murders: A Philosophical Inquiry* (Cambridge: Schenkman, 1974), pp., 3, 60, *passim.* See also Ed Sanders, *The Family* (New York: Dutton, 1971).
24. Vincent Bugliosi with Curt Gentry, *Helter Skelter: The True Story of the Manson Murders* (New York: Norton, 1974), pp. 240ff; Felton, *Mindfuckers,* pp. 62ff.

25. Bugliosi, p. 221; Felton, p. 27.
26. Bugliosi, pp. 221–222.
27. Jerry Rubin, *Do It!* (New York: Simon and Schuster, 1970), pp. 149–150.
28. Ibid., pp. 150–151.
29. Neville, *Play Power*, pp. 53–54.
30. Rubin, p. 122.
31. Ibid., pp. 122–123, 126, 127.
32. Nigel Young, *An Infantile Disorder? The Crisis and Decline of the New Left* (Boulder: Westview Press, 1977), p. 355.
33. *The Electric Kool-Aid Acid Test*, p. 326.
34. Richard Goldstein, "Love: A Groovy Idea While He Lasted," *The Village Voice*, October 19, 1967; reprinted in Kornbluth, p. 255.
35. *Weatherman*, p. 510.
36. Quoted in Christopher Bone, *The Disinherited Children: A Study of the New Left and the Generation Gap* (New York: Halstead Press, 1977), p. 159.
37. Massimo Teodori, ed., *The New Left: A Documentary History* (Indianapolis: Bobbs-Merrill, 1969), p. 364.
38. J. Bowrer Bell and Ted Robert Gurr, "Terrorism and Revolution in America," in Hugh Davis Graham and Ted Robert Gurr, eds., *Violence in America: Historical and Comparative Perspectives* (Beverly Hills: Sage Publications, 1979), p. 330.
39. Rubin, p. 122.

Chapter 6

1. Susan Sontag, "The Imagination of Disaster," in *Against Interpretation* (New York: Farrar, Straus, & Giroux, 1965).
2. Robert Warshow, "Movie Chronicle: The Westerner," in *The Immediate Experience* (Garden City, N.Y.: Doubleday Anchor, 1962).
3. Robert F. Moss, "The Brutalists: Making Movies Mean and Ugly," *Saturday Review*, October 1980, p. 14.
4. Michael Selzer, *Terrorist Chic: An Exploration of Violence in the Seventies* (New York: Hawthorn, 1979), p. xiv.
5. *Newsweek*, December 22, 1980, pp. 68–69.
6. See Graeme Newman, *Understanding Violence* (New York: J. B. Lippincott, 1979), p. 47.
7. Richard Maxwell Brown, "The American Vigilante Tradition," in *The History of Violence in America: Historical and Comparative Perspectives* (New York, 1969), pp. 154–217.
8. Newman, *Understanding Violence*, p. 46.
9. Frank Gruber, *The Pulp Jungle* (Los Angeles, 1967). See also Russel Nye, *The Unembarrassed Muse: The Popular Arts in America* (New York: Dial Press, 1970), p. 301.
10. George Orwell, "Raffles and Miss Blandish," quoted in John Fraser, *Violence in the Arts* (London: Cambridge University Press, 1974), p. 12.

11. Quoted in Fraser, *Violence in the Arts,* pp. 36–37.
12. *The Unembarrassed Muse,* p. 263.
13. Ibid., p. 264.
14. Mickey Spillane, *The Big Kill* (New York: Signet, n.d.), p. 41.
15. Philip French, *Westerns: Aspects of a Movie Genre* (New York: Oxford University Press, 1977), p. 172.
16. John G. Cawelti, *Adventure, Mystery, and Romance* (Chicago: University of Chicago Press, 1976), p. 254.
17. "The Brutalists," p. 14.
18. David A. Cook, *A History of Narrative Film* (New York: W. W. Norton, 1981), p. 627.
19. David Shaw, "Violent Movies Create Violent Kids," *Today's Health,* October 1974; reprinted in *Mass Media and the Popular Arts,* ed. by Fredric Rissover and David C. Birch (New York: McGraw-Hill, 1977), pp. 382–386.
20. *A History of Narrative Film,* p. 631.
21. Shaw, "Violent Movies Create Violent Kids," p. 384.
22. *Violence in the Arts,* p. 17.
23. See Nye, *The Unembarrassed Muse,* pp. 15–17.
24. Quoted in Stephen Farber, "The Bloody Movies: Why Violence Sells," *New West* (December 6, 1977); reprinted in *Mass Media: Forces in Our Society,* ed. by Francis H. Voelker and Ludmila A. Voelker (New York: Harcourt Brace Jovanovich, 3d ed., 1978), p. 286.
25. See John Brosnan, *The Horror People* (New York: New American Library, 1976), chap. 7.
26. Farber, "The Bloody Movies," p. 288.
27. Moss, "The Brutalists," p. 17.
28. Quoted in Farber, "The Bloody Movies," p. 283.
29. Moss, "The Brutalists," p. 17.
30. Farber, "The Bloody Movies," p. 288.
31. Shaw, "Violent Movies Create Violent Kids," p. 384.
32. Robert Brent Toplin, *Unchallenged Violence: An American Ordeal* (Westport, Conn.: Greenwood Press, 1975), p. 206.
33. *Violence and the Mass Media,* Vol. 9A, Mass Media Hearings: A Report to the National Commission on the Causes and Prevention of Violence (Washington, D.C., 1969), p. 202.
34. See James McKinley, *Assassination in America* (New York: Harper & Row, 1975), pp. 218–222.
35. Lawrence Donner, "Violence in the Media," *Rage * Hate * Assault and Other Forms of Violence,* ed. by Denis J. Madden and John R. Lion (New York: Spectrum Publications, 1976), p. 36.
36. Toplin, *Unchallenged Violence,* p. 197.
37. Charles E. Silberman, *Criminal Violence, Criminal Justice* (New York: Random House, 1978), pp. 62–63.
38. Farber, "The Bloody Movies," p. 283.
39. Ibid., p. 285.
40. Peter J. Boyer, "'Birthday' Shock Ads Skewer a Big Audience," *Honolulu Ad-*

vertiser (*Los Angeles Times* Service), September 12, 1982.

41. Ibid.
42. Susan Sontag, "Notes on 'Camp,' " *Against Interpretation: and Other Essays* (London: Eyre & Spottiswoode, 1967).
43. Quoted in Farber, "The Bloody Movies," p. 286.
44. Ibid.
45. *Terrorist Chic,* p. xv.
46. "The Bloody Movies," p. 286.
47. *Newsweek,* August 30, 1982, p. 61.
48. A few movie (and TV-movie) titles from the seventies will serve to illustrate the zoophobic theme: *Jaws, Willard, The Swarm, SSSSSS, The Howling, Piranha, Tarantulas: The Deadly Cargo, Wolfen,* and *Day of the Animals.*
49. Pauline Kael, *Reeling* (Boston: Little, Brown, 1976), p. 310.
50. Ibid., p. 311.
51. "The Brutalists," p. 17.
52. Quoted in Ashley Montagu, *The Nature of Human Aggression* (New York: Oxford University Press, 1976), p. 29.
53. Neil P. Hurley, "Hollywood's New Mythology," *Forum for Correspondence and Contact* (New York: International Center for Integrative Studies), November 1982, p. 37.
54. Thomas Hobbes, *Leviathan* (New York: Oxford University Press, 1947 [orig. ed. 1651]), Part 1, Chap. XIII.
55. See, e.g., the contributions by Susan Griffin, Robin Morgan, and Diana E. H. Russell in *Take Back the Night,* edited by Laura Lederer (New York: Morrow, 1980).
56. H. J. Eysenck & D. K. B. Nias, *Sex, Violence and the Media* (New York: St. Martin's Press, 1978), p. 63.
57. Quoted in Eysenck and Nias, ibid., p. 54.
58. Peter Watson, *War on the Mind: The Military Uses and Abuses of Psychology* (New York: Basic Books, 1978), p. 38.
59. *Sex, Violence, and the Media,* p. 55.
60. Christopher Lasch, *The Culture of Narcissism* (New York: W. W. Norton, 1978); Jim Hougan, *Decadence: Radical Nostalgia, Narcissism, and Decline in the Seventies* (New York: Morrow, 1975); Tom Wolfe, "The 'Me' Decade and the Third Great Awakening," *New York,* August 23, 1976, pp. 26–40; Peter Marin, "The New Narcissim," *Harper's,* October 1975.
61. Mark Crispin Miller, "Books and the Arts: Turned On, Tuned Up, Burned Out," *The Nation,* vol. 29 (August 25, 1979), pp. 149–152.
62. Quoted in Selzer, *Terrorist Chic,* p. 113.
63. Paul Hendrickson, quoted in Selzer, pp. 113–114.
64. Perry Lang and Paul Liberatore, "Punks Rock to 'Slam-Dancing,' " *San Francisco Chronicle,* August 18, 1981.
65. Toplin, *Unchallenged Violence,* p. 6.
66. Jim Miller, "Some Future," *New Republic,* vol. 180 (March 24, 1979), p. 26.
67. *San Francisco Chronicle,* August 18, 1981.

68. Edward Meadows, "Pistol-whipped," *National Review*, vol. 29 (November 11, 1977), p. 1311.
69. Miller, "Some Future," p. 28.
70. Quoted in Selzer, *Terrorist Chic*, p. 119.
71. Harold Schechter, *The New Gods: Psyche and Symbol in Popular Art* (Bowling Green, Ohio: Bowling Green University Popular Press, 1980), chap. 3.
72. C. G. Jung, "On the Psychology of the Trickster-Figure," in Paul Radin, *The Trickster: A Study in American Indian Mythology* (New York: Schocken Books, 1971), pp. 206, 196.
73. *Funk & Wagnalls Standard Dictionary of Folklore, Mythology and Legend*, ed. by Maria Leach (New York: Funk & Wagnalls, 1949), vol. I, p. 192.
74. Ibid., vol. II, p. 1124.

Chapter 7

1. William Heyliger, *Captain of the Nine* (1912); quoted in Russel Nye, *The Unembarrassed Muse: The Popular Arts in America* (New York: Dial Press, 1970), p. 76.
2. "We play our games with the same tenacious ferocity with which we fight a war in Vietnam and with as little reason or sense. We are taught from the cradle that we have never lost a war and that winning is everything, tying is like kissing your sister and losing is nothing." Sports columnist Leonard Shechter, quoted in Don Atyeo, *Blood and Guts: Violence in Sports* (New York: Paddington Press, 1979), p. 247.
3. Cf. Philip Goodhart and Christopher Chataway, *War Without Weapons* (London: W. H. Allen, 1968); Mike Holovak and Bill McSweeney, *Violence Every Sunday* (New York: Coward, McCann, 1967); Ira Gittler, *Blood on the Ice* (Chicago: Henry Regnery, 1974); Stan Fischler, *Slashing!* (New York: Warner, 1975); Roger Ingham, *Football Hooliganism* (London: Inter-Action Imprint, 1978); David Robins and Philip Cohen, *Knuckle Sandwich* (Middlesex: Penguin, 1978); Ivan N. Kaye, *Good Clean Violence* (Philadelphia: Lippincott, 1973); Paul Hoch, *Rip Off the Big Game* (New York: Doubleday, 1972); Paul Gardner, *Nice Guys Finish Last* (London: Allen Lane, 1974); Jerry Kramer, ed., *Lombardi: Winning is the Only Thing* (Cleveland: World, 1970); Arnold J. Mandell, *The Nightmare Season* (New York: Random House, 1976). See also Thomas Tutko and William Bruns, *Winning is Everything and Other American Myths* (New York: Macmillan, 1976); Gerhard Vinnai, *Football Mania* (London: Ocean Books, 1973); Ray Nitschke and Robert W. Wells, *Mean on Sunday* (Garden City: Doubleday, 1973); Dave Meggyesy, *Out of Their League* (New York: Warner, 1971); Gary Shaw, *Meat on the Hoof* (New York: St. Martin's 1972); Arnold R. Beisser, *The Madness in Sports* (New York: Meredith, 1967).
4. Neil D. Isaacs, *Jock Culture U.S.A.* (New York: Norton, 1978), p. 17.

5. Quoted In Atyeo, *Blood and Guts*, p. 248.
6. Johan Huizinga, *Homo Ludens: A Study of the Play Element in Culture* (Boston: Beacon, 1955), p. 13.
7. Ibid., p. 7.
8. Ibid., p. 13.
9. Ibid., p. 8.
10. E.g., Roger Callois, *Man, Play, and Games* (New York: Free Press, 1961); Allen Guttmann, *From Ritual to Record: The Nature of Modern Sports* (New York: Columbia University, 1978), p. 6f; Eric Dunning, ed., "General Introduction," *The Sociology of Sport* (London: Frank Cass, 1971); John W. Loy, Jr., "The Nature of Sport: A Definitional Effort," John W. Loy, Jr. and Gerald S. Kenyon, eds., *Sport, Culture, and Society* (New York: Macmillan, 1969), pp. 56–70; Brian M. Petrie, "Sport and Politics," Donald W. Ball and John W. Loy, eds., *Sport and Social Order* (Reading, Mass.: Addison-Wesley, 1975), p. 190.
11. *Homo Ludens*, p. 95.
12. Ibid., p. 89.
13. Ibid., pp. 89–90.
14. Ibid., p. 96.
15. Ibid., p. 90.
16. Ibid., p. 101.
17. Ibid., p. 199.
18. Elias's theory of sport was an outgrowth of a larger work, *The Process of Civilization*, first published as *Ueber den Prozess der Zivilisation* (Basle, 1939).
19. *The Sociology of Sport*, p. 84.
20. Norbert Elias, "The Genesis of Sport," *The Sociology of Sport*, p. 100.
21. Ibid., p. 102.
22. Ibid., p. 103.
23. See Atyeo, *Blood and Guts*, p. 183.
24. See Tutko and Bruns, *Winning Is Everything and Other American Myths*, p. 4.
25. Ibid., p. 5.
26. *Blood and Guts*, p. 221.
27. Ibid., p. 222.
28. Ibid., p. 254.
29. Bob Rubin, "Jets' Protection of Blinka 'Maddening, Depressing,'" *The Honolulu Advertiser*, December 3, 1982.
30. Atyeo, *Blood and Guts*, p. 277.
31. Beisser, *The Madness in Sports*, pp. 9–10.
32. *Winning Is Everything and Other American Myths*, p. 131.
33. Jacques Ellul, *The Technological Society* (New York: Knopf, 1964), p. 383.
34. Quoted in Atyeo, *Blood and Guts*, p. 279.
35. Stephen Potter, *One-Upmanship* (New York: Holt, 1952).
36. Dick Weiss (Knight-Ridder Newspapers), *The Honolulu Advertiser*, April 1, 1983.
37. Atyeo, *Blood and Guts*, pp. 254–255.
38. *Out of Their League*, p. 6.
39. Atyeo, p. 249.

40. Ibid.
41. See Gitler, *Blood on the Ice.*
42. Atyeo, pp. 270–272.

Epilogue

1. Jonathan Schell, *The Fate of the Earth* (New York: Knopf, 1982).
2. Robinson Jeffers, "Shine, Perishing Republic," *A Little Treasury of Modern Poetry,* ed. by Oscar Williams (New York: Scribner's Sons, 1946), p. 446.
3. See Christopher Lasch, *The Culture of Narcissism* (New York: Norton, 1978); Sigmund Koch, "Psychology Cannot Be a Coherent Science," *Psychology Today,* September 1969, reprinted in Floyd W. Matson, editor, *Without/Within: Behaviorism and Humanism* (Belmont: Brooks/Cole, 1973), pp. 80–91; Peter Marin, "The New Narcissism," *Harper's,* October 1975; Tom Wolfe, "The 'Me' Decade and the Third Great Awakening," *New York,* August 23, 1976; Kurt W. Back, *Beyond Words: The Story of Sensitivity Training and the Encounter Movement* (Baltimore: Penguin Books, 1973).
4. Key works include Abraham H. Maslow, *Toward a Psychology of Being* (New York: Van Nostrand, 1962); Gordon W. Allport, *Becoming* (New Haven: Yale, 1955); Erich Fromm, *Man for Himself* (New York: Rinehart, 1947); Carl R. Rogers, *On Becoming a Person* (Boston: Houghton Mifflin, 1961); Ernest G. Schachtel, *Metamorphosis* (New York: Basic Books, 1959); Rollo May, *Love and Will* (New York: Norton, 1969); Carl G. Jung, *The Undiscovered Self* (New York: Mentor, 1959); Charlotte Buhler, *Values in Psychotherapy* (New York: Free Press, 1962); James F. T. Bugental, *The Search for Authenticity* (New York: Holt, Rinehart, and Winston, 1965); René Dubos, *So Human an Animal* (New York: Scribner's, 1968); Amadeo Giorgi, *Psychology as a Human Science* (New York: Harper & Row, 1970). See also Ashley Montagu, *The Direction of Human Development* (New York: Harper & Row, 1955); Floyd W. Matson, *The Broken Image* (New York: Braziller, 1964).
5. See, for example, the contributions by 19 scientists to *Man and Aggression,* edited by Ashley Montagu (New York: Oxford University Press, 2d ed., 1973). See also Ashley Montagu, *The Nature of Human Aggression* (New York: Oxford University Press, 1976).
6. Alan McGlashan, *Savage and Beautiful Country: The Secret Life of the Mind* (New York: Hillstone, 1967), p. 56.

INDEX

About the Authors

Ashley Montagu is the author or editor of over sixty books on such varied subjects as anatomy and physiology, psychology, anthropology, race, evolution, and heredity, love, aggression and touching, human development, sexuality, the history of science, the dangers of pollution, the anatomy of swearing, and the dolphin in human history. Among his classic works are *The Natural Superiority of Women, Man's Most Dangerous Myth: The Fallacy of Race, Human Evolution, The Elephant Man, Touching, Anthropology and Human Nature, Life Before Birth, On Being Human,* and *The Nature of Human Aggression.* He is author of the critically acclaimed *Growing Young* and, with Floyd Matson, of *The Human Connection,* published by McGraw-Hill. He is the writer and director of the film "One World or None," described as one of the best documentaries ever made.

Floyd Matson has written widely in the fields of psychology, communication, and social thought. He has taught in Japan and Korea as well as at the University of California (Berkeley), where he obtained his Ph.D. in political science, and the University of Hawaii, where he is presently a professor of American Studies. Among his books are *The Broken Image, The Idea of Man,* and (with Ashley Montagu) *The Human Connection.*

2800
± 800
——
3600 March 10, 84
   7 0
 T 650
 W 1300
 M 0